Contents

Three Turk Plays from Early Modern England

Three Turk Plays
from Early Modern England

SELIMUS,
A CHRISTIAN TURNED TURK,

and

THE RENEGADO

Edited by Daniel J. Vitkus

COLUMBIA UNIVERSITY PRESS

NEW YORK

Columbia University Press
Publishers Since 1893
New York
Chichester, West Sussex

Copyright © 2000 Columbia University Press
All rights reserved
Library of Congress Cataloging-in-Publication Data
Three Turk plays from early modern England : Selimus, A Christian turned Turk,
and The renegado / edited by Daniel J. Vitkus.
   p. cm.
Includes bibliographical references.
ISBN 978-0-231-11028-0 (cloth : acid-free paper) — ISBN 978-0-231-11029-7 (pbk.)
   1. English drama—17th century.   2. Selim I, Sultan of the Turks, 1470–
1520 Drama.   3. Christianity and other religions—Islam Drama.   4. Turkey—
History—Selim I, 1512–1520 Drama.   5. Muslim converts from Christianity
Drama.   6. Greene, Robert, 1558?–1592—Authorship.   7. Islam—
Relations—Christianity Drama.   8. Converts from Islam Drama.   9. Islamic
countries Drama.   10. Tunis (Tunisia) Drama.   I. Vitkus, Daniel J.
II. Daborne, Robert, d. 1628.   Christian turned Turk.   III. Massinger, Philip,
1583–1640. Renegado.   IV. Selimus.
PR1263.T484   1999
822'.4080351—dc21   99–26526

Three Turk Plays from Early Modern England

For Jane

Introduction

~

THREE TURK PLAYS
FROM EARLY MODERN ENGLAND

Shakespeare's *Othello* explodes onto the stage with frantic dialogue and "haste-post-haste" action, conveying both erotic and martial "heat" (1.2.37–40). Cries of "What ho!" and "Thieves, thieves!" rouse Brabantio from sleep to discover that he has been "robbed" of his daughter by the Moor (1.1.78–85). Meanwhile, another robbery is in progress: the same cry, "What ho, what ho, what ho!" (1.3.12), is raised by messengers bearing urgent news to the city fathers of Venice. "The Turk" intends to take Cyprus from them, and the Moor is needed to fight the Turk: "Valiant Othello, we must straight employ you / Against the general enemy Ottoman" (1.3.49–50), announces the duke. In such a time of crisis, the "general care" of Venice must take precedent over Brabantio's "particular grief" (1.3.55–56). The Senate approves Othello's elopement, and by the end of the first act the Moor and his new bride are on their way to Cyprus.

The rising action of Shakespeare's tragedy encourages the audience to anticipate a heroic, epic-scale drama of love and war, with Desdemona and Othello cast in the mold of Marlowe's Zenocrate and Tamburlaine. In both *Tamburlaine the Great, Part I* and *Othello, the Moor of Venice*, a bold warrior converts crisis to opportunity by means of decisive action and rhetorical bravado. Like Tamburlaine, Othello audaciously woos above his station and claims an aristocratic bride for his own in "mighty lines" that defy his social superiors. In the case of Othello, the woman is willing, but both men use their rhetorical ability and sense of timing to legitimize what might otherwise have been condemned as an act of connubial piracy. Though Brabantio makes it clear that he considers Othello nothing more than a "foul thief" (1.2.62), the Venetian Senate supports Othello's theft, and Desdemona becomes, in Iago's words, a "lawful prize" (1.2.51).

I

Othello, like Marlowe's Tamburlaine, leads an army against the ultimate enemy of Christendom—the mighty Turk of Istanbul. But Othello's victory over the Ottoman forces comes without the expected confrontation: between acts 1 and 2 the Turks "are drowned" (2.1.18), and so the fearsome Ottoman invaders never take the stage in Shakespeare's play. Instead the Turks are defined as a menace that is kept, for the time being, beyond the boundaries of Christendom.[1] In act 2, however, the threat of Turkish aggression reappears in a new form, internalized and embodied by the Christian soldiers on Cyprus. When Othello asks, "Are we turned Turks, and to ourselves do that / Which heaven hath forbid the Ottomites?" (2.3.169–70), he refers to the incorporation of the Turks' stereotypical features, which include aggression, lust, suspicion, murderous conspiracy, sudden cruelty masquerading as justice, merciless violence rather than "Christian charity," wrathful vengeance instead of turning the other cheek. These are the "Turkish" qualities that will eventually contaminate Othello himself.[2] In the course of his tragic metamorphosis, Othello "turns Turk," betrays his love, and traduces the Christian state of Venice. He returns to the spiritual condition of reprobation that was identified with the "pagan" Moors and the "infidel" Turks.

According to anti-Islamic tales told in the West, the violence and cruelty of Turks and Moors was enacted in both public and private—on the field of battle and within the palace walls. Shakespeare's tragic hero is a Moorish warrior whose public militarism becomes, in the privacy of his bedroom, a version of the sultan's overprotective absolutism in his imperial harem. By the time Othello murders Desdemona, he has converted to erotic, Islamic evil and conformed to the European stereotype of the irascible, libidinous Muslim. He becomes a representative of the Venetians' greatest foe, the "malignant Turk" (5.2.351), and his suicide is a final effort to punish himself for his reversion to such an identity.

In *Othello* (1604), Turkish cruelty and violence are threatened and then displaced, but there were many other plays performed in the Elizabethan and Early Stuart theater that brought Turkish villains to center stage, representing Islamic culture in the form of Moorish or Turkish characters. The best known of these plays are Marlowe's *Tamburlaine, Parts I & II* (1587–88) and his *Jew of Malta* (1589). Examples of Islamic might, murderousness, and wealth are also found in George Peele's *Battle of Alcazar* (1588) and *Soliman and Perseda* (1590), Robert Greene's *Alphonsus, King of Aragon* (1588) and *Orlando Furioso* (1589), *The Famous History of the Life and Death of Captain Thomas Stukeley* (1596), Thomas Dekker's *Lust's Dominion* (1600), Thomas Heywood's *The*

Fair Maid of the West, Part I (1602), Thomas Goffe's *The Courageous Turk* (1618) and *The Raging Turk* (1618), John Fletcher and Philip Massinger's *The Knight of Malta* (1618), Thomas Middleton and William Rowley's *All's Lost by Lust* (1620), as well as the three plays printed in this volume.[3] These theatrical representations of Islamic power took the stage during a time when the Turkish empire was expanding rapidly. From the fifteenth to the eighteenth century, the Ottomans posed a sustained threat to Christian rule in Europe. For London theatergoers, the Turk was not an imaginary bogey, and the Turk plays in this volume are not simply fantasies about fictional demons lurking at the edges of the civilized world. These plays and other early modern writings dealing with the Turks express an anxious interest in Islamic power that is both complicated and overdetermined.

English images of Islamic culture often exhibited exaggeration and demonization, but increasingly these images were based on real contact with Muslim peoples in the Mediterranean. Queen Elizabeth herself maintained diplomatic relations and official correspondence with Moroccan and Turkish rulers. Her primary purpose was to request loans or military aid from these Islamic potentates or encourage trade, not to chastise them for their infidel ways. With the establishment of the Levant Company in 1581, and subsequently, the rapid development of English commerce throughout the Mediterranean, the power of Islam became directly visible to those who followed the sea for a living. A seafaring people with growing commercial connections to the Mediterranean world, the English felt the force of Islam as it affected their maritime economy. Both the Ottoman galleys of the Eastern Mediterranean and the Barbary pirate ships from North African ports were known to English seamen venturing through the straits of Gibraltar. Some of these cross-cultural encounters were mutually profitable, while other meetings with Muslim vessels involved robbery and the taking of captives, who were ransomed or sold into slavery. By the early seventeenth century, English commerce in Muslim entrepôts such as Constantinople, Aleppo, Alexandretta, Tunis, Tripoli, and Algiers was expanding rapidly. Muslim-sponsored piracy had become a serious problem both in the Northeast Atlantic and in the Mediterranean, where English merchant ships were sailing with greater regularity after trade pacts with both the Barbary principalities and the Ottoman sultanate were signed.[4]

During the early seventeenth century, Muslim power was brought home to British soil when the Barbary pirates began to raid the English coastline and take captives, on several occasions hauling their victims out of their homes and churches in the West country and carrying them off to be sold into slavery or held for ransom. In October 1617, a Turkish pirate ship was captured in the Thames estuary.[5] During this period the threat of Muslim pirates in the Atlantic and the Mediterranean increased to a crisis level, and the number of English captives held in Barbary soared.[6]

While the Barbary pirates attacked English shipping in the West, Ottoman armies were invading Austria in the East. The long arms of "the Turk" seemed to be encircling Europe. The Holy Land was in their possession, and "Turkish" vessels of one kind or another regularly raided the coasts of Italy, Spain, and France. The Turks and Moors of the Barbary ports (principally Tunis, Algiers, and Tripoli) sailed throughout the Mediterranean and preyed upon the Christians, who were never united against their Muslim foes (despite ceaseless talk about mounting a general crusade).

It should be noted, however, that piracy in the early modern Mediterranean was not an illegal practice undertaken by "wicked" pirates against "honest" merchants. Rather, it was a free-for-all whereby any intimidating ship or group of ships encountering a vulnerable ship flying another flag could take advantage and plunder the less fortunate vessel, rifling its cargo, and perhaps capturing its crew and selling them into slavery. Some captives taken by the Muslims—especially those who had little hope of being ransomed—converted to Islam. Many Christian sailors and ship captains also chose to "take the turban," formally joining the Muslim religious community in order to enjoy the freedom and protection of the Barbary principalities of the North African coast. In many cases, the temptation of lucrative employment motivated Christian sailors and soldiers to turn Turk and become renegade pirates or, in some instances, to join the Ottoman army or navy as technical advisers.[7] At the same time, crews of Christian corsairs from ports in Italy and Malta roamed the Mediterranean and attacked both Christian and Muslim targets.

During the seventeenth century, pirates based in North Africa continued to plague English maritime traffic.[8] Renegade freebooters posed a threat to both church and commerce, and the English rulers tried to adopt a strategy that would reduce corsair activity and prevent conversions to Islam. A great deal of diplomatic negotiation was conducted between the English court, the Barbary regencies, and the Ottoman sultanate—consisting mainly of the English asking the Ottomans to restrain the Barbary pirates' predations on English shipping—but force was also used. In 1612, for example, twelve pirates were executed on the same day: all were hanged publicly at Wapping. During the years that followed, the problems of piracy and captivity led the English monarchs James I and Charles I to mount attacks on the Barbary ports where these activities were based. Vice Admiral Sir Robert Mansell led an unsuccessful assault on Algiers in 1621, and Captain William Rainsborough's 1636 Sallee expedition took advantage of a civil war in Morocco to intervene and redeem about three hundred captives. Back in England, the "distressed wives" of almost two thousand English mariners had petitioned the court in 1625, asking for help in redeeming their husbands, who were held captive in Sallee in Morocco.[9]

The religious and political authorities in England suspected that there were pirates and renegades who led double lives, returning home when they wished and going unpunished for their apostasy. Renegades who did convert were described as "atheists," a term that implied not a denial of God's existence, but referred in early modern parlance to anyone who did not conform to orthodox religious practice. Sometimes an "atheist" was simply someone guilty of treasonous, criminal behavior. Islamic tyrants like Selimus and renegades like Ward were both described as atheists. The complex set of religious and political transgressions implied by the pirates' conversion to Islam was denounced as an irrational and unnatural crime, but it was also romanticized as a spectacular form of deviance from social and religious norms. There is a large gap, however, between the real experience and meaning of religious conversion for renegade seamen and the sensationalized representation of the Christian who "turns Turk." For those who became Muslims in order to join the Barbary pirates, conversion was probably a mere formality and involved little obligation in terms of religious practice. The formal ceremony of conversion to Islam is staged in the central scene of *A Christian Turned Turk* as an anti-Islamic fantasy, more a scare tactic to discourage potential converts than an accurate depiction of a religious rite. Because Christians in Europe did not practice circumcision at the time, this feature of Islamic custom was viewed with horror as an atavistic ritual performed by barbarians. The idea of adult circumcision was conflated and confused with the idea of castration. In this way, turning Turk was associated with becoming a eunuch. This was a misconception of real practices: there were slaves in the Islamic world who had been taken as boys from non-Muslim communities, castrated, and raised as Muslim servants in Muslim households or courts. We see the association of circumcision with emasculation or castration in the scene portraying Ward's conversion, and in the comic efforts of Gazet to become "an eunuch" in *The Renegado*.[10]

While the spectacle of circumcision and conversion was being staged in

London, sermons were being preached to congregations that included large
numbers of English mariners, warning these worshippers against conversion
and threatening eternal damnation for those who turned Turk. Protestant
divines exhorted their listeners to endure torture or even Christian martyrdom before converting to Islam.[11] For renegades who came home and wished
to confess their apostasy and be reinstated in the Church of England, there
were pardons available, but only after ritual penance was undergone. In 1635,
a standard "Form of Penance and Reconciliation of a Renegado" was pro-
mulgated by Bishop Hall and Archbishop Laud and employed for the rein-
tegration of returned apostates.[12]

Englishmen were converting to Islam, "Turkish" pirates were interfering
with international trade, and the Ottoman empire was asserting itself mili-
tarily and economically. In these ways, Turkish power and Muslim peoples
affected English society directly and increasingly. And yet, despite more extensive contact between Englishmen and Muslims, English representations
of Islamic society written at this time continue to paint an inaccurate picture. In scripts for the stage and in other accounts, the facts about Islamic or
Ottoman culture and its power are often imbedded within or distorted by
demonizing fantasies. Furthermore, the historical reality of the Ottoman
threat and real anxieties about the Turks were rarely represented or expressed
without the accompaniment of anti-Islamic polemic.

The demonization of Islam is a long and deeply rooted tradition in the
West—it spans centuries, from the early medieval period to the end of the
twentieth century, and harks back to a tradition of representations that describe the Eastern empires and invading hordes that came before Islam, such
as the Assyrians and the Persians of the ancient world. The classical and biblical stereotypes that are embedded in the tradition of Western humanism
were further shaped and solidified by the historical experience of "holy war"
that began with the rise of Islam, continued during the period of the Cru-
sades, and persisted in the era of Spanish *reconquista* and Ottoman imperial-
ism. During the Islamic conquests of the seventh and eighth centuries, and
later at the time of the Ottoman expansion, the Europeans were dominated
by Islamic power and awed by its culture. One prominent scholar claims that
"the creation of the distorted image of Islam was largely a response to the
cultural *superiority* of the Muslims, especially those of al-Andalus."[13] During
the early modern era, the Christians of Spain, Portugal, England, and other
nations were establishing their first permanent colonies in the New World

while simultaneously facing the threat at home of being colonized by the Ottoman Turks.

Many of the images of Islam produced by European culture in the early modern period are imaginary resolutions of real anxieties about Islamic wealth and might. The Christian West's inferiority complex, which originated in the trauma of the early Caliphate's conquests, was renewed and reinforced by the emergence of a new Islamic power, the Ottoman Turks, who achieved in 1453 what the Ummayid armies had failed to accomplish in 669 and 674—the capture of Constantinople. A series of Ottoman invasions and victories followed, including Athens in 1459, Otranto in 1480, Rhodes in 1522, Budapest in 1526, the siege of Vienna in 1529, Cyprus in 1571, and Crete in 1669.

In England, the long history of military aggression and cultural competition between Christians and Muslims served as the basis for the prevailing conception of Islamic culture during the sixteenth and seventeenth centuries. An English writer, Richard Knolles, in his *History of the Turks* (1603), refers to them as "the scourge of God and present terror of the world."[14] Even in England, the fear of Turkish expansion was strongly felt at this time, and any news of a Christian victory against Islam was cause for rejoicing.[15] In 1565, when Ottoman forces abandoned their long siege of Malta, a "form of thanksgiving" was issued by the archbishop of Canterbury that was to be read in all English churches every Sunday, Wednesday, and Friday.[16] Five years later, in 1570, Christians throughout Europe celebrated and performed prayers of thanks for the victory at Lepanto. But when the defeat of the Turkish fleet proved to be only a temporary setback to Ottoman expansion, a sense of dread returned. A short time later, in 1575, Thomas Newton wrote of the renewed Turkish menace: "They [the Saracens and Turks] were . . . at the very first very far from our clime and region, and therefore the less to be feared, but now they are even at our doors and ready to come into our houses"[17] Thirty years later there was still cause for alarm: an English tract on the Ottomans, printed in 1597, declares that "the terror of their name doth even now make the kings and princes of the West, with the weak and dismembered relics of their kingdoms and estates, to tremble and quake through the fear of their victorious forces."[18]

Despite such apprehensions about a shrinking Christendom, the English attitude toward the Ottoman threat was not simply and universally one of fear and loathing. As long as the Turkish expansion was at the expense of Roman Catholic powers, it was not, from the Protestant point of view, an altogether negative phenomenon. The Turks were often seen by the Protestants as a scourge sent by God to punish Roman papal pride, and some Protestant writers expressed a hope that the rival powers of pope and sultan would annihilate each other, leaving a power vacuum that might be filled by an expansion of the Protestant Reformation. Protestants often described the opposition to Roman Catholic rule and religion as a crusade against the "second Turk," the anti-Christ, or the Eastern "whore of Babylon." Luther is quoted as saying in *Table Talk* that "Antichrist is at the same time the Pope and the Turk. A living creature consists of body and soul. The spirit of Antichrist is the Pope, his flesh the Turk. One attacks the Church physically, the other spiritually."[19] In a 1587 sermon at Paul's Cross in London, William Gravet, a Protestant divine, also made the case for a link between pope and Turk, claiming that "the pope's supremacy and Mahumet's sect began both about one time (as is to be seen in the histories) and that was somewhat more than 600 years after Christ," and therefore "Mahumetism may go cheek by jowl with them."[20] This connection became a commonplace feature of Protestant historiography.[21]

Whatever the explanation for the rise of Islam and its resurgence under Turkish rule, it was a unified imperial force that put a weak and divided Christendom to shame. In England and throughout Europe, Christians described Islamic power as a clear and present danger. The Turks seemed capable of converting the entire world to their religion:

> They do think . . . that they are bound by all means as much as in them lieth, to amplify and increase their religion in all parts of the world, both by arms and otherwise: And that it is lawful for them to enforce and compel, to allure, to seduce, and to persuade all men to the embracing of their sect and superstitions: and to prosecute all such with fire and sword, as shall either oppose themselves against their religion, or shall refuse to conform and submit themselves to their ceremonies and traditions. And this they do to the intent the name and doctrine of their Prophet Mahomet may be everywhere, and of all nations, reverenced and embraced. Hence it is that the Turks do desire nothing more then to draw both Christians and others to embrace their religion and to turn Turk.[22]

For the anonymous author just quoted, and for the early modern Europeans in general, the prospect of conversion to Islam—by the sword or otherwise—

was a sensational subject that inspired anxious fascination.[23] English readers were offered numerous descriptions of the "Great Turk" and his court, and the quantity of material printed on the Ottomans and their culture and religion increased enormously during the seventeenth century. The account of Islamic doctrine and practice that appears in early modern texts bears little resemblance to the religion it purports to describe. In popular fiction and drama, pagan Saracens and idol-worshipping Moors alike pay homage to "Mahomet," "Mawmet," "Mahoun," or "Mahound," a deity who is often made part of a heathen pantheon that also includes Apollin, Termagant, and other devilish idols. One such representation of the "paynim knights" who worship Mahound is seen in a metrical romance entitled *The Sowdone of Babylon*. In this text, when the "sowdone" (i.e. "sultan") Laban is defeated by the Romans, one of his councilors says to him, "To tell the truth, our gods hate us. Thou seest, neither Mahoun nor Apollin is worth a pig's bristle." When the sultan has the idols brought before him, he tells them: "Fie upon thee, Apollin. Thou shalt have an evil end. And much sorrow shall come to thee also, Termagant. And as for thee, Mahound, Lord of all the rest, thou art not worth a mouse's turd."[24] He then has the idols beaten with sticks and thrown out of his tent.

While Muslims (or "Mahometans," as they were often called) were inaccurately depicted as pagans who had made an idol of their prophet, there was also a tendency to ignore their religious identity in favor of a label that signified a "barbaric" ethnicity. As Bernard Lewis points out,

> Europeans in various parts of the continent showed a curious reluctance to call the Muslims by any name with a religious connotation, preferring to call them by ethnic names, the obvious purpose of which was to diminish their stature and significance and to reduce them to something local or even tribal. At various times and in various places, Europeans called the Muslims Saracens, Moors, Turks, or Tatars, according to which of the Muslim peoples they have encountered.[25]

The Europeans' confusion of various Eastern ethnicities and their misunderstanding of Islamic religious practices were accompanied by a distorted picture of the Prophet Mohammed. When he was not depicted as an idol, Mohammed was described as a renegade and a fraud, and his religion was denounced as a heresy founded on deceit and spread by violence.

Late medieval and early modern accounts of the life of the Prophet and the establishment of Islam claim either that Mohammed was a Roman Catholic cardinal who was thwarted in his ambition to become pope, or that he was a poor camel driver who learned from a heretical Syrian monk to cobble together a new religion from fragments of Christian and Jewish doctrine.[26] These polemical biographies assert that he seduced the Arabian people by fraudulent "miracles" and black magic, convincing them by means of "imposture" that he was God's chosen prophet. The Koran is usually described in terms of contempt. The anti-Islamic propaganda directed against the Prophet and his Book are typified in a polemical dialogue written by William Bedwell, one of the first truly learned Arabists in England. The title of his tract, printed in 1615, gives a sense of the Western European attitude toward Islam: *Mohammedis Imposturae: That Is, A Discovery of the Manifold Forgeries, Falsehoods, and Horrible Impieties of the Blasphemous Seducer Mohammed: with a demonstration of the insufficiency of his law, contained in the cursed Alkoran.*

In Bedwell's text and elsewhere, Islam was narrowly defined and caricatured as a religion of violence and lust that advocated aggressive jihad in this world, and promised sensual pleasure as a reward in the next world. But if the doctrines of Islam were so obviously worthy of scorn, what could account for the rapid and widespread growth of Islam? Force of arms and successful military aggression, violent conversion by the sword—these are often cited by Christian writers in the early modern era as explanations for the astonishing achievement of the Islamic conquests. The early Arab Muslims are described as powerful bandits and plunderers, united by a voracious appetite for booty. According to Leo Africanus, a Moor who converted to Christianity during the early sixteenth century,

> there is nothing that hath greatlier furthered the progression of the Mahumetan sect than perpetuity of victory and the greatness of conquests. . . . In that the greatest part of men, yea, and in a manner all (except such as have fastened their confidence upon the cross of Christ and settled their hope in eternity) follow that which best agreeth with sense, and measure the grace of God by worldly prosperity.[27]

This is a standard argument made by Christian writers who needed to explain away the spectacular success of the Muslim conquerors. The notion that the victories of Islam were signs of divine favor was unacceptable, and so the rise of Islam and the expansion of the Ottoman empire were explained instead as a divine chastisement or "scourge" to punish backsliding Christians. This account of Christian defeat was founded upon biblical precedent: the ancient

Hebrew prophets had explained the sufferings and defeats of the Israelites as divine punishment for breaking their covenant with their god. The anxious question, "Whose side is God on?" is handled with irony in Marlowe's *Tamburlaine* plays; the same issue is raised in all three of the texts in this volume. In *A Christian Turned Turk*, for example, when Ward is being persuaded to forsake the Christian faith, Benwash, himself a convert, argues that if Islam "were so damnable / As others make it" (7.38–39), then God would have destroyed it long ago rather than allow it to prosper.

The early modern attitude toward Islam and its people is manifest not only in English accounts of Islamic theology or Turkish belligerence, but is also present in a fundamental and well-established set of stereotypes found in literature and art. In many fictional narratives, the unity of truth and the survival of Christian virtue are predicated upon the struggle against an evil empire in the East—an entity that is sometimes pagan, sometimes Islamic, and sometimes a confusion of the two. While depicting Islam and Christianity engaged in a Manichaean struggle, the early modern demonization of Islam tends to focus upon the overwhelming, absolute power of Islamic culture. In these representations, this unlimited power is often embodied in an Islamic ruler, sultan, or king whose authority over his subjects is compared to a cruel master's control over his slaves. It is therefore, by definition, an unjust, tyrannical, and oppressive rule. In *Selimus, Emperor of the Turks*, The Ottoman sultan Selimus, with his insatiable lust for power, is a typical example of this kind of oriental despotism.

The early modern images of Islam are contradictory, however, and may contain both positive and negative features. The Ottoman sultan was seen as a figure of tyranny, pride, and pomp leading an evil empire in a violent effort to conquer Christendom and extinguish the true faith. At the same time, Turkish accomplishments were admired, even envied, by some European observers. Sir Henry Blount, for example, writes in an account of his travels in the Levant: "He who would behold these times in their greatest glory could not find a better scene than Turkey. . . . [The Turks] are the only modern people, great in action . . . whose empire hath so suddenly invaded the world, and fixed itself such firm foundations as no other ever did."[28] For Blount and many others in England, the vast wealth, absolute hegemony, and steadfast discipline of the Islamic ruler and his loyal, united followers were cause for wonder and esteem.[29]

Closely related to the stereotypical conception of Turkish rule are the ideas of immense wealth and sensual luxury. These tend to be personal features of the Eastern potentate, but these images also refer to commercial realities—

particularly the huge profits to be made by trading in the ports of the southern and eastern Mediterranean, which include Tunis and Constantinople—the settings for the plays contained in this volume. Valuable luxury goods came to Europe from the East, including silk, carpets, spices, gold, and incense. English writers from Mandeville to Milton wrote of the spectacular wealth and exotic splendor to be found in the courts of African and Asian princes.[30] Accounts of vast riches are found in many early modern "descriptions" of foreign lands and palaces. The seraglio of the "Great Turk" in Istanbul was a focal point for European fantasies about sexual and economic excess.[31] Such images of Oriental wealth provided material for the spectacle of Renaissance theater and court masque. In Robert Greene's heroic play *Orlando Furioso* (1594), to cite one example, Orlando plans to defeat his Saracen foes and return to France for a wedding, his ship laden with luxury goods:

> Our sails of sendal spread into the wind;
> Our ropes and tacklings all of finest silk,
> Fetched from the native looms of laboring worms,
> The pride of Barbary, and the glorious wealth
> That is transported by the Western bounds;
> Our stems cut out of gleaming ivory;
> Our planks and sides framed out of cypress wood,
> . . . So rich shall be the rubbish of our barks,
> Ta'en here for ballast to the ports of France,
> That Charles himself shall wonder at the sight.
>
>   (lines 1586–1601)

This fabulous example of venture capitalism is a fanciful exaggeration, but such fictions were based upon the lucrative adventures of real merchants such as Roger Bodenham, whose 1550 voyage to Crete and Chios is recorded in Hakluyt's *Principal Navigations* (1598–1600) and includes hairbreadth escapes and skirmishes with Turkish galleys.[32]

The Mediterranean was the setting for many stories and "true reports" about Islamic power at sea and in commercial ports controlled by the Ottomans. Printed accounts of Turkish or Barbary galleys attacking Christian merchantmen confirmed the traditional association of Islam with acts of violence, treachery, cruelty, and wrath. In literature and legend, Saracens, Turks, and Moors frequently appear as ranting, fanatical killers who practice treachery, oath breaking, double-dealing, slavery, and piracy. From the Saracen knights of medieval romance to the Barbary pirates and Turkish pashas of early modern report, Western tales have depicted an Islamic predilection for the taking, imprisoning, and enslaving of captives.

There were also numerous printed narratives describing the exploits of renegades and pirates who had willingly joined the Moors and become part of the privateering communities in Algiers, Tunis, Tripoli, Sallee, and other North African ports.[33] These fascinating traitors and apostates were thought to have succumbed to the sensual temptations offered by life in Islamic society. The private life of wealthy Arabs, Moors, and Turks was said to be one of hidden sin, and their houses and palaces were supposedly designed for the indulgence of sensual and sexual pleasure. In European descriptions of Islamic society, the harem, polygamy, and concubinage were frequently presented as if they were universally practiced by the Muslims. As Samuel Chew has observed, "The interest of Europeans centered with a natural though often prurient curiosity upon the Seraglio . . . because in it were practiced, or were reported to be practiced, barbarous cruelties and extravagant sensualities which were none the less frequently described for being characterized as indescribable."[34] Courtly, upper-class customs—especially those of the Ottoman ruling class—were best known by European readers; published reports that offered a peep into the harem produced an image of Islamic sexuality that made the Ottoman sultan's palace a proverbial site for sexual excess, sadistic entertainment, and private, pornographic spectacle. In Shakespeare's *King Lear*, when Edgar, in his disguise as Poor Tom, recites his catalogue of courtly sins, he claims that he had "in women, out-paramoured the Turk" (3.4.92). Not only the Turk of Istanbul, but all Muslims of the ruling class were thought to be aggressively promiscuous. Mullisheg, the sultan of Fez in Heywood's *Fair Maid of the West*, demands quantity, quality, and variety in the supply of his harem:

> . . . what's the style of king
> Without his pleasure? Find us concubines,
> The fairest Christian damsels you can hire
> Or buy for gold, the loveliest of the Moors
> We can command, and Negroes everywhere.
> Italians, French, and Dutch, choice Turkish girls
> Must fill our Alkedavy, the great palace
> Where Mullisheg now deigns to keep his court.
>
> (4.3.27–34)

These lines demonstrate the link between cross-cultural commerce and sexual exchange that is frequently made in English representations of Islamic culture.

Both excess and repression are emphasized in Western accounts of Islamic sexuality. The notion of a veiled, hidden lust that masquerades as virtue and chastity is often a characteristic of the Islamic woman in English Renaissance texts. In *The Renegado,* the Ottoman princess Donusa embodies this contradiction. She acknowledges that Islam's sexual code "Allows all pleasure" (1.2.50), but with tyrannical pride she rejects a series of noble Muslim suitors. When she does fall in love, it is with a young Venetian gentleman, Vitelli, who she pursues aggressively and seduces with her power, beauty, and wealth. Vitelli succumbs to this temptation, as does Ward in Daborne's play. Voada, in *A Christian Turned Turk,* exemplifies the negative model of Islamic femininity. She is the beautiful but treacherous Muslim temptress whose true motives are cupidity and lust. Her allure is too much for Ward, bringing on his conversion and ruin. Voada is portrayed as essentially evil, while Donusa is a virtuous Muslim (like the stereotypical "good pagan") whose essential goodness has been corrupted by her false religion. As such, she is convertible: Donusa becomes a Christian and is "saved" by the love of a good Christian man.

The association of Islam and sexual sin drew upon and exaggerated certain Muslim beliefs and practices. In medieval and early modern accounts of Islam, "Mahomet's paradise" is described as a false vision of sexual and sensual delights with its nubile houris, rivers of wine, and luxurious gardens. One such account of Islamic eschatology is in *The Travels of Sir John Mandeville,* in which the author approves the Islamic belief in heaven, hell, and divine judgment, and goes so far as to acknowledge substantial compatibility between Islamic and Christian doctrine. But he finds the Muslims' description of paradise to be one of their greatest errors:

> if they are asked what paradise they are talking about, they say it is a place of delights, where a man shall find all kinds of fruit at all seasons of the year, and rivers running with wine, and milk, and honey, and clear water; they say they will have beautiful palaces and fine great mansions, according to their deserts, and that these palaces and mansions are made of precious stones, gold and silver. Every man shall have four score wives, who will be beautiful damsels, and he shall lie with them whenever he wishes, and he will always find them virgins.[35]

The erotic rewards of the Islamic afterlife were frequently condemned by Christian writers who also asserted that the attraction of conversion to Islam—and the reluctance of Muslims to convert to Christianity—was based primarily upon the greater sexual freedom permitted under Islamic law. Christian authors also saw a connection between the alleged sexual excesses of the Muslims or Turks and those attributed to the Moors or Black Africans, who are frequently described in the Western tradition as a people naturally given to promiscuity.[36] Whether imagined as a dark-skinned African Moor, or a robed and turbaned Turk, the external appearance of the Islamic Other was often read as a sign of spiritual darkness or barbaric ignorance. This point may be linked to one more aspect of Western stereotyping—the representation of Saracens, Moors, and Turks as embodiments of evil. The stereotype of the devilish Moor or cruel Turk was sometimes employed to demonstrate the supposed iniquity of Islam, and to portray Muslims as agents of Satan. Such representations occur frequently in popular culture, including the public theater, or in societies that had little direct contact with Islamic culture. It was difficult for more learned Europeans, or those who lived in closer proximity to lands ruled by Muslims, to demonize Islam in such a crude way. As Jack D'Amico has observed,

> [T]he problem of containing Islam, politically and intellectually, was made more difficult by those respects in which Islamic culture was actually superior. . . . A more potent and seductive foe, Islam, had to be represented as a dangerous distortion of the true Church, a parody of civilization, its Mohammed a false prophet, its Jihad a perversion of the Crusade, its book, the Koran, a collection of errors and lies that mocked the Bible.[37]

Nonetheless, there were Europeans who rejected both the popular and the learned demonizations of Islam; not all Europeans believed in the accuracy of the negative stereotypes. Some who traveled to the Islamic world and observed the achievements and institutions of that culture with their own eyes, were inspired to praise rather than revile what they saw. One such traveler was the Frenchman Jean Thevenot, who went to Turkey in 1652 and observed:

> There are many in Christendom who believe that the Turks are great devils, barbarians, and people without faith, but those who have known

them and who have talked with them have quite a different opinion; since it is certain that the Turks are good people who follow very well the commandment given to us by nature, only to do to others what we would have done to us.[38]

And the French philosopher Jean Bodin, writing in the sixteenth century, reported that

[t]he king of the Turks, who rules over a great part of Europe, safeguards the rites of religion as well as any prince in the world. Yet, he constrains no one, but on the contrary permits everyone to live as his conscience dictates. What is more, even in his seraglio at Pera he permits the practice of four diverse religions, that of the Jews, the Christians, according to both the Roman and Greek rites, and that of Islam.[39]

Such views, however, were rare and were not usually shared by Europeans who did not have the chance to visit the Middle East. It was not until the second half of the seventeenth century that voices in favor of toleration and openness toward Islam were widely heard.[40]

Unfortunately, the demonization and misunderstanding of Islamic society and religion remain prevalent in Western culture. Today, many of these stereotypes continue to shape the image of Islam produced by the mass media in North America, Europe, and other parts of the world.[41] If we examine, in particular, the representation of Islam in American journalism during the last thirty years, we will find ample evidence for an unbroken tradition depicting Islamic people as violent, cruel, wrathful, lustful, and the like. With the end of the Cold War, America needed a new ideological bogey to serve as an alleged external threat; perhaps this explains the recent resurgence of anti-Islamic imagery, a revival that draws upon a venerable tradition of demonization that began in the medieval period and acquired some of its present features in the sixteenth and seventeenth centuries.

Selimus, Emperor of the Turks

The play's full title in the 1594 printed edition is *The First Part of the Tragical Reign of Selimus, sometime Emperor of the Turks, and grandfather to him that now reigneth.* Both the title page and the "epilogue" of the 1594 text promise a sequel in which the Ottoman tyrant Selimus will go on to accomplish prodigious conquests. Selim I, who reigned from 1512 to 1520 as Selim the Inexorable, did in fact go on to conquer Syria, Egypt, and western Arabia. There is no evidence, however, that a second play recounting these events and concluding with Selim's death was ever written. In 1638, the unsold stock of the 1594 edition was reissued with a new first page bearing the title, *The Tragedy of Selimus, Emperor of the Turks,* but the text remained unsupplemented.

The 1594 quarto does not specify authorship, but an attribution to Robert Greene was established at the end of the nineteenth century by Alexander Grosart and this has never been convincingly refuted. The evidence in favor of Greene, both internal and external, is strong, especially in the appearance of two passages from *Selimus* that are identified as Greene's in Robert Allott's *England's Parnassus* (1600).[42] This evidence, however, is not incontrovertible, and the play's attribution to Greene will always be, in some sense, "doubtful." Furthermore, we cannot be certain that Greene wrote the entire play himself; it is quite possible that sections of the play were written by other playwrights working with Greene or by other authors who revised and perhaps added to the manuscript that went to the printer. It has been suggested by Kenneth Muir and other scholars that the portions of the play written in stanzaic verse are by a different hand than those in blank verse, or that the 1594 printed text represents a revised version of Greene's original. Despite these uncertainties and qualifications, I believe that Grosart and his supporters are correct. The play exhibits both a form and a content that is consistent with Greene's other writings, and so I will assume that Greene is at least the main author of the play.[43]

Robert Greene was born and baptized at Norwich in 1558. He enrolled in 1575 as a sizar at St. John's College, Cambridge University, where he took a B.A. in 1578, and an M.A. from Clare Hall in 1583. From 1585 until his death in 1592 he was living and working in London as a prolific writer of poetry, prose romances, moral tales, "coney-catching" pamphlets, and plays. Along with Marlowe and others, Greene is usually named as one of the "university wits," a group of writers with university degrees from Oxford or Cambridge who came to London in the 1580s and began writing scripts for the public playhouses. Greene made a precarious living from his writing, and his autobiographical works describe a life of poverty and dissipation. He was a vigorous participant in some of the literary quarrels of his day and is famous for calling Shakespeare "an upstart crow, beautified with our feathers" in his *Groatsworth of Wit* (1592). *Selimus* and *Alphonsus of Aragon* (ca. 1588) were probably Greene's earliest plays. Later plays include *Orlando Furioso* (1589), *Friar Bacon and Friar Bungay* (1589–90) and *James IV* (ca. 1590). *Selimus* was probably written soon after Marlowe's *Tamburlaine* plays were first staged during the winter of 1587–88. Greene's own remarks in the preface to his *Perimedes the Blacksmith* (published 29 March 1588) indicate a calculated attempt to compete with and imitate the bombastic new style established by Marlowe in the wildly popular blank verse drama that was "daring God out of heaven with that atheist Tamburlaine."[44] Greene most likely composed the play in early 1588, when it was added to the repertoire of the Queen's Men. There is evidence that when plague restricted performance in London from 1592 to 1594, the company took *Selimus* on tour in the provinces.[45]

Marlowe's *Tamburlaine* plays, with Edward Alleyn in the title role, made huge profits for Philip Henslowe's company, the Lord Admiral's Men. The Queen's Men were their rivals and competitors. Following the trend set by Marlowe, the Queen's Men also began to perform plays that featured exotic settings and conquering, blustering antiheroes in the Tamburlaine mold. In *Selimus*, as in *Alphonsus, King of Aragon*, Greene indulges in heavy-handed imitation of Marlovian drama. Greene must have hoped that the success of his *Selimus* would be like that of *Tamburlaine, Part I*, and that a sequel would be demanded. This sequel, *Selimus, Part II*, would present the sultan's foreign campaigns of conquest and would end with his death.

Greene's main sources for his plot were early modern descriptions of the Ottoman court and historical narratives that chronicled the career of Selim himself. The two most important sources—texts that Greene almost certainly drew upon—are Thomas Newton's 1575 translation of Augustino Curione's *Sarracenicae Historiae libri III* (Basel, 1567) and Peter Ashton's 1546 translation of Paolo Giovio's *Comentarii della cose de Turchi* (Florence, 1531).[46] The plot of *Selimus* is based on the events described by Giovio in chapters nine ("Of Bayazet the second, the ninth emperor of the Turks") and ten ("Of Selimus the tenth emperor of the Turks"). Greene may well have consulted other sixteenth-century descriptions of the Ottoman court, as there were numerous works available that dealt with this subject.[47]

Greene's play is based upon historical events that took place between January 1511 and April 15, 1513 (the date of the battle of Yenişehir). The drama presents the brutal exploits of the Ottoman prince, Selimus, who overthrows and poisons his father Bajezet and murders his older brothers, Acomat and Corcut, to gain sole rulership of the Ottoman empire. In Greene's dramatization, these events are not always represented with historical accuracy. It was not accepted as a certainty, for example, that Selimus was responsible for his father's death, or that Bajezet was poisoned. In the play, Selimus' early career is depicted in a sensationalized and simplified form: Greene's Selimus is a monster and a caricature, a prodigy of egotism without compassion. Selim the Inexorable did in fact kill his own brothers, his nephews, and later, all of his own sons except his handpicked successor, Suleiman. He was a harsh and unprincipled sovereign who was feared and hated by many of his own subjects. Greene's Selimus goes further in vice: he is also a self-declared atheist who denounces religion as a "bugbear." Like Tamburlaine, Selimus is never defeated or punished for his "unnatural" actions or bold blasphemies. The play is a study in monomaniacal cruelty, revealing a merciless Machiavel at work. Despite his irreligious statements and murderous actions, Selimus is triumphant at the end and, having set his house in order, he decides to rest before carrying out a series of foreign campaigns.

Until recently, *Selimus* has been of interest mainly to readers of early modern theater because of its connection to the drama of Christopher Marlowe and its imitation of Marlovian language and plot. Critics have noted the influence of both Spenser and Marlowe in *Selimus*, and they have also seen significant connections between three texts—Greene's *Selimus*, the anonymous tragedy *Locrine* (printed in 1595), and Shakespeare's *King Lear*, with *Selimus* exerting a palpable influence on Shakespeare's great tragedy. This influence is most striking in the similarity between Selimus' cruel treatment of the wise old counselor, Aga, whose eyes are put out while a character named Regan looks on, and the blinding of Gloucester in *King Lear*.[48]

When placed next to the other two plays in this volume, *A Christian Turned Turk* and *The Renegado*, *Selimus* clearly represents an earlier phase in the development of the London theater. At the time that Greene wrote *Selimus*, most Elizabethan plays were still rooted in the deep structures of traditional homiletic drama. David Bevington has shown how Marlovian theater developed and diverged from this tradition, and *Selimus* followed very closely the pattern defined by Marlowe's phenomenal success.[49] *Selimus, Emperor of the Turks* exhibits many of the typical features of the Elizabethan tyrant play and the neo-Senecan spectacle of wrath, revenge, and violence, complete with grisly acts of mutilation performed on stage. Its dramatic structure is derived from the conventions established in homiletic tyrant plays like *Cambyses, Horestes, Gorboduc*, and *Titus Andronicus*, plays that enact a providential punishment for tyranny, cruelty, and irreligious behavior. Greene's play, in imitation of Marlowe's *Tamburlaine, Part I*, violates generic expectations for the providential punishment of tyranny and blasphemy. Like the *Tamburlaine* plays, *Selimus* works against conventional expectations for the providential fall of the proud tyrant.

Another feature of *Selimus* that marks it as a play written around 1590 is the formal, static quality of its language, organized in long, set pieces of blank or rhyming verse, sometimes in the form of stichomythic dialogue. It is written mostly in iambic pentameter lines, including many that rhyme. This is in contrast to the more dynamic, colloquial language of the later plays by Daborne and Massinger. The stern militarism and moralizing of *Selimus*, expressed in a rigid prosodic pattern, is relieved only in the scenes featuring Bullithrumble, who speaks in prose and sings a comic ditty. The sudden appearance of this English, Christian clown in the Islamic world of the Ottoman empire is an example of the seriocomic clowning that was common on the tragic stage of the 1580s and 1590s. Bullithrumble is the direct descendant of Hob and Lob in Preston's *Cambyses* (composed during the 1560s) and a precursor of Shakespeare's country fools. The part of the shepherd Bullithrumble may well have been written for Richard Tarleton, the famous slapstick comedian who performed with the Queen's Men.

When Bullithrumble meets the philosopher-prince in hiding, Corcut, we are shown a scene from an old tale well known in the native English tradition: a persecuted prince or knight is forced to seek solace and safety in the pastoral world (like the Duke in Shakespeare's *As You Like It*). English audiences must have delighted in witnessing this homespun English fool appear in the deadly serious world of Islamic foreigners. Suddenly, a familiar bit of English clownery is incongruously thrust into the world of imperial politics, intruding upon the murderous intrigues of the Turkish court. Unlike Corcut or Acomat, Bullithrumble is able to escape death easily—he simply turns tail and runs like the coward and survivor he is.

Greene's play does not emphasize the erotic element that is often highlighted in Western representations of Islamic culture and is central to the other two Turk plays in this volume. The Turkish women in *Selimus* act only as supporters of their husbands' and male relatives' honor, offering defiance to the enemies of their men and soliciting pathos from the audience when they become victims. Greene's focus throughout is on the militarism of the Turks and on the actions and passions produced by the lust for power. Erotic urges or temptations do not interfere with or complement Selimus' desire to eliminate all other competitors for the imperial crown. Selimus never hesitates in his effort to mount the Ottoman throne over a pile of dead bodies, and he commits parricide, fratricide, and massacre to achieve his goal.

Turkish sultans were known in the West as great warriors and conquerors, but they were also famous for killing the other members of their nuclear family and for suddenly ordering the execution of trusted advisors. Many early modern descriptions of the Ottoman sultan and his court depict the Turkish ruling class as cruel, murderous, and arbitrary. Of course this was not mere fiction but was based on historical fact; the actions of the Turkish royal family gave the anti-Islamic polemicists of Western Europe plenty of material to confirm their preconceived notions of oriental despotism. The Great Turk became a European bogey partly on the strength of a dynastic track record of executions, poisonings, strangulations, and general familicide. *Selimus* is a play about a family at war with itself and a political order that achieves internal peace only through internecine slaughter and attrition. Once Selimus eliminates all rivals for the Ottoman throne, he can pause before turning his inexorable will toward conquest, and this is as much closure as the plot provides.

It was not only the horrid events inside the seraglio that thrilled and chilled Elizabethans, but also a sense of the Great Turk as an epic-scale conqueror and his armies as a horde of cruel and fearless fighters. Elizabethans reacted to the news of the Turkish conquests in Europe and the Mediterranean with fear and fascination. They knew that the Turks were a real threat and that their continued expansion had pushed the borders of Christendom back even further since the days of Selim I. In 1588, when Greene's play was first performed, the problem of a foreign invasion mounted by an "evil empire of religious heretics" was very much on the minds of Londoners preparing for the Spanish armada to invade their shores. The theater of Marlowe and Greene projected anxieties about Philip of Spain and his power into the exotic distance of Anatolia or Persepolis. Simon Shepherd has shown how plays like *Tamburlaine* and *Selimus* also expressed widespread concerns in Elizabethan England about royal succession and monarchical tyranny.[50]

The tyranny of Selimus is amplified by his blasphemous rejection of divine right, a principle he dismisses with the scorn of a monomaniacal atheist.[51] Selimus' faith is in his own ability to succeed by means of his Machiavellian willpower. He is triumphant, even glorified, at the end of the play despite his blasphemous assertion that "The names of gods, religion, heaven and hell" are "mere fictions" created by those in power to "strike / Into our mind a certain kind of love. . . . To keep the quiet of society" (2.98–115). Perhaps the most striking passages from Greene's play are the speeches in which Selimus derides the basic precepts of religious faith, providence, and morality. In one such passage, he plainly denies the very existence of God:

> I count it sacrilege for to be holy,
> Or reverence this threadbare name of "good."
> Leave to old men and babes that kind of folly;
> Count it of equal value with the mud:
> Make thou a passage for thy gushing flood,
> by slaughter, treason, or what else thou can.
> And scorn religion—it disgraces man.
>
> (2.15–21)

For Elizabethan theatergoers, these lines would have been disturbingly transgressive, providing electrifying moments for the audience, who gasped to hear such fearless defiance of divine law, and became increasingly uneasy later in the play as Selimus' sins went unpunished. Despite these anxieties, it was easier for an English audience to countenance the staging of such sin when it came from an Islamic character. The English stage had a long tradition of representing Middle Eastern tyrants who blustered and boasted of their wrongdoing, but Selimus and his lack of moral principle were affiliated with a clear and present danger to Christendom—he could not be mocked as lightheartedly or dismissed as easily as a bogey from long ago and far away, such as a Herod or a Cambyses.

At the end of the play Selimus announces that he will pause to enjoy the well earned rest of a "weary, wandering traveler" (29.35), but he also speaks a warning that may have resonated with ominous meaning for a London audience that was living under the threat of a Spanish invasion and conversion by the sword: "And now to you, my neighbor emperors / That durst lend aid to Selim's enemies: / . . . Egypt and Persia, Selimus will quell / Or he himself will sink to lowest hell" (29.67–71). This vow rings with irony because the Turkish atheist has specifically rejected the notion of an afterlife. For London audiences there would be a further irony in the knowledge that Selimus was to be successful in conquering Persia and Egypt. They knew that the Ottoman armies would make good on their sultan's parting boast, that Selimus would go on to risk all and win. The English audience could only take comfort from their belief that, whatever the worldly success of Selimus had been, his ultimate fate was to be damned "to lowest hell."

A Christian Turned Turk

The author of *A Christian Turned Turk* was born between 1580 and 1583 and was named after his father, Robert Daborne, Senior (1551?–1612). The father was a London merchant who invested in overseas trade ventures to Spain and elsewhere, which may account for Daborne's knowledge of seafaring life and piracy. Little is known of Daborne's early life. By 1609 he was married to an Anne Younger, with children, and living in his father-in-law's house in Shoreditch. There is some evidence that he had previously attended Cambridge University and graduated with a Master of Arts degree.[52]

Daborne's earliest known involvement in the London theater business was his association with the theatrical entrepreneur and musician Philip Rosseter and others in a reorganization of the Queen's Revels Children at the Whitefriars playhouse.[53] On 4 January 1610 a warrant was issued for Robert Daborne and "others the queen's servants . . . to bring up and practice children in plays by the name of the Children of the Queen's Revels."[54] By early 1613, Daborne was writing for Philip Henslowe's company, the Lady Elizabeth's Men. A series of letters from Daborne to Henslowe written between April 1613 and July 1614 have been preserved among the Dulwich manuscripts collection.[55] These letters record Daborne's collaboration with other playwrights working for Henslowe, including Philip Massinger, and they testify to an intimate relationship between playwright and patron that involved Henslowe in Daborne's financial problems.[56] After the death of his father, Daborne and his family became entangled in a complex series of legal disputes over debt, inheritance, and the sale of inherited property. Apparently the cost of these legal proceedings impoverished the playwright, who on one occasion appealed to Henslowe to bail him out of debtor's prison. These letters to Henslowe indicate that Daborne, like others who worked for Henslowe's theater, became legally and financially "bound" to his employer. Daborne's correspondence with Henslowe is wheedling and plaintive, full of promises and excuses for delays in delivering the latest scripts.[57] While Henslowe may have helped him with loans, these debts also put Daborne under pressure to repay Henslowe by providing more plays or parts of plays for his employer and creditor.

Although Daborne wrote a series of plays for Henslowe, only two texts are extant. One is *A Christian Turned Turk,* and the other is *The Poor Man's Comfort.*[58] The title page declares that this second play "was divers times acted in Drury Lane with great applause." It is a pastoral tragicomedy set in Arcadia, with disguised aristocrats and virtuous shepherds as its characters. It was performed at the Red Bull by Queen Anne's company some time between 1615 and 1617 and, perhaps, after 1617 at Beeston's Cockpit in Drury Lane.[59] Little else is known of Daborne's career as a playwright. In 1618 he left London and went to Ireland, where he served as a clergyman until his death in 1628.

The 1612 quarto edition is the only known version of *A Christian Turned Turk.* There is no evidence that it was ever reprinted. The date of composition must be between 1609—when Daborne's principal sources were first available—and 1612—when the quarto was printed. The play was probably written for performance by Rosseter's Queen's Revels company at the indoor Whitefriars Hall theater located just outside the city walls near the Inns of Court. Daborne's business associations at the time with Robert Keysar, a goldsmith and theater manager-entrepreneur (to whom Daborne owed money in 1608), and Philip Rosseter suggest that Daborne was working for the companies managed by Keysar and Rosseter—the Blackfriars Boys, the King's Revels Boys, and subsequently the primarily adult company, the so-called Queen's Revels Children, a company that re-formed from a merger of the other two after the long plague closure of 1609–10.[60]

Daborne based the plot of *A Christian Turned Turk* on events recounted in two pamphlets, both printed in 1609: Andrew Barker's *True and Certain Report of the Beginning, Proceedings, Overthrows, and now present Estate of Captain Ward and Dansiker, the two late famous Pirates* . . . (London, 1609) and the anonymous *News from Sea, Of Two Notorious Pirates, Ward . . . and Dansiker* (London, 1609). Barker's narrative condemns Ward as a renegade, traitor, and thief. Nonetheless, in spinning a good rags-to-riches yarn, Barker's *Report* makes Ward into an attractive antihero. This ambivalent attitude toward piracy is present in both pamphlet accounts. We see a positive image conveyed, for example, by the words of another pirate, William Graves, who had served under Ward's command: "[T]hese last three years, quoth he, [Ward] is grown the most absolute, the most resolute, and the most undauntedest man in fight, that ever any heart did accompany at sea. And if his actions were as honest as his valor is honorable, his deeds might be dignified in the chronicles with the worthiest."[61] It was not only his bravery and resolution, but also his extraordinary ascent from poverty to luxury that made

Ward an appealing antihero. He was born in Faversham in Kent, and in *News from Sea* his humble origins are described: "[H]is parentage was but mean, his estate low, and his hope less."[62] In 1603, having settled in Plymouth, he found employment as a common seaman serving on a royal ship—the *Lion's Whelp*—in the Channel Squadron. Within two years he had become a wealthy freebooter cruising the Mediterranean and commanding a powerful ship of two hundred tons with thirty-two guns and a crew of one hundred.

In 1606 Ward reached an agreement with the Ottoman commander of the Janissaries in Tunis, Cara Osman (this is the "Crosman" of *A Christian Turned Turk*), to use Tunis as the base for his piratical operations. There followed a spectacular series of raids on Christian ships, culminating in the capture of the six hundred-ton Venetian argosy, the *Reniera e Soderina*, near Cyprus in 1607. This great ship was carrying a cargo of cotton, cinnamon, indigo, and silk worth more than £100,000. After each raiding expedition Ward would return to Tunis and sell his booty to Cara Osman at very low prices. Cara Osman would then resell at a huge profit.

Thomas Mitton, who had spent three years in Tunis and had served under Ward's command, gave this testimony to the admiralty court:

> [T]he said Carosman is the only aider, assister and upholder of the said Ward in his piracies and spoils for that he (the said Ward) hath no other place to victual save only at Tunis, and at Tunis he could not victual but by the means of Carosman who graunteth him (the said Ward) warrants to take up and buy victuals at Tunis and the country thereabouts. And the reason that moveth the said Carosman so to do is because when Ward taketh any prize Carosman buyeth his goods of him at his own price.[63]

Born and raised a lowly fisherman, Ward became a roving king of the sea with his own private navy, beholden to no Christian monarch.

The negative portrait of Ward in Barker's *True and Certain Report* and *News from Sea* can be contrasted, to some degree, with the daring figure celebrated in several popular ballads (see Appendix 1). These ballads praise Ward's audacity and celebrate his victories over foreign ships, but they reserve some condemnation for his awesome crimes against God and the English king. Passages such as the following, from a ballad printed in 1609, indicate the popular perception of Ward's accomplishments:

The riches he hath gained,
And by bloodshed obtained,
Well may suffice for to maintain a king;
His fellows all were valiant wights,
Fit to be made prince's knights,
But that their lives do base dishonors bring.[64]

Barker's pamphlet confirms the stories of Ward's "royal" status, reporting that Ward "lives there in Tunis in a most princely and magnificent state. His apparel both curious and costly, his diet sumptuous, and his followers seriously observing and obeying his will."[65] *News from the Sea* tells its readers that Ward "hath built a very stately house, far more fit for a prince, than a pirate," and claims that the viceroy of Tunis has allowed him a personal guard of twelve Turkish janissaries. Furthermore, "[h]is respect and regard is reported to be such with the Great Turk, as he is made equal in estimate with the Bashaw."[66]

The ambivalence displayed in these representations of Ward's exploits is similar to the mixture of acclaim and opprobrium bestowed by English writers upon the "luxurious" Islamic rulers of the Middle East. The renegade captain Ward is "orientalized" in these reports; he takes on many of the features of the stereotypical oriental despot—wealth, luxury, tyranny, sensual and sexual vices, and so on. He is an "admirable villain," a paragon of wealth and valor who exemplified the success and autonomy that may be achieved through an unruly masculine virtue that is willing and able to defy the rules laid down by the Christian authorities.

Barker's biography of Ward condemns the pirate leader in the same way that Islamic potentates were stereotyped and demonized on religious grounds. Barker accuses Ward and his followers of monstrous sins including "concupiscence and covetousness," "sodomy," and "atheism." *News from Sea* also describes a sensationally sinful man whose crew of renegades are "pampering and fatting themselves with the poison of their souls."[67] While Barker's text sometimes acknowledges the boldness and bravery of his exploits at sea, it reviles Ward's onshore behavior in Islamic territory, where "he was diverted and abased to most vile actions, clothing his mind with the most ugly habiliments that either pride, luxury, or cruelty can produce from the blindness of unruly desires."[68]

Daborne used these sources freely, adding many details that were not included in the pamphlets. Daborne's play clearly echoes, however, the moralizing providentialism found in the pamphlets. In *News from the Sea* there are many passages lamenting the power of death, fortune, and destiny to control human beings and limit their aspirations and enterprises. Similar sentiments are expressed throughout Daborne's play, and it seems likely that the playwright drew some inspiration from the proverbial wisdom offered in passages such as this: "nothing is there in this world but is transitory like ourselves: our life is not permanent; no more is our fortunes. We have joy in this minute and sorrow in the next."[69]

The most notable difference between the "true reports" and Daborne's playscript is in the staging of the pirate's demise. The pamphlet sources acknowledge that in 1609 the real John Ward was alive and well. In 1608 a Venetian who had been to Tunis described Ward, who was about fifty-five years old at the time. This description does not sound much like the swashbuckling blusterer and passionate lover of Daborne's play: "Very short and with little hair, and that quite white, bald in front; swarthy face and beard. Speaks little, and almost always swearing. Drunk from morn till night. Most prodigal and plucky. Sleeps a great deal, and often on board when in port. The habits of a thorough 'salt.' A fool and an idiot out of his trade."[70] Ward lived to the age of seventy and never committed the tragic suicide that is dramatized in Daborne's play.

The apogee of Ward's career came in 1607; in the years that followed, his ships suffered a series of setbacks. These circumstances led Ward to initiate negotiations with various authorities for a formal pardon. The Venetian ambassador to England, Zorzi Gustinian, reported in October 1607 that Ward had formally applied to James I for a pardon, offering, in exchange for his own amnesty and that of three hundred followers, to return ships, guns, and commodities valued at more than thirty thousand crowns, and to cease all piratical activities.[71] Pirates who asked for pardon often received generous terms, especially if they made the traditional statements of repentance and agreed to pay fines.[72] After several unsuccessful attempts to obtain amnesty on his desired terms (first from James I, later from the grand duke of Florence), Ward resumed piratical operations from his base in Tunis. There he formally converted to Islam and married a second wife, a renegade woman from Palermo. (He had left behind a wife in England, to whom he tried to send money.) According to the Scottish traveler William Lithgow, who claims to have visited Tunis in 1616, Ward had built a "fair palace beautified with rich marble and alabaster stones," and lived there with a group of "English runagates, whose lives and countenances were both alike, even as des-

perate as disdainful."[73] Ward continued his career as an active pirate in sub-
sequent years, but not with the same success or notoriety. He is reported to
have ransomed and freed Englishmen enslaved in Algiers and Tunis. Apparently, he never returned to England and died in Tunis, probably during an
outbreak of the plague in 1623.

Ward was not the only English corsair to prosper under Islamic sponsor-
ship. Other English renegades went further than Ward and became powerful
admirals in the Turkish navy. Most notable among them is Sampson Denball,
another English convert to Islam who, after the assassination of Cara Osman
in 1610, took the name Ali Reis and became admiral of the galleons of Youssef
Dey, the Turkish ruler who succeeded Cara Osman.

The period immediately before and after the staging of *A Christian Turned
Turk* was one in which piracy strongly affected English trade through the
Straits of Gibraltar. It was a commercial crisis that continued throughout
the early decades of the seventeenth century. James I issued a series of royal
proclamations against piracy, including a proclamation that accuses "Captain
John Ward and his adherents, and other English pirates" of "diverse great and
enormous spoils and piracies" (see appendix 2). Andrew Barker wrote in his
dedicatory epistle, warning English authorities about the Barbary pirates' in-
creasing "success at sea":

> It is most lamentable to report how many ships of London and other
> parts of England have been taken and made prey unto them, [and]
> without the help of [English renegades], the Turks by no means could
> have governed and conducted them through their unskillfulness and
> insufficiency in the art of navigation. Yet of late, to my woeful experi-
> ence, I can witness they have been so readied by the instruction of our
> apostate countrymen (I mean of Ward and others, who have been their
> commanders) to tackle their ships, to man and manage a fight, that if it
> do not please God to move the heart of his Majesty and other Christian
> princes and states to join together for their speedy suppression and the
> disjointing of their late strengthened forces, which continually increas-
> eth by the ships of England and Holland which they daily surprise, it
> will be discommodious to the state, and so dangerous to the common-
> wealth, in succeeding times, that Christendom must expect no traffic
> at sea.

England, France, Holland, and Spain all raised fleets and carried out search-
and-destroy missions against the Barbary pirates during the first two decades

of the seventeenth century. The targets of those raids, located along the Barbary coast of North Africa, included Tunis, the setting for both *A Christian Turned Turk* and Massinger's *The Renegado*.

English sailors who turned Turk were condemned for their crimes against Christianity, but piracy itself was not necessarily considered an evil pursuit. Many English Protestant pirates saw their activities as a continuation of justifiable hostility against Roman Catholic Spain, even after James had made peace with Spain in 1604. An aggressive and patriotic impulse carried over from that earlier era during which the English crown had sponsored and encouraged privateers who preyed upon Spanish shipping.[74] After 1603, high unemployment among English seamen encouraged them to pursue an unlawful livelihood at sea; there were fewer legitimate jobs, and many of these were badly paid and toilsome. According to Barker, it was just this sort of nostalgia for the Elizabethan freebooting days that Ward invoked during his successful mutiny on the *Lion's Whelp*, the royal vessel he took over when he first turned pirate. He reportedly urged the other discontented sailors to recover their former liberties:

> 'Zblood, what would you have me say? Where are the days that have been, and the seasons that we have seen, when we might sing, swear, drink, drab, and kill men as freely as your cakemakers do flies? When we might do what we list, and the law would bear us out in't? Nay, when we might lawfully do that we shall be hanged for and we do now? When the whole sea was our empire, when we robbed at will, and the world but our garden where we walked for sport?[75]

Life on a pirate ship, even as a low-ranking crew member, was much freer and more profitable than serving as a seaman on a law-abiding merchantman, and piracy was preferable to life under the miserable conditions aboard royal ships. According to one historian, "Sailors on merchantmen could not expect [to earn] more than £10 a year, whereas a pirate [crew member] could hope to make as much from one prize."[76] Given the difficult circumstances of most Englishmen employed as sailors, to turn pirate or even to become a renegade was understandable and appealed to many seamen who were offered the opportunity.

Furthermore, what constituted a "criminal" act of piracy on the high seas was not clear in the early modern era. Accusations and counteraccusations of piracy were bandied about by various powers in the Mediterranean and elsewhere, but the norm was a sphere of economic activity in which might made right. Every encounter with another ship or group of ships was potentially dangerous. There were opportunities for the profitable taking of booty, but there was also the danger that a more powerful adversary would come along. Everything depended upon the identities and relative technical advantages of the converging ships. Traders and merchantmen habitually combined commerce and theft. Pillage was a routine, legitimate part of any commercial venture or voyage of "exploration." The Age of Discovery was also the Age of Plunder. A case in point is the famous voyage of Sir Francis Drake in *The Golden Hind.*

If the distinctions between pirate and privateer, outlaw and honorable seaman, renegade and loyal subject, were not clear or stable, it also seems that, despite official pronouncements, pirates were not stigmatized or universally condemned. In fact, there was clearly a sense of popular admiration for the exploits of some pirate captains. For patriotic Englishmen, piracy was not seen as essentially dishonest, especially if directed against foreigners, and larceny on the high seas could receive popular approbation and admiration as a sort of "Robin Hood" activity that did not harm the commonwealth and brought cheap goods into British markets. Pirates had little difficulty finding buyers for their stolen goods in the Mediterranean or the British Isles, and they were able to engage in open exchange with merchants in Ireland and the West country.

The Barbary corsairs roamed the main, but this did not deter English merchants from trading in the Barbary ports themselves. Sometimes merchants from France, England, or other European nations traded directly with pirates like Ward. John King of Limehouse, for example, reported that in 1608, while he was exchanging goods in Algiers, Ward came into the harbor with two prizes—a French ship laden with oil, cochineal, and hides, and a Spaniard with "alligant wines." In a case of friendly barter, the homesick English pirate gave the merchant a tun of red wine in exchange for a tun of beer.[77]

After the accession of James I in 1603, the English government began a prolonged effort to crack down on the institution of piracy. The king himself was particularly irritated by complaints that reached him at court about English freebooters like Ward. A number of James's royal proclamations articulate an official willingness (if not a workable policy) to reduce and punish these transgressions. There are also numerous depositions and records extant from the English High Court of Admiralty that attest to the predations of Ward and others and record the countermeasures taken by the English authorities. Though Ward remained free, many other pirates were captured and brought to the gallows at Execution Dock in Wapping, where the scaffold was built below the tide line, and the dead bodies were traditionally left to be covered by the waters of high tide three times before they were removed.

Once a pirate captain had made his fortune, it was tempting to quit while ahead, given the risks involved in continued piracy. With some accumulated wealth at his disposal, a successful corsair could easily buy a pardon from a king or an amenable Italian principality, such as Savoy, and retire in a courtly style. When English pirates were offered amnesty by the king in 1612, they were told that if they surrendered and promised to cease their predations they would be allowed to keep the wealth they had obtained from plunder.

The other famous pirate featured in Daborne's play, Simon Dansiker, did receive a royal pardon. (Dansiker was also referred to as Danseker, Dantziger, Danser or Dansker.) He, too, is a real historical figure and, like Ward, was the subject of popular ballads. Dansiker is often identified as a Dutchman, though he was in fact a Fleming from Dordrecht who began his career as a ship's master in Flushing, the Dutch port of Vlissingen.[78] In the Venetian reports he is often associated with or compared to Ward; they were the two most effective pirates in the Mediterranean-North Atlantic sphere in the first decade of the seventeenth century. An English supercargo reported in October 1608 that Dansiker was operating just outside the Straits of Gibraltar with a fleet of four pirate ships manned by Dutch, English, and "Turkish" crews, and that in one month's plundering he had captured twenty-nine ships off the coast of Spain, near San Lucar.[79] His base was Algiers, but word reached the English court in 1609 of his pardon by Henry IV, "on the condition that he quits piracy and his quarters in Algiers and goes to Marsailles."[80] In October, Giacomo Vendramin, a Venetian living in Florence, reported that "Danziker has revolted against the Algerines and slain one hundred Turks and freed three hundred slaves. He then went to Marseilles where he took booty to the value of four hundred thousand crowns. He was met by the Duke of Guise with every sign of joy. . . . There will be trouble. This is expected to be the utter ruin of Ward. God grant it be so."[81] In 1609 Dansiker did leave Algiers for Marseilles, where he accepted a royal pardon, went into French service as a privateer, and continued to attack English and Spanish shipping. Dansiker traveled to the French court with the duke of Guise, who was then the governor of Provence, and reportedly repaid the duke for his support at court with a large bribe. When the Spanish ambassador to the French court protested the capture of a Spanish galleon by Dansiker, the king refused to punish Dansiker and "held that he [Henry IV] had rendered a service to Spain and other nations by clearing the sea of such a famous pirate." [82] The French king may have been plotting to employ Dansiker in a naval attack on the Genoese, but after Henry IV was assassinated Dansiker returned to Marseilles, where he reportedly planned to attack Algiers while flying the French flag. [83]

There are conflicting reports about the death of Dansiker, but one story matches, to a limited degree, the version of Dansiker's death staged in Daborne's play. In 1609 Antonio Foscarini, the Venetian ambassador in Paris, received letters from Marseilles confirming that Dansiker had led a French fleet against Algiers, but when he came ashore to parley with the local bey, "he was deceived by the Bey of the pirates, made prisoner and has paid by his death for his excessive credulity and the thousands of murders he committed in former times." [84] News of Dansiker's death may have reached London just before Daborne's play was first staged. [85]

The historical record confirms what both of the pirate plays printed here show—that relations between English renegade pirates and their Turkish overlords were not always harmonious. Problems intensified after a series of incidents that occurred during the early seventeenth century. Both *A Christian Turned Turk* and *The Renegado* feature renegade pirates who regret their apostasy and turn against their Muslim masters. These representations of renegades betraying and delivering crippling blows to their Muslim sponsors are imaginative expressions of political, military, and economic ambitions that were achievable only to a limited degree. Christian armies and navies deployed against the Barbary pirates in the seventeenth century scored a few small successes and experienced several large-scale defeats. Occasionally Christian ships raided North African harbors intending to cripple the Muslim maritime economy, but this was contrary to the promotion of peaceable, profitable commerce, and business was normally conducted in a posture of humble submission to Muslim port authorities and their policies.

In 1609, however, Don Luis Fajardo, a Spanish admiral, accomplished a mission of sabotage in the harbor at Goletta, where he destroyed much of the Tunis pirate fleet by sending in fire ships at night. [86] This attack may be what Daborne had in mind when he has Dansiker and some other pirates blow up the pirate ships in the Tunisian harbor. Two years later, in September 1611, Captain Gifford, an English renegade based in Algiers, offended by the way that the dey of Algiers had handled the purchase of Gifford's prize, succeeded in setting the harbor on fire and destroying most of the Algerine fleet. This made things difficult for Ward, who arrived in Algiers soon after, at a time when English pirates were no longer trusted. Consequently, Ward was forced to leave Algiers for Tunis.

In Tunis and other places under Islamic rule in the Mediterranean, renegades were able to gain considerable freedom, wealth, and authority—to a degree that would have been nearly impossible for English seamen serving on English merchant vessels. Le Sieur de Brèves, a Frenchman who visited Tunis in 1606, observed:

> The great profit that the English bring to the country, their open-handed ways and the excessive debauches in which they spend their money before leaving town and returning to the war (for that is what brigandage at sea is called), has made them cherished and supported by the janissaries above all nations. No one else is noticed but them; they carry their swords at their sides and run drunk together through the town, without ordinary Christian people, usually outspoken by nature, daring to stand up against them. They sleep with the wives of the Moors and when discovered, buy their way out of being shot; the penalty which others have to suffer without remission. In short, every kind of debauchery is allowed them: even that which is not tolerated among the Turks themselves.[87]

In return for this favorable treatment, English, French, and Dutch renegades helped teach Moors and Turks about the latest nautical and military technologies. From them, Turkish shipbuilders gained important knowledge about building and sailing the new "round ships" or "galliots" that were faster and more maneuverable. Renegades living among the Muslims also shared information about how to manufacture guns and cannons used on ships and on the battlefield. Captain John Smith, in the last chapter of his *Travels*, describes how "the Moors knew scarce how to sail a ship. . . . those [renegades] were the first that taught the Moors to be men of war," and explains how seamen who had served lawfully against Spain turned renegade after James made peace.[88] Lithgow confirms Smith's assertion:

> For true it is, the natural Turks were never skillful in managing of sea battles, neither were they expert mariners, nor experienced gunners, if it were not for our Christian runnagates, French, English, and Flemings (and they are too subtle, accurate, and desperate fellows) who have

taught the Turks the art of navigation, and especially the use of munition, which they both cast to them and then become their chief cannon-
eers, the Turks would be as weak and ignorant at sea as the silly Ethio-
pian is unexpert in handling of arms on land. For the private humor of
discontented castaways is always an enemy to public good, who from
the society of true believers are driven to the servitude of infidels, and
refusing the bridle of Christian correction, they receive the double yoke
of despair and condemnation. Whose terror of a guilty conscience, or
rather blazing brand of their vexed souls, in forsaking their Faith, and
denying Christ to be their Saviour, ramverts most of them, either in
a torment of melancholy, otherwise in the ecstasy of madness: which
indeed is a torturing horror that is sooner felt than known and cannot
be avoided by the rudeness of nature, but by the saving grace of true
felicity.[89]

Lithgow's account, like that of Daborne's play, exaggerates in order to demonize the renegades. In truth, many of these pirates who had turned Turk were
accepted, contented members of the thriving corsair communities at Tunis,
Algiers, Sallee, and other ports. Once they returned home to port with their
booty, they usually sold these goods to Jewish or Muslim merchants. These
merchants often resold the stolen commodities to Christian merchants. Local
rulers from Morocco to Egypt tolerated and encouraged the pirates to operate
out of their ports because the trade resulting from plunder was good for the
local economy. As time went on, some of these ports, including Tunis, came
to rely upon freebooting and the slave trade as the mainstay of their economy.
These ports not only served as harbors for the corsair community, but they
also became trading centers where merchants from all over the Mediterranean
could buy and sell. The commodities bought and sold included human beings—captives who were taken and sold in the slave markets. If a merchant
ship surrendered peaceably to the Barbary corsairs, the pirates would usually
not take the crew captive as part of the spoils, but they would often do so if
the ship resisted. This piratical law of the sea, like Tamburlaine's colored tents
threatening the besieged city, is recorded in a letter from the masters of the
Charity and the *Pearl* (two English vessels captured by Ward and his confed-
erates) appended to *News from Sea:*

For this was a decree amongst them (which they had established should
stand irrevocable) that what Christian soever they met (be he of what

country soever) if he submitted not upon the first summons or durst be so hardy as to outdare them with the least blast of breath: if he were taken he should be a slave; if not taken, they would sink them in the sea.[90]

In both of Daborne's sources, there is mention of a group of discontented pirates under Ward who mutinied and stole a ship. Daborne's sources also describe a situation similar to the sea battle that occurs in the early scenes of *A Christian Turned Turk*, although Daborne does not follow the original story closely.

According to Barker and *News from Sea*, Ward was far crueler than Dansiker. The difference between them is illustrated in an incident recounted in *News from Sea*. After being robbed by Ward's men and then ransacked by his Turkish collaborators, the English ship *Charity* was released—but without ammunition or food. Five days later the *Charity* encountered "Captain Dansker of Argier" in a well-armed man-of-war. Dansiker, however, proves to be "an honest pirate" who "scorned to rob an hospital, to afflict where was misery before, or to make prey of them had nothing left."[91] He let the *Charity* go, an act that was not motivated by mercy alone, as he had already captured two richly laden ships (a Flemish and an English merchant) and had his hands full. Dansiker also acceded to the request of some of the English victims to be placed on shore: "when he not only condescended to their request, but also gave them four shillings apiece, to carry them up into the country of Spain."[92] The authors of a letter printed in *News from Sea* conclude that "Ward makes prey of all, and Dansker hath compassion of some: the one contemning to be charitable to any; the other holding it hateful to take any thing from them who labor in continual danger to maintain their lives. And we have heard that the like cause as this was the falling out betwixt these two pirates. For certain they are now at difference."[93] When pirates like Dansiker or Ward took a prize, the people on board that ship were often taken prisoner and brought back to the corsair's home port. Ransoms would be arranged for some while other captives would be sold into slavery. Many of the captives enslaved by Muslims would be encouraged to turn Turk. Some English Christians willingly converted to Islam in order to pursue the career of "Turkish" piracy, while others converted in order to better their lot after having lost hope of being ransomed or "redeemed." In addition to the English renegades, there were some English held in North Africa as slaves who remained Christian. By the 1620s there were thousands of English captives there. In 1624 a petition was presented to the House of Lords concerning, "the humble and lamentable

complaint of above 1,500 poor captive souls, now under the miserable oppres-
sion of the Turks in Argier, Tunis, Sally, and Tituane."[94] Parliament ordered
a general collection of monies throughout England for the redemption of the
captives, and the king issued letters patent for that purpose.

When captives were brought to the slave markets of Algiers or Tunis to be
sold, Jewish merchants sometimes acted as middlemen and were known to
purchase both slaves and other commodities obtained by piracy. These merchants were part of the Jewish communities that thrived under the relatively
tolerant rule of the Ottoman empire. In the late fifteenth and early sixteenth
centuries, a period of intensified anti-Semitic persecution had begun, resulting in the expulsion and migration of Jews from Iberia, Germany, and other
parts of western Europe. Large numbers of Jewish refugees migrated to the
Ottoman empire during that time and, by the early seventeenth century, had
become well established in many cities under Turkish rule. The Ottoman
conquest of Syria, Palestine, and Egypt in 1517 encouraged Jewish immigra-
tion to these areas. Tunis was reconquered by the Turks in 1574. During the
sixteenth century, "the Ottoman Jewish communities emerged as the fore-
most centers in the world, rivaled, perhaps, only by those of Poland and Lith-
uania."[95] The Ottoman empire appealed to Jewish immigrants because of its
religious tolerance, cultural pluralism, and multiethnic society, as well as the
economic opportunities it provided. Jewish citizens of the Ottoman empire
enjoyed much more freedom than their co-religionists under contemporary
Christian rule, and some Jews were even granted a tax-exempt status for their
service to the Turkish state, or for performing administrative duties within
the Jewish community itself. The Ottoman authorities came to regard Jewish
residents as economically productive and politically dependable. Their mana-
gerial and entrepreneurial skills were employed by the expanding bureaucracy
of the Turkish empire, especially in the areas of tax collection, custom farm-
ing, banking, and minting. In Istanbul, Jews were the third largest ethnic
group after the Turks and Greeks, and they played an important role in international trade throughout the empire.

This alliance between Muslims and Jews under Ottoman rule raised many
Jewish merchants and dignitaries to impressive positions of power and wealth.
When Ottoman officials were sent to administer distant provinces, it was a
frequent practice to hire a local Jew to serve as a private banker, commercial
agent, and financial advisor.[96] The relationship between Benwash and the
Muslim officials in *A Christian Turned Turk* represents an awareness of this
kind of special relationship between Ottoman viceroys and Jewish entrepre-

neurs. Since it was customary for a Jew to hold the office of merchant-banker to the janissary corps, and of chief financier and purveyor for the Ottoman military elite, these Jewish officials must have been on close terms with powerful janissary officers. We see in *A Christian Turned Turk* the triangular trade relationship of the western European renegade, the Ottoman overlord, and the Jewish middleman—all of them profiting from piracy that targeted Christian shipping in the Atlantic and Mediterranean.

Scholars of Mediterranean history have argued that the important role Jews played in building the Ottoman Empire (what Avigdor Levy has termed "the Jewish-Ottoman symbiosis") contributed significantly to Western anti-Semitism. Anti-Semitism and anti-Muslimism are both assumed by the plays in this volume. Abraham, the Jew who appears in *Selimus*, is a figure from a long-standing anti-Semitic tradition representing Jews as treacherous "cunning men"—herbalists, apothecaries, or physicians with special skills in both healing and poisoning. But Benwash in *A Christian Turned Turk* is a new kind of caricature, whose characteristics reflect the role of Jewish merchants in the Mediterranean economy, which the English were coming to know more intimately by the early seventeenth century.[97]

Daborne's play exhibits European anti-Semitism with a twist: a Jewish merchant converts to Islam in order to protect his wife from the sexual predations of the Muslims in Tunis. The traditional stereotype of the Jew as a trickster and miser is drawn upon, and certainly Marlowe's Barabas is an important model for Daborne's Benwash, especially in the scene during which his house burns down. Benwash's concern for his wife and his wealth are a rewriting of Barabas's frenzied concern for his daughter and his ducats. But Benwash is not a father figure like Barabas or Shylock; rather, he is a husband and cuckold. The erotic significance of conversion to Islam is highlighted in his own conversion. He, too, is a renegade, but his Muslim status is not stressed.

In *The Jew of Malta*, Barabas, who is loyal to neither Christians nor Turks, makes the following statement: "They say we are a scattered nation." The culture of early modern England describes Jews as parasitical vagabonds, both outcast and invasive. According to the western European representations of the time, they occupy no stable national or geographical position—they are a kind of "runagate" people, subversive of both the social and economic order, and economically aggressive as well. A typical articulation of this anti-Semitic stereotype is this reference made in passing by Nicolas de Nicolay, a French traveler in the early modern Mediterranean: "this detestable nation of the Jews

are men full of malice, fraud, deceit, and subtle dealing, exercising execrable
usuries amongst the Christians and other nations without any consciences or
reprehension, but have free licence, paying the tribute: a thing which is so
great a ruin onto the country and people whereto they are conversant."[98] Since
the expulsion of the Jews from England by Edward I in 1290, the only people
of Jewish origin permitted to reside in England were "conversos" from Spain
and Portugal, or other Jews who had turned Christian. But even these people
were considered by the English to be radically unalterable in their essential
Jewishness. An English theologian, Andrew Willet, wrote in 1590: "A Jew . . .
whether he journeys into Spain, or France, or into whatever other place he
goes to, declares himself to be not a Spaniard or a Frenchman, but a Jew."[99]
Thus Benwash, though he has formally converted to Islam, is still identified
as "the Jew" of Tunis.

Although Daborne's stage Jew, Benwash, exhibits some new features that
refer to the special role of the Jewish community in the Ottoman economy
during the seventeenth century, it may also be said that the alliance of Benwash the Jew with Crosman the Turk is not only a representation of an economic relationship, but also of an ideological one. Recently, Alan and Helen
Cutler have argued that modern anti-Semitism finds its origins in the anti-
Muslimism of the late Middle Ages. The Cutlers have pointed to a tendency
in the Western Christian tradition "to associate Jew with Muslim . . . and to
consider the Jew an *ally* of the Muslim as well as an Islamic fifth columnist in
Christian territory."[100] Because of a perceived ethnolinguistic similarity and
because of their geographical proximity to the Muslims, the Christian crusad-
ers began to attack Jews as well as Muslims, and tended to affiliate and confuse these two groups. Medieval anti-Islamic polemics refer to a proverb, "A
Jew is not a Jew until he converts to Islam," which indicates the moral and
religious affinity perceived by hostile Christian authors.[101] Again this reminds
us of Daborne's Benwash, whose essential and unchanging Jewish identity is
merely confirmed by his conversion to Islam. Ironically, Benwash turns Turk
to prevent the lustful Turks from seducing his wife and is then cuckolded by
a Christian fool and coward, Gallop.

Like Benwash, Ward turns Turk for a woman's sake, and both cases
demonstrate the conventional association of religious conversion with sexual
temptation. Ward's choice is clearly marked as the triumph of libido over both
faith and reason. Alizia tries to warn him against conversion: "Sell not your
soul for such a vanity / As that which you term 'beauty,' eye-pleasing idol!"
(7.207–8). But Ward cannot resist the charms of Voada, and for his crime he

will suffer death, defeat, and damnation—a providential punishment. Daborne's play is the tragedy of a man who puts love before religion and then despairs of God's mercy.

Dansiker is Ward's foil, a renegade pirate who returns to serve the Christian king of France and is pardoned. Unlike Ward, he seeks and receives mercy. Dansiker successfully proves his loyalty to Christendom when he achieves his mission of atonement, and assassinates Benwash before committing suicide to avoid torture and execution by the Turks. Ward's suicide, which follows immediately, is less heroic and more damnable. Like Othello at the end of Shakespeare's play, Ward kills the woman he loves and then turns his sword on himself, assuring and confirming his damnation. He dies cursing, offering himself as an example to all future pirates and renegades: "Let dying Ward tell you that heaven is just, / And that despair attends on blood and lust" (16.320–21). Daborne's fiction rewrites the biography of Ward to give force to the play's didactic function, but it is interesting to consider that London playgoers were probably aware that Ward was still alive and prospering, a reality that may have tinged the tragic ending with irony.

The Renegado

Philip Massinger, the author of *The Renegado*, was baptized on 24 November 1583 at the parish church of St. Thomas in Salisbury. His father was Arthur Massinger, who served as a legal agent and steward in the household of Henry Herbert, second earl of Pembroke, at Wilton. Philip studied for several years at St. Alban's Hall, Oxford, but apparently left without taking a degree. Little is known of Massinger's doings until 1613 when, along with Richard Daborne and a third playwright, Nathan Field, he signed his name to a letter pleading for financial assistance from his employer, the playhouse owner and manager Philip Henslowe. Field, Daborne, and Massinger asked Henslowe for a loan to bail them out of debtor's prison. This "tripartite letter" is the first evidence of Massinger's activity as a playwright and indicates that he was working as one of Henslowe's team of writers at that time. Other records link the names of Massinger and Daborne, indicating that they both worked for Henslowe for many years, and that both lived during this time in continual poverty and debt.[102]

Although in 1613 he was undistinguished and impoverished, Massinger was later to become one of the leading dramatists writing for the English

stage. Following in the footsteps of William Shakespeare and John Fletcher, Massinger worked as principal playwright for the King's Men from
1625 until his death in 1640. He is the sole author of at least fifteen extant
plays, and he shared in the authorship of over twenty more as a reviser or
collaborator.[103]

The date of composition for *The Renegado* is late 1623 or early 1624. This
dating is supported by the record of Sir Henry Herbert's license for performance on 17 April 1624. The play was one of a series of comedies and tragi-
comedies that Massinger penned during these years for Christopher Beeston's
companies at the Phoenix playhouse, also known as the Cockpit. *The Renegado* was staged for the first time during the brief period—December 1623 to
October 1626—when Massinger had left the King's Men and was writing
for the Lady Elizabeth's Men, and then for Queen Henrietta's Men.[104] *The
Renegado* may have been performed initially by the Lady Elizabeth's Company, who were based at the Cockpit from the summer of 1622 until the public theaters were temporarily closed following the death of James I in March
of 1625.[105]

Unlike Daborne's *A Christian Turned Turk,* which seems not to have been
a success on the London stage, *The Renegado* was well received by seventeenth-century playgoers. The frontispiece of the 1630 edition says that it was
"often acted by the Queen's Majesty's servants, at the private playhouse in
Drury Lane." This refers to performances staged by Queen Henrietta's Men
at the Cockpit. There is evidence that it was frequently performed during the
1630s and up until the closing of the theaters in 1642: for example, *The Renegado* was still in demand in 1639 when Beeston deemed it worthy of inclusion
in a list of plays protected against performance by any other London companies.[106] It was then revived on the Restoration stage by the King's Men, who
mounted a production in 1662.

Some of the sources Massinger consulted when composing *The Renegado*
were available only in Spanish. These include several works by Cervantes: the
most striking parallels are with Cervantes's comedy *Los baños de Argel* (*The
Prisons of Algiers*), which was published in *Ocho comedias y ocho entremeses nue-
vos* (1615). Massinger's play also draws upon "The Captive's Story" from *Don
Quixote, Part 1,* which was translated and printed in English in 1605, and from
"The Liberal Lover," published in the *Novelas ejemplares* in 1613. These texts,
engendered by Cervantes' personal experience as a captive in Algiers, provided ideas for the plot set in Tunis, another center for piracy and slavery.
Massinger also consulted several contemporary tracts describing Islamic cul-

ture, most notably Biddulph's *The Travels of Certain Englishmen into Africa, Troy, Bythnia, Thracia, and to the Black Sea* (1609), George Sandys' *Relation of a Journey* (1615), and Richard Knolles's *General History of the Turks* (1603).[107]

The play's setting, the Barbary pirate community of Tunis, is the same as that of Daborne's Turk play. Most of the scenes in Massinger's play take place in the viceregal palace where the lustful and tyrannous Asembeg rules in the name of the Great Turk, but the first scene of *The Renegado* occurs in the common marketplace, where Christian merchants are permitted to sell their wares openly and publicly. Within this sphere of commerce and exchange, the desire for profit leads to other lusts, and the market becomes a site of temptation and potential contamination.

As in Daborne's play, religious conversion is offered as an erotic temptation. *The Renegado* also dramatizes the conventional association of Islam and sexual sin: Vitelli's priestly mentor, Francisco, warns Vitelli about the sexual aggression of Muslim women:

> . . . these Turkish dames
> (Like English mastiffs that increase their fierceness
> By being chained up), from the restraint of freedom,
> If lust once fire their blood from a fair object,
> Will run a course the fiends themselves would shake at
> To enjoy their wanton ends (1.3.8–13).

Despite this admonition, Vitelli fails when he is put to the test. Posing as a merchant selling cheap goods in the market, he gains the attention of the beautiful Ottoman princess, Donusa. When she unveils herself before him, Vitelli beholds her as a "wonder." Later, when secretly admitted to her quarters (a "forbidden place / Where Christian yet ne'er trode"), Vitelli is awed by her beauty, power, and wealth (2.4.32–33). Her exotic charms and social status reverse the normative dynamic of power and gender, compelling Vitelli to submit to a woman's will.

At first, Massinger's play seems to offer a rewriting of Daborne's plot, but Vitelli repents and resists temptation. Francisco, Vitelli's Jesuit mentor, chastises him for his sexual liaison with Donusa, and rather than converting to Islam for love, Vitelli eventually succeeds in converting Donusa to Christianity. It is interesting that Massinger's Christian *raisonneur* has the same name as Daborne's—Francisco. This similarity, among others, indicates that Massinger may have been consciously responding to the earlier play, rewriting it

with a happier ending. In *The Renegado,* the tragic Ward-Voada relationship is reconfigured in the happy outcome of the Vitelli-Donusa relationship.
Donusa herself resembles a conventional figure from the romance tradition—
the virtuous Saracen maiden. The stock situation involves an Islamic princess
who is converted to Christianity after falling in love with a virtuous Christian
knight.

While Christianity was tolerated under Islam, for a Muslim to turn Christian was considered apostasy under Islamic law and was a capital crime. Even
today, Islamic law and custom do not permit a Christian man to marry a
Muslim woman unless he first converts to Islam. On the other hand, a Muslim man is permitted to marry a woman who wishes to remain Christian after
marriage. This was noted by Harry Cavendish, an Englishman who visited
Constantinople in 1589: "No Christian man may have to do with a Turkish
woman, but she shall die for it if it be known, but a Turk may have as many
Christian women as he will." [108] This perception of Muslim sexual standards
informs Massinger's play, especially in those scenes that dramatize the murderous jealousy of the Islamic potentates, Asembeg and Mustapha, who discover the relationship of Donusa and the Christian Vitelli. They carry out
the will of the Great Turk, Amurath, whose judgments are conveyed in a
sinister "black box" and then read publicly. The Ottoman sultan commands
the execution of his own niece because she commits the crime described by
Cavendish.

Donusa's power and independence as a Muslim woman are contrasted
with the slavery of Vitelli's sister, Paulina, who has been sold to Asembeg.
She becomes the captive object of Asembeg's raging lust, and only a sacred
charm with protective powers prevents the viceroy from raping her. Grimaldi,
the play's "renegado," was the pirate who captured Paulina and sold her to
Asembeg. He eventually returns to the Christian fold, but only after his ill-
gotten wealth is confiscated by the Turks, and not without a harrowing spiritual struggle. Grimaldi (like Ward) is an unruly man of blunt speech who is
punished by his Muslim masters for his bitter insolence. Like Dansiker, he
repents before it is too late and comes to serve the Christian cause again. His
moral recovery is preceded, however, by a steep descent into despair. Grimaldi's desperate condition is brought on by a guilty conscience that leads
him to believe he deserves damnation. Grimaldi's spiritual struggle reflects
the seventeenth-century understanding of religious conversion and its psy-
chology. There were well known cases involving apostates who attempted to
rejoin Christianity but were agonized or destroyed by remorse and hopeless-

ness. Most notable was the case of the Italian lawyer, Francis Spira, who publicly renounced his Protestantism at St. Mark's in Venice, and then came to believe that God had abandoned him. He threatened suicide and became convinced that he was possessed by the Devil. Finally, despite the ministrations of various priests, he died of starvation.[109] The Spira story was widely disseminated and was certainly known to Massinger, who may have been thinking of Spira's recantation in St. Mark's when he has his apostate, Grimaldi, commit an act of blasphemy in the same church. Grimaldi experiences the sufferings and near madness of Spira, but in the end he is rehabilitated and restored to sanity by Francisco.

Restored to Christian virtue, Grimaldi becomes the reformed renegade that neither Ward, nor even Dansiker, could be. Grimaldi's unruly masculinity is recuperated for the service of Christendom, and he aids in the escape plot that concludes the play. When Vitelli and Donusa are about to be executed, Paulina suddenly offers herself to Asembeg; by doing so, she is able to delay their execution. The play's conclusion stresses the definitive Turkish vice of lust, which proves a weak point for the Christians to exploit. All of the Christians escape, leaving Asembeg in a state of despair, facing torture and death at the hands of the Ottoman authorities—a fate that in Daborne's play was the lot of Ward and Dansiker. Both Donusa and Grimaldi forsake Islam, escaping from Tunis with their bodies and souls intact. Thus *The Renegado* might have been subtitled "A Turk Turned Christian": Massinger's tragicomedy rewrites *A Christian Turned Turk* and reverses the outcome of Daborne's tragedy by affirming the power of Christianity to "redeem" both Muslims and renegades.

Conclusion: Mediterranean Multiculturalism

The three Turk plays in this volume, along with the other multicultural Mediterranean plays performed on the London stage, offered their audiences an exhilarating, frightening spectacle. Audiences were given a vicarious sense of the dangerous but potentially profitable exchanges that took place in the Mediterranean world, where identity, status, and freedom were always at risk, and where conquest and conversion threatened. English theatergoers who lived in London, where foreign trade was becoming more important with each passing year, were increasingly aware of the power of the "Grand Seigneur" in Turkey, and of the complex manifestations of Islamic domination in the maritime sphere and in central Europe. Their perception of Islamic culture and people is not, however, the "orientalism" described by Edward Said, with its essentializing binary opposition of Western self to Eastern other.[110] The analogy to individual consciousness as it is presented in Said's *Orientalism* reduces a web of unstable signifiers to a monolithic signified called "the oriental other." In the early modern period there is not yet a construct such as Said's "Orient"; it is a far more confused and complicated set of images and conceptions we see articulated, for example, in the drama of sixteenth and seventeenth-century England.

The complexity and instability of early modern identity is inscribed in the Turk plays printed in this volume. In these texts the question of identity is a vexed one. The plays present a plurality of others—Turk, Moor, Jew, Christian, renegade, heretic, pagan. The Mediterranean world is represented in these three plays without clear national borders or neat ethnic categories. Rather, these texts display a disorderly set of shifting categories that attempt to make sense of the porous cultural mélange that made up the Islamic Mediterranean.

The realm of the Turks was exciting and alluring: it was a place where huge profits could be made from a single successful voyage, but it was also replete with the risks, both imaginary and real, of conversion and contamination. English merchants sought commercial contact and exchange, but the transculturation they witnessed and reported sometimes seemed frightening to them. Coming from a place where only Christianity was tolerated (and exactly what kind of Christianity was always a troubled question), it was difficult to accept a social order in which Christians, Jews, and Muslims of various sects were living side by side in relative harmony. These exotic hybridities and fluidities of identity provided fascinating but troubling subject matter for a group of plays performed at the public playhouses.

Greene's *Selimus* is tightly focused on one character, an Ottoman sultan whose tyranny and atheism comprise an "admirable" example of power pursued and attained without moral constraint. The murderous, self-serving audacity of Selimus is the absolute opposite of the political ideal of "commonwealth," and during a period when Spanish invasion forces menaced England, Selimus' presence on the London stage would certainly have reminded spectators of the threat to the English Protestant commonwealth posed by another demonized despot, Philip of Spain. In *A Christian Turned Turk* and *The Renegado*, the threat to an autonomous English Protestant identity is not concentrated in a single, monstrous potentate. Instead, the danger to the Christian commonwealth is both interiorized and complicated. In the seventeenth century, Muslim power is represented as a more complex and various force because commercial interests brought more Englishmen into direct contact with Islamic culture throughout the Mediterranean region. Trade with the Turk and peace with Spain had changed the cross-cultural context. The seventeenth-century interest in the renegade or the temptation of conversion indicates a shift in the modes of representation used to depict Islamic culture. A comparison of *Selimus* and contemporary tyrant plays of the Armada era to later Turk plays reveals this transition from a simpler structure of representation to a more complicated, multiplex sense of cultural vertigo. Greene's play stresses the demonization of Muslim power in the form of the evil tyrant, while the other two plays printed here offer a more complex web of relations. This web threatens to entrap or convert those Englishmen who traveled to Islamic lands to pursue trade and profit. Islamic tyranny is still present in characters like Daborne's Governor of Tunis and Massinger's Asembeg, but it is the figure of the convert, not the tyrant, that occupies the center of the two later works. In these "renegade" plays, Christian men of virtue and talent are tempted by Islamic wealth and Muslim women: they undergo an internal battle between will and appetite, with their souls at stake. For Ward, Danseker, Vitelli, and Grimaldi, the interior struggle against lust, cupidity, and false faith leads either to "redemption" or to death and damnation.

Notes

1. In 1603, when *Othello* was first performed, English audiences knew that the Venetian attempts to protect Cyprus had failed. Cyprus had been conquered in 1571 and remained firmly in Turkish hands. The menace of Muslim power lurks offstage in several of Shakespeare's plays set in the Mediterranean, including *Othello, Twelfth Night, Much Ado About Nothing,* and *The Taming of the Shrew.*

2. For further analysis of Othello as a figure whose tragic fall is a "conversion" to "Turkish" cruelty, violence, etc., see Daniel J. Vitkus, "Turning Turk in *Othello:* The Conversion and Damnation of the Moor," *Shakespeare Quarterly* 48 (Summer 1997): 145–76.

3. A full account of such plays may be found in chapter 4 ("Moslems on the London Stage") of Samuel Chew's *The Crescent and the Rose: Islam and England during the Renaissance* (Oxford: Oxford University Press, 1937; reprinted New York: Octagon, 1965), 469–540.

4. See Fernand Braudel, *The Mediterranean and the Mediterranean World in the Age of Philip II,* 2 vols. (London: Collins, 1972), 1:626.

5. *Calendar of State Papers, Domestic,* 1611–18, 427. See David D. Hebb, *Piracy and the English Government, 1616–1642* (Scolar Press, 1994), 149.

6. According to David D. Hebb's recent assessment, "[B]y the early seventeenth century the character of the operations of the Barbary pirates had changed dramatically." Increasingly, they used "tall ships" instead of galleys, and they began to move out of the western Mediterranean into the Atlantic, taking captives as far north as Iceland. Pirates from the Barbary ports captured "on average, seventy to eighty Christian vessels a year between 1592 and 1609" (Hebb, *Piracy,* 15).

7. See Nabil Matar, "'Turning Turk': Conversion to Islam in English Renaissance Thought," *Durham University Journal* 86 (1994): 37.

8. Important studies of Mediterranean piracy during this period include the following: Alberto Tenenti, *Piracy and the Decline of Venice, 1580–1615* (London: Longmans, 1967); John B. Wolf, *The Barbary Coast: Algiers Under the Turks, 1500 to 1830* (New York: Norton, 1969); Peter Earle, *Corsairs of Malta and Barbary* (London: Sidgwick & Jackson, 1970); and Godfrey Fisher, *Barbary Legend: War, Trade, and Piracy in North Africa, 1415–1830* (Oxford: Clarendon, 1957).

9. *Calendar of State Papers, Domestic,* 1623–25, 516. For an interesting look at this petitioning in the context of Caroline politics, see Nabil Matar's "Wives, Captive Husbands, and Turks: The First Women Petitioners in Caroline England," in *Explorations in Renaissance Culture* 23 (1997): 111–28.

10. Cf. Clem in *The Fair Maid of the West, Part I,* who offers to accept the "cutting honor" of becoming chief eunuch under the Moorish sultan Mullisheg. At the end of the play he runs onstage pursued by a razor-wielding Moor and exclaiming, "No more of your honor, if you love me! Is this your Moorish preferment, to rob a man of his best jewels?" (5.2.126–7). Quoted from the text edited by Robert K. Turner (Lincoln: University of Nebraska Press, 1967).

11. See, for example, the two sermons published together in Edward Kellett, *A Returne from Argier. A Sermon Preached at Min[e]head in the County of Somerset the 16. of March, 1627, at the re-admission of a relapsed Christian into our church.* [Includes "A Returne from Argier, A Sermon . . . by Henry Byam," with a separate title page.] (London, 1628).

12. The "Form of Penance . . . of a Renegado" is reprinted in *The Works of Joseph Hall,* 12 vols. (Oxford: D. A. Talboys, 1837–39), 12:346–50.

13. W. M. Watt, in *Muslim-Christian Encounters: Perceptions and Misperceptions* (London: Routledge, 1991), 88.

14. Richard Knolles, *History of the Turks* (London, 1603). Knolles's characterization of Turkish culture draws upon the stereotype described in C. A. Patrides, "'The Bloody and Cruell Turke': The Background of a Renaissance Commonplace" (*Studies in the Renaissance* 10 (1963): 126–35.

15. See chapter 3, "'The Present Terror of the World,'" in Chew, *The Crescent and the Rose.*

16. *A Short Forme of Thanksgiving to God for the Delyverie of the Isle of Malta* (1565), reprinted in *Liturgical Services of the Reign of Queen Elizabeth: Liturgies and Occasional Forms of Prayer set forth in the Reign of Queen Elizabeth*, William K. Clay, ed. (Cambridge: Parker Society, 1847): 527–35.

17. In the dedication to his English translation of Coelius Augustinius Curio, *A Notable History of the Saracens* (London, 1575).

18. Anonymous, *The Policy of the Turkish Empire* (London, 1597) sig. A3v.

19. Cited in Kenneth M. Setton, "Lutheranism and the Turkish Peril," *Balkan Studies* 3:1 (1962), 151.

20. William Gravet, *A Sermon Preached at Paules Cross . . . intreating of the holy Scriptures, and the use of the same* (London, 1587), 50–51.

21. See, for example, the discussion of the Turks' rise to imperial power in John Foxe, *Actes and Monuments*, 2 vols. (London, 1596), 1: 675 ff.

22. *The Policy* sig. B4v–B5r.

23. See Nabil Matar, "Turning Turk."

24. Cited in Chew, 392.

25. Cited in Bernard Lewis, *Islam and the West* (London: Oxford, 1993), 7.

26. On the polemical biography of Mohammed, see chapter 3, "The Life of Muhammed" in Norman Daniel, *Islam and the West: The Making of an Image* (Edinburgh University Press, 1960); the section on "'Makomet and Mede': The Treatment of Islam," in Dorothee Metlitzki, *The Matter of Araby in Medieval England* (New Haven: Yale, 1977), 197–210; and chapter nine, "The Prophet and his Book," in Chew.

27. Leo Africanus, *The History and Description of Africa*, Robert Brown, ed., John Pory, trans., 3 vols. (London: Hakluyt Society, 1896), 3:1019.

28. *A Voyage into the Levant* (London, 1636), 2–3.

29. See, for example, R. M., *Learne of a Turke; or instructions and advise sent from the Turkish Army at Constantinople to the English army at London* (London, 1660).

30. For more information on the movement of merchant ships and commodities between Europe and the Middle East during this period, consult T. S. Willan, "Some Aspects of English Trade with the Levant in the Sixteenth Century," *English History Review* 70 (1955): 399–410; and Ralph Davis, "England and the Mediterranean, 1570–1670," *Essays in the Economic and Social History of Tudor and Stuart England in Honour of R. H. Tawney*, F. J. Fisher, ed., (London: Cambridge, 1961), 117–37.

31. See, for example, Robert Withers, *A Description of the Grand Signor's Seraglio, or the Turkish Emperor's Court* (London, 1650).

32. Reprinted in Richard Hakluyt, *Voyages and Discoveries*, Jack Beeching, ed. (NY: Penguin, 1972), 52–55.

33. For an account of how these renegades were represented in English culture, refer to Nabil Matar, "The Renegade in English Seventeenth-Century Imagination," *Studies in English Literature* 33 (1993): 489–505.

34. Chew, 192. For a few more summaries of such accounts see Chew, 192–95.

35. *The Travels of Sir John Mandeville,* C. W. R. D. Moseley, ed. (London: Penguin, 1983), 104.

36. See Jack D'Amico, *The Moor in English Renaissance Drama* (Tampa: University of South Florida Press, 1991), 63 ff; and Eldred Jones, *Othello's Countrymen: The African in English Renaissance Drama* (London: Oxford, 1965), 1–26.

37. D'Amico, 75–76.

38. Cited in Bernard Lewis, *Islam and the West,* 80.

39. Cited in Paul Coles, *The Ottoman Impact on Europe* (New York: Harcourt, Brace, 1968), 151.

40. See, for example, the authors cited in Nabil Matar, "Islam in Interregnum and Restoration England," *The Seventeenth Century* 6.1 (Spring 1991): 57–71.

41. Edward Said has made this point eloquently and persuasively in his book, *Covering Islam: How the Media and the Experts Determine How We See the World* (New York: Pantheon, 1981). See also John L. Esposito, *The Islamic Threat: Myth or Reality?* (Oxford: Oxford University Press, 1992) for a more recent treatment of the subject.

42. See Alexander B. Grosart's introduction to *Selimus, Emperour of the Turkes* in the first volume of *The Life and Complete Works in Prose and Verse of Robert Greene,* 15 vols. (London, Watson and Viney, 1881–86; reprint, New York: Russell & Russell, 1964), 71–77 (page citations are to the original edition). Grosart cites the two passages quoted by Allott: 3.56–62 and 10.19–23. Grosart further developed his argument for an attribution to Greene in the introduction to his 1898 edition of *Selimus.* See Robert Greene, *The Tragical Reign of Selimus, Sometime Emperor of the Turks,* Alexander B. Grosart, ed. (London: J. M. Dent, 1898): 9–21.

43. Anyone wishing to enter the tangled web of attribution studies and pursue this question further may begin by consulting these articles: Peter Berek, "*Locrine* revised, *Selimus,* and Early Responses to Tamburlaine," *Research Opportunities in Renaissance Drama* 23 (1980): 33–54; Irving Ribner, "Greene's Attack on Marlowe: Some Light on *Alphonsus* and *Selimus,*" *Studies in Philology* 52 (1955): 162–71; Kenneth Muir, "Who Wrote *Selimus?,*" *Proceedings of the Leeds Philosophical and Literary Society,* Literary and Historical Section, vol. 6, part 6 (February 1949): 373–76.

44. *Perimedes the Blacke-Smith* (London, 1588) sig. A3v.

45. See Gerald M. Pincess, "Thomas Creede and the repertory of the Queen's Men, 1583–1592," *Modern Philology* 67 (1970): 321–30; Scott McMillan, "The Queen's Men in 1594: A Study of 'Good' and 'Bad' Quartos," *English Literary Renaissance* 14 (1984): 55–69.

46. Augustino Celio Curione, *Sarracenicae Historiae* (Basel, 1567), translated by Thomas Newton as *A Notable Historie of the Saracens* (London, 1575); Paolo Giovio, *Comentarii della cose de Turchi* (Florence, 1531), translated by Peter Ashton as *A Shorte treatise upon the Turkes Chronicles, compyled by Paulus Jovius bishop of Lucerne, and dedicated to Charles the V. Emperour* (London, 1546). Giovio's text was originally published

in Latin as Paulus Jovius, *Rerum Turicarum commentarius ad Invictissimum Caesarem Carolum V. Imperatorem Augustum,* and then translated into Italian.

47. Other contemporary texts that were available to Greene in English include the following: Frauncis Billerbege, *Most rare and straunge discourse of Amurathe the Turkish Emperor that now is: Of his personne, and how hee is governed* (London, 1582); Franciscus de Billerby, *Most rare and straunge discourses, of Amurathe then Turkish emperor* (London, 1584); Hugh Goughe, *The Ofspring of the house of Ottomano* (London, 1553); Antoine Geuffroy, *Briefve description de la court du Grant Turc et ung sommaire du regne des Othmans* (Paris, 1543); *The order of the great Turckes courte, of hys menne of warre, and of all hys conquestes, with the summe of Mahumetes doctryne,* translated by Richard Grafton (London, 1544); Benedetto Ramberti, *Libri tre della cose de Turchi* (Venice, 1539), translated as *The order of the Great Turke's court* (London, 1542); *Two very notable Commentaries, The One of the Originall of the Turcks and Empire of the house of Ottomano, written by Andrewe Cambine, and thother of the warres of the Turcke against Scanderbeg . . . translated out of the Italian into English by John Shute* (London, 1562).

48. See Frank G. Hubbard, "Locrine and Selimus," *Shakespeare Studies by the Department of English of the University of Wisconsin* (Madison, 1916), 17–35.

49. Bevington's masterful survey of the homiletic tradition is *From "Mankind" to Marlowe: Growth of Structure in the Popular Drama of Tudor England* (Cambridge: Harvard University Press, 1962).

50. Simon Shepherd, *Marlowe and the Politics of Elizabethan Theatre* (Brighton, Sussex: Harvester Press, 1986).

51. The issue of atheism in *Selimus* has been given serious attention in Jonathan Dollimore's *Radical Tragedy* (Brighton: Harvester, 1984), 87 ff.

52. The title page of Daborne's only other extant play, *The Poor Man's Comfort* (printed in 1655), refers to the author as "Robert Dauborne, Master of Arts," and Cambridge University records confirm the matriculation of a "Robert Dauburne" as a sizar at King's College in 1598.

53. See Andrew Gurr, *The Shakespearian Playing Companies* (Oxford: Clarendon, 1996), 356–65.

54. Cited in the article by A. H. Bullen in the *Dictionary of National Biography* (1888). For further biographical information on Daborne, consult Mark Eccles, "Brief Lives: Tudor and Stuart Authors—Robert Daborne," *Studies in Philology* 79 (1982): 28–36; A. E. H. Swaen, "Robert Daborne's Plays," *Anglia* 20 (1898): 153–256; Wayne H. Phelps, "The Early Life of Robert Daborne," *Philological Quarterly* 59:1 (Winter 1980): 1–10.

55. See *Henslowe's Diary,* Walter Greg, ed., 2 vols. (London: A. H. Bullen, 1904–08), 2:141–43; or R. A. Foakes' facsimile edition of *The Henslowe Papers* (New York: AMS Press, 1975), MS 70–99, p. 102.

56. Other writers employed by Henslowe at that time include Nathan Field, Fran-

cis Beaumont, John Fletcher, and Cyril Tourneur. See the records of Henslowe's correspondence in George F. Warner, *Catalogue of Manuscripts and Muniments of Alleyn's College of God's Gift at Dulwich* (London: Longmans, Green, 1881), pp. 37–49, 51, 141, 339.

57. In one of his letters begging for more cash, Daborne tells Henslowe that if he does not buy Daborne's newest play at the right price, Daborne will sell it to the King's Men—Henslowe's competition! Records and letters indicate that Daborne was a close associate of Philip Henslowe during that time. In fact Daborne's second wife, Francis, was present at Henslowe's deathbed, demanding the return of some of Daborne's "writings." Mrs. Daborne was one of the last to see Henslowe alive. The papers were handed over to her, and she was reportedly told by Henslowe, "I know you and with all my heart do freely forgive all that you owe me" (Greg, 2:20). Henslowe died on 6 January 1616.

58. *The Poor Man's Comfort. A Tragicomedy* (London, 1655). Other plays by Daborne are mentioned in the Henslowe papers but are not extant: the *Tragedy of Machiavel and the Devil*, possibly a reworking of the earlier "matchevell" recorded by Henslowe as being performed by Strange's Men in February 1591 or 1592 (Greg, 2:152); *The Arraignment of London* (or *The Bellman of London*), with Tourneur; *The Owl* and *The She-Saint.*

59. The *Annals of English Drama*, Alfred Harbage, S. Schoenbaum, and S. S. Wagonheim, eds., 3d edition (London: Routledge, 1989), assigns 1617 as the date of composition. It has been edited as a doctoral dissertation by Sister Marie E. McIlvaine (University of Pennsylvania, 1934).

60. Other plays staged by the Queen's Revels at this time include Jonson's *Epicoene* and revivals of Chapman's *Revenge of Bussy D'Ambois*, as well as the work of other playwrights known to have collaborated with Daborne, such as Field, Beaumont, and Fletcher. See Gurr, *Playing Companies*, 359.

61. Andrew Barker, *Atrve and certaine report of . . . the Estate of Captaine Ward and Danseker, aht two late famous Pirates* (London, 1609), 14.

62. *Newes from Sea, Of Two Notorious Pyrates, Ward . . . and Dansekar* (London, 1609), sig. A2r.

63. Cited in C. M. Senior, *A Nation of Pirates: English Piracy in Its Heyday* (New York: Crane, Russak & Co., 1976), 90. See Senior, 90–91 for an account of Carosman and Ward's relationship.

64. "The Ballad of Ward and Danseker" was listed in the Stationers' Register on 3 July 1609. It is reprinted in *The Roxburghe Ballads*, vol. 6, 784–5.

65. Barker, 16.

66. *News from Sea*, sig. B3r.

67. Ibid.

68. *News from Sea*, sig. A4r.

69. *News from Sea*, sig. D2r.

70. *Calendar of State Papers and Manuscripts, Existing in the Archives and Collections of Venice* (hereafter referred to as CSPV),1607–10, vol. 11 (London, 1904), 141.

71. *CSPV* 1607–10, 11:49.

72. One of the English corsairs who served under Ward, Captain Bishop, surrendered and declared, "I will die a poor labourer in mine own country, if I may, rather than be the richest pirate in the world." *CSPV, Ireland, 1611–14,* 91.

73. Lithgow goes on to say, "Yet old Ward their master was placable, and joined me safely with a passing land conduct to Algier; yea, and diverse times in my ten days staying there, I dined and supped with him. . . ." *The Totall Discourse of the Rare Adventures* (London, 1632), 358.

74. The opening sentence of King James's 1605 "Proclamation for revocation of mariners from foreign services":

> Within this short time since the peace concluded between us and the King of Spain and the Archduke our good brothers, it hath appeared unto us that many mariners and seafaring men of this realm, having gotten a custom and a habit in the time of the war to make profit by spoil, do leave their ordinary and honest vocation and trading in merchantly voyages . . . and do betake themselves to the service of diverse foreign states . . . to have thereby occasion to continue their unlawful and ungodly course of living by spoil, using the services of those princes but for color and pretext, but in effect making themselves no better than pirates to rob both our own subjects their countrymen and the subjects of other princes our neighbors.

Stuart Royal Proclamations, Paul L. Hughes and James F. Larkin, eds., vol. 1 (New Haven: Yale University Press, 1988), 108, no. 50.

75. Barker, 4.

76. Senior, 41.

77. Cited in C. L'Estrange-Ewan, *Captain John Ward, Arch-Pirate* (privately printed, 1939), 9.

78. His career can be traced in the *CSPV,* vols. 11 and 12, 1607–10 and 1610–13. See esp. 11:348.

79. *CSPV,* 11:348.

80. *CSPV,* 11:575, p. 312.

81. *CSPV,* 11:687, p. 375.

82. *CSPV,* 11:724, p. 391.

83. *CSPV,* 11 916, p. 492; 12:59, pp. 45–6.

84. *CSPV,* 12:156, p. 105.

85. A similar account of Danseker's demise is given by Lithgow, who claims that in February 1616 Danseker was tricked and executed by the bashaw of Tunis (*Rare Adventures,* 381–82).

86. *CSPV,* 11:629, p. 346.

87. Cited in Senior, 95–96.

88. Captain John Smith, *The True Travels, Adventures, and Observations of Captaine John Smith . . . from . . . 1593 to 1629* (London, 1630), 59.

89. *Rare Adventures,* 188–89.

90. *News from Sea,* sig. C2r.

91. *News from Sea,* sig. D2v.

92. *News from Sea,* sig. D3r.

93. *News from Sea,* sig. D2v–3r. The 1609 ballad "The Song of Dansekar the Dutchman" also reports that "Ward and Dansekar / begin greatly now to jar / About dividing of their goods. . . ."

94. *Lords' Journals,* vol. 3, 411–13.

95. Avigdor Levy, *The Jews of the Ottoman Empire* (Princeton: Darwin Press, 1994), 12.

96. Levy, 29.

97. See James Shapiro, *Shakespeare and the Jews,* chapter 6, "Race, Nation, or Alien?" (New York: Columbia University Press, 1996).

98. De Nicolay, translated by T. Washington the Younger, *Navigations and Voyages Made into Turkie* (London, 1585), 131.

99. Cited in Shapiro, 168.

100. Alan and Helen Cutler, *The Jew as Ally of the Muslim: Medieval Roots of Anti-Semitism* (South Bend, Indiana: University of Notre Dame Press, 1986), 2.

101. Cited in Cutler, 98.

102. See Thomas A. Dunn, *Philip Massinger: The Man and the Playwright* (London: printed for the University College of Ghana, 1957), 15–16; Donald S. Lawless, *Philip Massinger and His Associates,* monograph no. 10 (Muncie, Indiana: Ball State University, 1967), 3–4.

103. There were other plays, now lost, some of which were preserved in manuscripts collected by John Warburton (1682–1759), but many of these were destroyed when Warburton's cook used them to line pie bottoms. See *The Plays and Poems of Philip Massinger,* Philip Edwards and Colin Gibson, eds., 5 vols. (Oxford: Clarendon Press, 1976), 1:xxvi–xxvii.

104. See Dunn, 28–29.

105. See Gurr, 405–408, for a reconstruction of the Lady Elizabeth's Men's repertory during this time. Also helpful are Edwards and Gibson's introduction to their text of *The Renegado* in *The Plays and Poems of Philip Massinger* (2:7–9); and T. J. King, "Staging of Plays at the Phoenix in Drury Lane, 1617–42," *Theatre Notebook* 19 (1964–65): 146–66.

106. See Edwards and Gibson, 2:8.

107. See Edwards and Gibson's "Introduction" in the first volume of their edition,

pp. ii–iv; Warner G. Rice, "The Sources of Massinger's *The Renegado*," *Philological Quarterly* 11 (1932): 65–75.

108. *Mr. Harrie Cavendish, his journey to and from Constantinople, 1589, by Fox, his servant*, A. C. Wood, ed., *Camden Miscellany* vol. 17, no. 2, (London: Royal Historical Society, 1940), 24–25 [from a ms].

109. See the article by Michael MacDonald on "'The Fearefull Estate of Francis Spira': Narrative, Identity, and Emotion in Early Modern England," *Journal of British Studies* 31 (January, 1992): 32–61.

110. Edward Said, *Orientalism* (New York: Vintage, 1978).

BYZANTIVM NVNC C

CASTEL *bdut diue Ha*
elefara del gran Torcho

LAVLACA

ARSENALE

OTOMAN ORCAN AMVRAT AIAZIT MAHOMET MVRATES

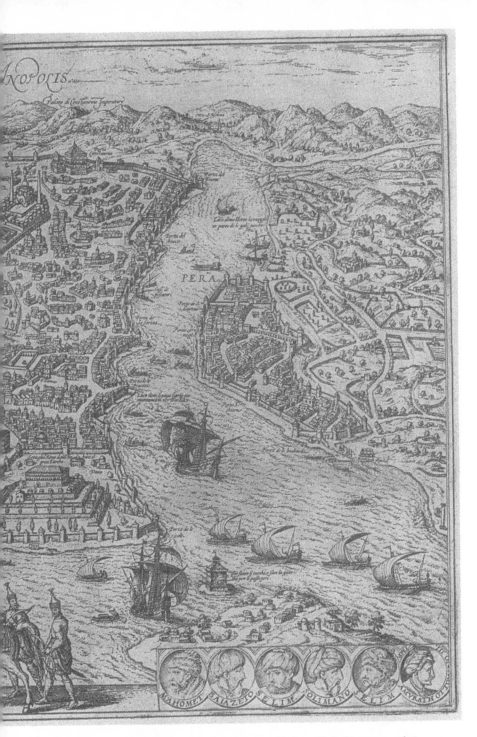

A view of Constantinople, from Georg Braun, *Civitates Orbis Terrarum*, vol. 6 (Cologne, 1606–18).

TVNES

NOVA   AR

Collimur Fosfa Christianorum

STAG

CASTRA   T   VR
CA
C

GVLET

CLA   SSIS

TVNETIS VRBIS, AC NOVAE EIVS ARCIS,
ET GVLETAE. QVAE PHILIPPO HISPAN:
REGI PARENT VT A TVRCIS, ET MAV:
RIS, SELIMO. THRACIAE REGE, ANNO
CHRISTI, Ɔ Ɔ ꞮƆ LXXIV. MENSE IV:
LIO, ET AVGVSTO. FIXIS CASTRIS OP:
PVGNABANTVR. EFFIGIES.

A map of Tunis and its fortified harbor, Goletta, showing the 1535 attack launched by
Charles V. From Georg Braun, *Civitates Orbis Terrarum*, vol. 2 (Cologne, 1606–18).

MOLDAVIA

AVSTRIA.

MVN
GARIA

VALACHIA

MARE MAGIORE, ol PONTVS

ITALIA

SLAVONIA

Venetia

Roma

Napol

MACEDONIA

ALBANIA

Messina

SICILIA

Malta

MARE MEDITERRANEVM

AFRICAE OCCIDENS.

Regni Tunc
tum
pars.

P.Magn

Sinus magnus

BARCHA

AEGYPTVS.

Memphis

NOSTRAE REG-
NI PARS

Libyæ deserta.

And C. Raguses, olim Barrium Prouin-
erant patrum nostrarum memoria,
Regis Tunetani, et Soldani Ægypti &
finibus, hodie vero Solimannorum imperi,
un huiusque, & vltra detinebant

AFR= ICAE

P

TVRCICI IMPE-
RII DESCRIPTIO.

Concordia paruæ res crescunt.
Discordia maxime dilabuntur.

A map of the Ottoman empire, from Abraham Ortelius, *Theatrum Orbis Terrarum* (Antwerp, 1959).

An engraved portrait of Bajazet II, from Richard Knolles, *The General History of the Turks* (London, 1603).

An engraved portrait of Selimus I, from Richard Knolles, *The General History of the Turks* (London, 1603).

An engraved portrait of "Tomombeius, The Last Sultan of Egypt" (in Greene's play
he is called "Tonombey"), from Richard Knolles, *The General History of the Turks*
(London, 1603).

A woodcut from the title page of *Ward and Danseker, Two Notorious Pirates*
(London, 1609), showing "Turkish" pirates assaulting another ship.

Wards Skiffe when he was a Fiſherman.

The charity of London of M. Megs twice taken.

These images are printed next to each other in Ward and Danseker, *Two Notorious Pirates* (London, 1609) to illustrate a contrast between Ward's humble beginnings as a fisherman and his later success as a pirate taking rich prizes like the *Charity*.

A Gentlewoman of the Turks being within her house or Sarail.

"A gentlewoman of the Turks being within her house or sarail [seraglio]," from Nicolas de Nicolay, *The Navigations, Peregrinations and Voyages Made into Turkey*, T. Washington, trans. (London, 1585).

The Ianissarie going to the warres.

"The janissary going to the wars," from Nicolas de Nicolay, *The Navigations, Peregrinations and Voyages Made into Turkey,* T. Washington, trans. (London 1585).

Aga captaine generall of the Ianiſſaries.

"Aga captain-general of the janissaries," from Nicolas de Nicolay, *The Navigations, Peregrinations and Voyages Made into Turkey,* T. Washington, trans. (London, 1585).

A Merchant Iewe.

"A merchant Jew," from Nicolas de Nicolay, *The Navigations, Peregrinations and Voyages Made into Turkey*, T. Washington, trans. (London, 1585).

THE
First part of the Tra=

gicall raigne of Selimus, sometime Emperour of the Turkes, and grandfather to him
that now raigneth.

Wherein is showne how hee most vnnaturally
raised warres against his owne father *Baiazet*, and pre-
uailing therein, in the end caused him to
be poysoned:

Also with the murthering of his two brethren,
Corcut, and *Acomat*.

As it was playd by the Queenes Maiesties
Players.

LONDON
Printed by Thomas Creede, dwelling in Thames
streete at the signe of the Kathren wheele,
neare the olde Swanne.
1594.

Selimus, Emperor of the Turks

The First Part of the Tragical Reign of Selimus,
Sometime Emperor of the Turks,
and grandfather to him
that now reigneth.

Wherein is shown how he most unnaturally
raised wars against his own father Bajazet,
and prevailing therein,
in the end caused him to be poisoned.

Also with the murthering of his two brethren,
Corcut and Acomat.

As it was played by the Queen's Majesty's Players.

LONDON
PRINTED BY THOMAS CREEDE, DWELLING IN THAMES
STREET AT THE SIGN OF THE CATHERINE WHEEL,
NEAR THE OLD SWAN.
1594.

Dramatis Personae

~

Bajazet	*emperor of the Turks.*
Selimus (or Selim)	*youngest son of Bajazet, and soldan of Trebizond; later, emperor of the Turks.*
Acomat	*son of Bajazet and soldan of Amasia.*
Corcut	*son of Bajazet and soldan of Magnesia.*
Mustaffa	*imperial councilor and son-in-law of Bajazet.*
Aga	*follower of Bajazet.*
Cherseoli	*follower of Bajazet.*
Cali Bassa	*Turkish courtier.*
Hali Bassa	*Turkish courtier and brother of Cali Bassa.*
Mahomet	*prince of Natolia and son of Bajazet's deceased son Alemshae.*
Sinam Bassa	*follower of Selimus.*
Ottrante	*a Tartar lord and ally of Selimus.*
Occhiali	*follower of Selimus.*
Regan	*follower of Acomat.*
Tonombey	*son of the soldan of Egypt, ally of Acomat.*
Vizier	*follower of Acomat.*
Beylerbey of Natolia	*follower of Prince Mahomet.*

---

soldan] i.e., sultan, a title given to the ruler of a province within the Ottoman empire.

Trebizond] An area in Asia Minor on the Black Sea. It had been an autonomous kingdom from 1204 until 1461, when it was conquered by the Ottomans.

Amasia] an area in northeast Asia Minor bordering the Black Sea, formerly the Roman province of Pontus.

Magnesia] ancient name for Manisa, a city in western Turkey.

Aga] really a Turkish title, not a name, given to the chief officer in command of the janissaries.

Bassa] a form of "Bashaw," i.e., the modern title "Pasha," which was given to officials of high rank in the Ottoman empire.

Aladin	*son of Acomat.*
Amurath	*son of Acomat.*
Bullithrumble	*a Christian shepherd.*
Abraham	*the Jew.*
Zonara	*sister to Mahomet.*
Solyma	*sister to Selimus and wife of Mustaffa.*
Queen of Amasia	*wife of Acomat.*

Soldiers, Messengers, Page, Janissaries.

Janissaries] an elite corps of the Turkish military made up of soldiers who were captured or purchased as slaves when young and then trained in military discipline and the Islamic faith.

Prologue

No feignèd toy nor forgèd tragedy,
Gentles, we here present unto your view;
But a most lamentable history
Which this last age acknowledgeth for true.
5   Here shall you see the wicked son pursue
His wretched father with remorseless spite
And daunted once, his force again renew,
Poison his father, kill his friends in fight.
You shall behold him character in blood
10   The image of an unplacable king,
And like a sea or high resurging flood,
All obstant lets, down with his fury fling.
Which if with patience of you shall be heard,
We have the greatest part of our reward.

Exit.

---

9   **character**] inscribe, personify.
10   **unplacable**] implacable.
12   **obstant lets**] opposing obstacles.

SCENE 1.
COURT OF THE OTTOMAN EMPEROR, BAJAZET,
AT BYZANTIUM.

Enter Bajazet (Emperor of Turkey), Mustaffa, Cherseoli, and the janissaries.

BAJAZET: Leave me, my lords, until I call you forth,
For I am heavy and disconsolate.

Exeunt all but Bajazet.

So, Bajazet, now thou remain'st alone,
Unrip the thoughts that harbor in thy breast
5   And eat thee up; for arbiter here's none
That may descry the cause of thy unrest
Unless these walls thy secret thoughts declare;
And princes' walls, they say, unfaithful are.
Why, that's the profit of great regiment,
10   That all of us are subject unto fears,
And this vain show and glorious intent
Privy suspicion on each scruple rears.
Aye, though on all the world we make extent,
From the south pole unto the northern bears,

---

9   **regiment**] power, rule.
13   **make extent**] seize.
14   **northern bears**] the constellations Ursa Major and Minor.

15 And stretch our reign from East to Western shore,
    Yet doubt and care are with us evermore.
    Look how the earth, clad in her summer's pride,
    Embroidereth her mantle gorgeously
    With fragrant herbs and flowers gaily dyed,
20 Spreading abroad her spangled tapestry:
    Yet under all a loathsome snake doth hide.
    Such is our life: under crowns cares do lie.
    Oh, who can take delight in kingly throne?
    Public disorders joined with private cark,
25 Care of our friends and of our children dear,
    Do toss our lives, as waves a silly bark.
    Though we be fearless, 'tis not without fear,
    For hidden mischief lurketh in the dark,
    And storms may fall, be the day ne'er so clear.
30 He knows not what it is to be king
    That thinks a scepter is a pleasant thing.
    Twice fifteen times hath fair Latona's son
    Walked about the world with his great light
    Since I began—would I had ne'er begun—
35 To sway this scepter. Many a careful night
    When Cynthia in haste to bed did run,
    Have I with watching vexed my agèd spright!
    Since when, what dangers I have overpassed
    Would make a heart of adamant aghast.
40 The Persian Sophy, mighty Ismael,
    Took the Levant clean away from me;
    And Caraguis Bassa (sent his force to quell)
    Was killed himself, the while his men did flee.
    Poor Hali Bassa having once sped well
45 And gained of him a bloody victory
    Was at the last slain fighting in the field,°

---

24 cark] care, sorrow.
26 silly bark] helpless little boat.
32 Latona's son] Apollo, i.e., the sun.
37 spright] spirit.
44 Hali Bassa] the Ottoman Grand Vizier, Hadim Ali Pasha. He was the father of the Hali Bassa
and Cali Bassa who appear in the play.

Charactering honor in his batt'red shield.
Ramirchan the Tartarian emperor,
Gathering to him a number numberless
50   Of big-boned Tartars, in a hapless hour
Encountered me; and there my chiefest bless,
Good Alemshae (ah, this remembrance sour!),
Was slain, the more t'augment my sad distress.°
In leesing Alemshae, poor I lost more
55   Than ever I had gainèd theretofore.
Well may thy soul rest in her latest grave,
Sweet Alemshae, the comfort of my days!
That thou might'st live, how often did I crave!
How often did I bootless prayers raise
60   To that high power that life first to thee gave!
Trusty wast thou to me at all assays;
And dearest child, thy father oft hath cried
That thou hadst lived, so he himself had died.
The Christian armies, oftentimes defeated
65   By my victorious father's valiance,
Have all my captains famously confronted,
And cracked in two our uncontrollèd lance.
My strongest garrisons they have supplanted,
And overwhelmed me in sad mischance;
70   And my decrease so long wrought their increase,
Till I was forced conclude a friendly peace.
Now all these are but foreign damages
Taken in war, whose die uncertain is;
But I shall have more home-born outrages,
75   Unless my divination aim amiss.
I have three sons, all of unequal ages,
And all in diverse studies set their bliss:
Corcut, my eldest, a philosopher;
Acomat pompous, Selim a warrior.

---

48   **Ramirchan**] probably refers to a leader of the Krim Tatars, Ottoman vassals who formed an alliance with Selim I.
54   **leesing**] losing.
67   **uncontrollèd lance**] previously undefeated army (perhaps referring specifically to "lancers" or cavalry).

80   Corcut in fair Magnesia leads his life
In learning arts and Mahound's dreaded laws.°
Acomat loves to court it with his wife,
And in a pleasant quiet joys to pause;
But Selim follows wars in dismal strife
85   And snatcheth at my crown with greedy claws;
But he shall miss of that he aimeth at,
For I reserve it for my Acomat.
For Acomat? Alas, it cannot be!
Stern Selimus hath won my people's heart;
90   The janissaries love him more then me
And for his cause will suffer any smart.
They see he is a friend to chivalry,
And sooner will they from my faith depart,
And by strong hand, Bajazet, pull thee down
95   Than let their Selim hop without the crown.
Ah, if the soldiers overrule thy state
(And nothing must be done without their will),
If every base and upstart runagate°
Shall cross a prince and overthwart him still,
100   If Corcut, Selimus, and Acomat
With crowns and kingdoms shall their hungers fill;
Poor Bajazet, what then remains to thee
But the bare title of thy dignity?
Aye, and unless thou do dissemble all
105   And wink at Selimus' aspiring thought,
The bassas cruelly shall work thy fall,
And then thy empire is but dearly bought.
Ah, that our sons, thus to ambition thrall,
Should set the law of nature all at nought.
110   But what must be cannot choose but be done.
Come, Bassas, enter; Bajazet hath done.

---

81   **arts and Mahound's dreaded laws**] liberal arts (not "fine" arts) and the religious laws of Islam
("Mahound" was used in English to refer to the Prophet Mohammed).
95   **hop**] limp, go haltingly.
99   **overthwart**] obstruct.

[Mustaffa, Cherseoli, and the Janissaries] enter again.

CHERSEOLI: Dread emperor, long may you happy live,
    Loved of your subjects and feared of your foes!
    We wonder much what doth your Highness grieve
115   That you will not unto your lords disclose.
    Perhaps you fear lest we, your loyal peers,
    Would prove disloyal to your Majesty
    And be rebellious in your dying years.
    But mighty prince, the heavens can testify
120   How dearly we esteem your safety.
MUSTAFFA: Perhaps you think Mustaffa will revolt
    And leave your Grace and cleave to Selimus,
    But sooner shall th'almighty's thunderbolt
    Strike me down to the cave tenebrious,
125   The lowest land, and damnèd spirits holt,
    Than true Mustaffa prove so treacherous.
    Your Majesty then needs not much to fear,
    Since you are loved of subject, prince and peer.
    First shall the sun rise from the Occident
130   And loose his steeds benighted in the East;
    First shall the sea become the continent,
    Ere we forsake our sovereign's behest.
    We fought not for you 'gainst Persian's tent,
    Breaking our lances on his sturdy crest;
135   We fought not for you 'gainst the Christian host,
    To become traitors after all our cost.
BAJAZET: Hear me, Mustaffa and Cherseoli.
    I am a father of a headstrong brood,
    Which if I look not closely to myself,
140   Will seek to ruinate their father's state,
    Even as the vipers in great Nero's fen
    Eat up the belly that first nourished them.

---

125 **holt**] hold, place of custody.
141 **great Nero's fen**] the marshes in the Campagna Romana, here associated with the Roman emperor Nero. It was believed that the first act of newborn vipers was to devour their mother.

You see the harvest of my life is passed,
And agèd winter hath besprent my head
145   With a hoarfrost of silver-colored hairs,
The harbingers of honorable eld.
These branchlike veins which once did guide my arms
To toss the spear in battellous array,
Now withered up, have lost their former strength.
150   My sons whom now ambition 'gins to prick
May take occasion of my weakened age
And rise in rebellious arms against my state.
But stay, here comes a messenger to us.

Sound [a trumpet] within. Enter a Messenger.

MESSENGER: Health and good hap to Bajazet,
155   The great commander of all Asia!
Selim the soldan of great Trebizond
Sends me unto your Grace, to signify
His alliance with the king of Tartary.
BAJAZET: Said I not, lords, as much to you before,
160   That mine own sons would seek my overthrow?
And see, here comes a luckless messenger
To prove that true which my mind did foretell.
Does Selim make so small account of us,
That he dare marry without our consent,
165   And to that devil, too, of Tartary?
And could he then unkind, so soon forget
The injuries that Ramir did to me,
Thus to confront himself with him 'gainst me?
CHERSEOLI: Your Majesty misconsters Selimus;
170   It cannot be that he, in whose high thoughts
A map of many valors is enshrined,
Should seek his father's ruin and decay.
Selimus is a prince of forward hope,

---

146   eld] old age.
150   to prick] "to drive or urge as with a spur" (*O.E.D.*).
169   misconsters] misconstrues.

Whose only name affrights your enemies;
175   It cannot be he should prove false to you.
BAJAZET: Can it not be? Oh yes, Cherseoli;
For Selimus' hands do itch to have the crown,
And he will have it—or else pull me down.
Is he a prince? Ah no, he is a sea,
180   Into which run nought but ambitious reaches,
Seditious complots, murther, fraud, and hate.
Could he not let his father know his mind,
But match himself when I least thought on it?
MUSTAFFA: Perhaps my lord Selimus loved the dame
185   And feared to certify you of his love
Because her father was your enemy.
BAJAZET: In love, Mustaffa? Selimus in love?
If he be, lording, 'tis not ladies' love
But love of rule and kingly sovereignty.
190   For wherefore should he fear t'ask my consent?
Trusty Mustaffa, if he had feared me,
He never would have loved mine enemy.
But this his marriage with the Tartar's daughter,
Is but the prologue to his cruelty,
195   And quickly shall we have the tragedy,
Which though he act with meditated bravery,
The world will never give him plaudity.
What, yet more news?

Sound [trumpets] within. Another Messenger enters.

MESSENGER: Dread emperor, Selimus is at hand.
200   Two hundreth thousand strong Tartarians
Armed at all points does he lead with him,
Besides his followers from Trebizond.
BAJAZET: I thought so much of wicked Selimus!
Oh forlorn hopes and hapless Bajazet!
205   Is duty then exiled from his breast,

---

174 **only name**] name alone.
197 **plaudity**] applause, approval.

Which Nature hath inscribed with golden pen,
Deep in the hearts of honorable men?
Ah Selim, Selim, wert thou not my son,
But some strange unacquainted foreigner,
210   Whom I should honor as I honored thee;
Yet would it grieve me even unto death,
If he should deal as thou hast dealt with me.
And thou my son, to whom I freely gave
The mighty empire of great Trebizond,
215   Art too unnatural to requite me thus.
Good Alemshae, hadst thou lived till this day,
Thou wouldst have blushed at thy brother's mind.
Come, sweet Mustaffa; come Cherseoli,
And with some good advice recomfort me.

Exeunt all.

SCENE 2.
SELIMUS' ENCAMPMENT NEAR ADRIANOPLE.

Enter Selimus, Sinam Bassa, Ottrante, Occhiali, and Soldiers.

SELIMUS: Now Selimus, consider who thou art.
Long hast thou marched in disguisèd attire,
But now unmask thyself and play thy part
And manifest the heat of thy desire;
5   Nourish the coals of thine ambitious fire.
And think that then thy empire is most sure
When men for fear thy tyranny endure.
Think that to thee there is no worse reproach
Than filial duty in so high a place.
10   Thou oughtst to set barrels of blood abroach
And seek with sword whole kingdoms to displace.
Let Mahound's laws be locked up in their case,
And meaner men and of a baser spirit
In virtuous actions seek for glorious merit.

Adrianople] modern-day Edirne, in European Turkey.

15 I count it sacrilege for to be holy
Or reverence this threadbare name of "good."
Leave to old men and babes that kind of folly;
Count it of equal value with the mud:
Make thou a passage for thy gushing flood
20 By slaughter, treason, or what else thou can;
And scorn religion—it disgraces man.
My father Bajazet is weak and old,
And hath not much above two years to live.
The Turkish crown of pearl and Ophir gold
25 He means to his dear Acomat to give;
But ere his ship can to her haven drive,
I'll send abroad my tempests in such sort
That she shall sink before she get the port.
Alas, alas, his highness' agèd head
30 Is not sufficient to support a crown.
Then Selimus, take thou it in his stead,
And if at this thy boldness he dare frown
Or but resist thy will, then pull him down:
For since he hath so short a time t'enjoy it,
35 I'll make it shorter, or I will destroy it.
Nor pass I what our holy votaries
Shall here object against my forward mind:
I reck not of their foolish ceremonies,
But mean to take my fortune as I find.
40 Wisdom commands to follow tide and wind,
And catch the front of swift Occasion
Before she be too quickly overgone.
Some man will say I am too impious,
Thus to lay siege against my father's life,
45 And that I ought to follow virtuous
And godly sons; that virtue is a glass
Wherein I may my errant life behold
And frame myself by it in ancient mold.
Good sir, your wisdom's overflowing wit
50 Digs deep with learning's wonder-working spade:

---

41 **Occasion**] personified as a woman who is bald except for a long shock of hair hanging down in front. When she comes near, one must "seize occasion" and grasp her forelock while it is in reach.

Perhaps you think that now forsooth you sit
With some grave wizard in a prattling shade.
Avaunt such glasses! Let them view in me
The perfect picture of right tyranny.
55   Aye, like a lion's look—not worth a leek
When every dog deprives him of his prey—
These honest terms are far enough to seek.
When angry Fortune menaceth decay,
My resolution treads a nearer way.
60   Give me the heart conspiring with the hand,
In such a cause my father to withstand.
Is he my father? Why, I am his son.
I owe no more to him than he to me.
If he proceed as he hath now begun
65   And pass from me the Turkish seigniory
To Acomat, then Selimus is free.
And if he injure me that am his son,
Faith, all the love 'twixt him and me is done.
But for I see the schoolmen are prepared
70   To plant 'gainst me their bookish ordinance,
I mean to stand on a sententious guard;
And without any farfetched circumstance
Quickly unfold mine own opinion
To arm my heart with irreligion.
75   When first this circled round, this building fair,
Some god took out of the confused mass
(What god I do not know, nor greatly care)
Then everyone his life in peace did pass.
War was not then, and riches were not known,
80   And no man said, "this, or this, is mine own."
The ploughman with a furrow did not mark
How far his great possessions did reach;
The earth knew not the share, nor seas the bark.

---

52   **wizard**] wise man.
52   **prattling shady**] shady retreat for idle talk.
69   **schoolmen**] scholars of philosophy and theology.
75   **this circled round**] the earth, with its concentric spheres.
83   **share**] ploughshare.

The soldiers entered not the battered breach,
85   Nor trumpets the tantara loud did teach.
There needed them no judge, nor yet no law,
Nor any king of whom to stand in awe.
But after Ninus, warlike Belus' son,
The earth with unknown armor did worry;
90   Then first the sacred name of king begun,
And things that were as common as the day
Did then to set possessors first obey.
Then they established laws and holy rites
To maintain peace and govern bloody fights.°
95   Then some sage man, above the vulgar wise,
Knowing that laws could not in quiet dwell,
Unless they were observed, did first devise
The names of gods, religion, heaven and hell,
And 'gan of pains and feigned rewards to tell:
100   Pains for those men which did neglect the law;
Rewards for those that lived in quiet awe.
Whereas indeed they were mere fictions,
And if they were not, Selim thinks they were;
And these religious observations,
105   Only bugbears to keep the world in fear
And make men quietly a yoke to bear.
So that religion (of itself a fable)
Was only found to make us peaceable.
Hence in especial come the foolish names
110   Of father, mother, brother, and such like:
For who so well his cogitation frames
Shall find they serve but only for to strike
Into our minds a certain kind of love.
For these names, too, are but a policy
115   To keep the quiet of society.
Indeed I must confess they are not bad
Because they keep the baser sort in fear;
But we, whose mind in heavenly thoughts is clad,
Whose body doth a glorious spirit bear
120   That hath no bounds but flieth every where;
Why should we seek to make that soul a slave,

To which dame Nature so large freedom gave?
Amongst us men, there is some difference
Of actions, termed by us good or ill:
125 As he that doth his father recompense
Differs from him that doth his father kill.
And yet I think, think other what they will,
That parricides, when death hath given them rest,
Shall have as good a part as have the best;
130 And that's just nothing: for as I suppose
In Death's void kingdom reigns eternal Night,
Secure of evil and secure of foes,
Where nothing doth the wicked man affright,
No more than him that dies in doing right.
135 Then since in death nothing shall to us fall,
Here while I live, I'll have a snatch at all;
And that can never, never be attained,
Unless old Bajazet do die the death.
For long enough the graybeard now hath reigned
140 And lived at ease while others lived uneath;
And now it's time he should resign his breath.
'Twere good for him if he were pressèd out:
'Twould bring him rest and rid him of his gout.
Resolved to do it, cast to compass it
145 Without delay or long procrastination.
It argueth an unmaturèd wit,
When all is ready for so strong invasion,
To draw out time; an unlooked for mutation
May soon prevent us if we do delay;
150 Quick speed is good where wisdom leads the way.
Occhiali?
OCCHIALI: My lord.
SELIMUS: Lo fly, boy, to my father Bajazet
And tell him Selim his obedient son
155 Desires to speak with him and kiss his hands;

---

140   **lived uneath**] barely lived.
142   **pressèd**] forced.
144   **cast to compass**] arrange a way to accomplish.

Tell him I long to see his gracious face,
And that I come with all my chivalry,
To chase the Christians from his seigniory:
In any wise, say I must speak with him.

Exit Occhiali.

160   Now Sinam, if I speed.
    SINAM BASSA: What then, my Lord?
    SELIMUS: What then? Why Sinam, thou art nothing worth!
        I will endeavor to persuade him, man,
        To give the empire over unto me.
165   Perhaps I shall attain it at his hands;
        If I cannot, this right hand is resolved
        To end the period with a fatal stab.
    SINAM BASSA: My gracious Lord, give Sinam leave to speak.
        If you resolve to work your father's death,
170   You venture life. Think you the janissaries
        Will suffer you to kill him in their sight
        And let you pass free without punishment?
    SELIMUS: If I resolve? As sure as heaven is heaven,
        I mean to see him dead—or myself king.
175   As for the bassas, they are all my friends,
        And I am sure would pawn their dearest blood
        That Selim might be emperor of Turks.
    SINAM BASSA: Yet Acomat and Corcut both survive
        To be revenged for their father's death.
180 SELIMUS: Sinam, if they (or twenty such as they)
        Had twenty several armies in the field,
        If Selimus were once your emperor,
        I'd dart abroad the thunderbolts of war
        And mow their heartless squadrons to the ground.
185 SINAM BASSA: Oh yet, my Lord, after your Highness' death,
        There is a hell and a revenging God.
    SELIMUS: Tush Sinam, these are school conditions,
        To fear the Devil or his cursèd dam!

---

187   school conditions] prohibitions set by theological theorists.

Thinkst thou I care for apparitions
190   Of Sisyphus and of his backward stone,
And poor Ixion's lamentable moan?
No, no! I think the cave of damnèd ghosts,
Is but a tale to terrify young babes,
Like devils' faces scored on painted posts
195   Or feignèd circles in our astrolabes.
Why, there's no difference when we are dead;
And death, once come, then all alike are sped.
Or, if there were, as I can scarce believe,
A heaven of joy and hell of endless pain,
200   Yet by my soul it never should me grieve,
So I might on the Turkish empire reign,
To enter hell and leave fair heaven's gain.
An empire, Sinam, is so sweet a thing,
As I could be a devil to be a king.
205   But go we, lords, and solace in our camp
Till the return of young Occhiali;
And if his answer be to thy desire,
Selim, thy mind in kingly thoughts attire.

Exeunt all.

SCENE 3.
ADRIANOPLE.

Enter Bajazet, Mustaffa, Cherseoli, Occhiali, and the janissaries.

BAJAZET: Even as the great Egyptian crocodile,
Wanting his prey, with artificial tears

---

190   **Sisyphus**] according to classical myth, a king of Corinth who suffered punishment in the under-world. He was condemned to push a heavy boulder to the top of a hill, but never to reach the top before it rolled back down again.
191   **Ixion**] mythical king of the Lapithae, punished in the underworld by Zeus, who ied him to an eternally revolving wheel.

And feignèd plaints his subtle tongue doth file
T'entrap the silly wand'ring traveler
5   And move him to advance his footing near,
That when he is in danger of his claws,
He may devour him with his famished jaws:
So playeth crafty Selimus with me.
His haughty thoughts still wait on diadems,
10   And not a step but treads to majesty.
The phoenix gazeth on the sun's bright beams;
The echinaeis swims against the streams.
Nought but the Turkish scepter can him please,
And there I know lieth his chief disease.
15   He sends his messenger to crave access
And says he longs to kiss my agèd hands,
But howsoever he in show profess,
His meaning with his words but weakly stands,
And sooner will the Syrtis' boiling sands
20   Become a quiet road for fleeting ships,
Than Selimus' heart agree with Selim's lips.
Too well I know the crocodile's feigned tears
Are but [the] nets wherein to catch his prey,
Which who so moved with foolish pity hears
25   Will be the author of his own decay.
Then hie thee, Bajazet—from hence away!
A fawning monster is false Selimus,
Whose fairest words are most pernicious.
Young man, would Selim come and speak with us?
30   What is his message to us, canst thou tell?
OCCHIALI: He craves, my Lord, another seigniory,
Nearer to you and to the Christians,
That he may make them know that Selimus
Is born to be a scourge unto them all.
35 BAJAZET: He's born to be a scourge to me and mine.
He never would have come with such an host

---

12   echinaeis] sea urchin.
19   Syrtis] an area of quicksand along the North African coast.

Unless he meant my state to undermine.
What though in word he bravely seem to boast
The foraging of all the Christian coast?
40 Yet we have cause to fear when burning brands
Are vainly given into a madman's hands.
Well, I must seem to wink at his desire,
Although I see it plainer then the light.
My lenity adds fuel to his fire,
45 Which now begins to break in flashing bright.
Then Bajazet, chastise his stubborn spright,
Lest these small sparkles grow to such a flame
As shall consume thee and thy house's name.
Alas, I spare when all my store is gone
50 And thrust my sickle where the corn is reaped.
In vain I send for the physician,
When on the patient is his grave dust heaped.
In vain—now all his veins in venom steeped
Break out in blisters that will poison us—
55 We seek to give him an antidotus.
He that will stop the brook must then begin
When summer's heat hath dried up his spring,
And when his pittering streams are low and thin;
For let the winter aid unto him bring,
60 He grows to be of watery floods the king;
And though you dam him up with lofty ranks,
Yet will he quickly overflow his banks.
Messenger, go and tell young Selimus,
We give to him all great Samandria,
65 Bordering on Belgrade of Hungaria,
Where he may plague those Christian runagates
And salve the wounds that they have given our states.°
Cherseoli, go and provide a gift,
A royal present for my Selimus;
70 And tell him, messenger, another time
He shall have talk enough with Bajazet.

---

58 pittering] making a soft, repeated sound.
66 runagates] fugitives, renegades.

Exeunt Cherseoli and Occhiali.

And now what counsel gives Mustaffa to us?
I fear this hasty reckoning will undo us.
MUSTAFFA: Make haste, my lord, from Adrianople walls,
75   And let us fly to fair Byzantium;
Lest if your son before you take the town,
He may with little labor win the crown.
BAJAZET: Then do so: good Mustaffa, call our guard
And gather all our warlike janissaries.
80   Our chiefest aid is swift celerity.
Then let our wingèd coursers tread the wind
And leave rebellious Selimus behind.

Exeunt all.

SCENE 4.
SELIMUS' ENCAMPMENT NEAR ADRIANOPLE.

Enter Selimus, Sinam Bassa, Occhiali, Ottrante and their Soldiers.

SELIMUS: And is his answer so, Occhiali?
Is Selim such a corsive to his heart,
That he cannot endure the sight of him?
Forsooth he gives thee all Samandria,
5   From whence our mighty Emperor Mahomet
Was driven to his country back with shame.°
No doubt thy father loves thee, Selimus,
To make thee regent of so great a land;
Which is not yet his own, or if it were,
10   What dangers wait on him that should it steer!
Here the Polonian he comes hurtling in
Under the conduct of some foreign prince,

---

75 **Byzantium]** ancient name for Istanbul.
2   **corsive]** corrosive.
11 **Polonian]** Polish (soldier).

To fight in honor of his crucifix!
Here the Hungarian with his bloody cross
15   Deals blows about to win Belgrade again.
And after all, forsooth Basilius
The mighty emperor of Russia,
Sends in his troops of slave-born Muscovites,
And he will share with us—or else take all!°
20   In giving such a land so full of strife,
His meaning is to rid me of my life.
Now by the dreaded name of Termagant
And by the blackest brook in loathsome hell,
Since he is so unnatural to me,
25   I will prove as unnatural as he.
Thinks he to stop my mouth with gold or pearl?
Or rusty jades fet from Barbaria?
No, let his minion, his philosopher,
Corcut and Acomat, be enriched with them!
30   I will not take my rest till this right hand
Hath pulled the crown from off his coward's head
And on the ground his bastards' gore-blood shed.
Nor shall his flight to old Byzantium
Dismay my thoughts, which never learned to stoop.
35   March, Sinam, march in order after him.
Were his steeds as swift as Pegasus
And trod the airy pavement with their heels,
Yet Selimus would overtake them soon.
And though the heavens do ne'er so crossly frown,
40   In spite of heaven shall Selim wear the crown.

Exeunt.

---

22 **Termagant**] Along with Mahound and Apollin, a member of a trinity of pagan idols identified in the Christian romance tradition as deities supposedly worshipped by Moorish or "Saracen" knights.
27 **rusty jades**] worn out horses.
27 **fet from Barbaria**] brought from Barbary in North Africa.

SCENE 5.
FIELD OF BATTLE NEAR CHIURLU.

Alarum within. Enter Bajazet, Mustaffa, Cherseoli, and the janissaries at one door, Selimus, Sinam Bassa, Ottrante, Occhiali, and their Soldiers at another.

BAJAZET: Is this thy duty, son, unto thy father?
So impiously to level at his life?
Can thy soul, wallowing in ambitious mire,
Seek for to rive that breast with bloody knife
5   From whence thou hadst thy being, Selimus?
Was this the end for which thou joindst thyself
With that mischievous traitor Ramirchan?
Was this thy drift to speak with Bajazet?
Well hoped I (but hope, I see, is vain)
10   Thou wouldst have been a comfort to mine age,
A scourge and terror to mine enemies;
That this thy coming with so great an host
Was for no other purpose and intent
Than for to chastise those base Christians
15   Which spoil my subjects' wealth with fire and sword.
Well hoped I the rule of Trebizond
Would have increased the valor of thy mind,
To turn thy strength upon the Persians.
But thou, like to a crafty polypus,
20   Dost turn thy hungry jaws upon thyself:
For what am I, Selimus, but thyself?
When courage first crept in thy manly breast
And thou beganst to rule the martial sword,
How oft said thou the sun should change his course,
25   Water should turn to earth, and earth to heaven,
Ere thou wouldst prove disloyal to thy father.
O Titan, turn thy breathless coursers back

Chiurlu] a city located sixty miles west of Byzantium/Istanbul.
s.d. **Alarum**] a call to arms, produced by drum and/or trumpet.
19 **polypus**] cuttlefish.
27 **Titan**] the sun.

And enterprise thy journey from the East.
Blush, Selim, that the world should say of thee
30   That by my death thou gaindst the empery.
SELIMUS: Now let my cause be pleaded, Bajazet,
For "father" I disdain to call thee now.
I took not arms to seize upon thy crown;
For that, if once thou hadst been laid in grave,
35   Should fit upon the head of Selimus
In spite of Corcut and of Acomat.
I took not arms to take away thy life:
The remnant of thy days is but a span,
And foolish had I been to enterprise
40   That which the gout and death would do for me.
I took not arms to shed my brothers' blood
Because they stop my passage to the crown;
For whilst thou liv'st Selimus is content
That they should live, but when thou once art dead,
45   Which of them both dares Selimus withstand?
I soon should hew their bodies in piecemeal,
As easy as man would kill a gnat;
But I took arms, unkind, to honor thee
And win again the fame that thou hast lost.
50   And thou thought'st scorn Selim should speak with thee,
But had it been your darling Acomat,
You would have met him half the way yourself.
I am a prince, and though your younger son,
Yet are my merits better than both theirs;
55   But you do seek to disinherit me
And mean t'invest Acomat with your crown.
So he shall have a prince's due reward
That cannot show a scar received in field.
We that have fought with mighty Prester John
60   And stripped th'Egyptian soldan of his camp,
Venturing life and living to honor thee,
For that same cause shall now dishonored be.

---

59   **Prester John**] mythical Christian king, believed to rule a kingdom in Ethiopia or China.

Art thou a father? Nay, false Bajazet,
Disclaim the title which thou dost not merit.
65 A father would not thus flee from his son
As thou dost fly from loyal Selimus.
Then Bajazet, prepare thee to the fight.
Selimus, once thy son but now thy foe,
Will make his fortunes by the sword and shield;
70 And since thou fear'st as long as I do live,
I'll also fear—as long as thou dost live.

Exit Selimus and his company.

BAJAZET: My heart is overwhelmed with fear and grief!
What dismal comet blazed at my birth,
Whose influence makes my strong unbridled son
75 Instead of love to render hate to me?
Ah bassas, if that ever heretofore
Your emperor ought his safety unto you,
Defend me now 'gainst my unnatural son:
Non timeo mortem: mortis mihi displicet author.

Exit Bajazet and his company.

SCENE 6.
FIELD OF BATTLE NEAR CHIURLU.

Alarum. Mustaffa beats Selimus in, then Ottrante and Cherseoli enter at diverse doors.

CHERSEOLI: Yield thee, Tartarian, or thou shalt die!
Upon my sword's sharp point standeth pale death,
Ready to rive in two thy caitiff breast.

---

77 **ought**] owed.
79 **Non timeo mortem: mortis mihi displicet author**] L., "I do not fear death: it is the cause of death that distresses me" (Ovid, *Metamorphoses*, 8:493).

OTTRANTE: Art thou that knight that like a lion fierce,
5   Tiring his stomach on a flock of lambs,
     Hast broke our ranks and put them clean to flight?
CHERSEOLI: Aye, and unless thou look unto thyself,
     This sword here, drunk in the Tartarian blood,
     Shall make thy carcass as the outcast dung.
10 OTTRANTE: Nay, I have matched a braver knight than you,
     Strong Alemshae, thy master's eldest son,
     Leaving his body naked on the plains;
     And Turk, the selfsame end for thee remains.

They fight. [Ottrante] killeth Cherseoli and flieth. Alarum. Enter Selimus.

SELIMUS: Shall Selimus' hope be buried in the dust?
15   And Bajazet triumph over his fall?
     Then oh, thou blindful mistress of mishap,
     Chief patroness of Rhamus' golden gates,
     I will advance my strong revenging hand,
     And pluck thee from thy ever-turning wheel.
20   Mars or Minerva, Mahound, Termagant,
     Or whosoe'er you are that fight 'gainst me,
     Come and but show yourselves before my face,
     And I will rend you all like trembling reeds.
     Well, Bajazet, though Fortune smile on thee
25   And deck thy camp with glorious victory,
     Though Selimus, now conquered by thee,
     Is fain to put his safety in swift flight;
     Yet so he flies, that like an angry ram,
     He'll turn more fiercely than before he came.

Exit Selimus.

---

16   **blindful mistress of mishap**] the goddess Fortune, Lady Luck.
17   **Rhamus**] a surname of Nemesis, classical goddess of divine retribution.

SCENE 7.
FIELD OF BATTLE NEAR CHIURLU.

*Enter Bajazet, Mustaffa, Soldier [carrying] the body of Cherseoli, and
Ottrante [held] prisoner.*

BAJAZET: Thus have we gained a bloody victory,
And though we are the masters of the field,
Yet have we lost more than our enemies.
Ah luckless fault of my Cherseoli!
5 As dear and dearer wert thou unto me
Than any of my sons, than mine own self.
When I was glad, thy heart was full of joy;
And bravely hast thou died for Bajazet.
And though thy bloodless body here do lie,
10 Yet thy sweet soul in heaven forever blest,
Among the stars enjoys eternal rest.
What art thou, warlike man of Tartary,
Whose hap it is to be our prisoner?
OTTRANTE: I am a prince. Ottrante is my name,
15 Chief captain of the Tartar's mighty host.
BAJAZET: Ottrante? Wast not thou that slew my son?
OTTRANTE: Aye, and if fortune had but favored me,
Had sent the sire to keep him company.
BAJAZET: Off with his head and spoil him of his arms,
20 And leave his body for the airy birds.

Exit one with Ottrante.

The unrevengèd ghost of Alemshae
Shall now no more wander on Stygian banks
But rest in quiet in th'Elysian fields.
Mustaffa, and you worthy men at arms
25 That left not Bajazet in greatest need,

---

19 **spoil**] strip.
23 **Elysian fields**] part of the classical underworld reserved for heroes.

When we arrive at Constantine's great tour,
You shall be honored of your emperor.

Exeunt all.

SCENE 8.
AMASIA.

Enter Acomat, Vizier, Regan and a band of Soldiers.

ACOMAT: Perhaps you wonder why Prince Acomat,
   Delighting heretofore in foolish love,
   Hath changed his quiet to a soldier's state
   And turned the dullest tunes of Hymen's song
5   Into Bellona's horrible outcries.
   You think it strange, that whereas I have lived
   Almost a votary to wantonness,
   To see me now lay off effeminate robes
   And arm my body in an iron wall.
10   I have enjoyed quiet long enough
   And surfeited with pleasure's surquidry.
   A field of dainties I have passèd through
   And been a champion to fair Cytheree.
   Now, since this idle peace hath wearied me,
15   I'll follow Mars and war another while
   And dye my shield in dolorous vermeil.
   My brother Selim through his manly deeds
   Hath lifted up his fame unto the skies,
   While we, like earthworms lurking in the weeds,
20   Do live inglorious in all men's eyes.
   What lets me, then? From this vain slumber rise

---

26 Constantine's great tour] tower in Byzantium (Istanbul) built by the Emperor Constantine.
4 Hymen] classical god of marriage.
5 Bellona] ancient Roman goddess of war.
11 surquidry] excessive pride.
13 Cytheree] Aphrodite, classical goddess of love.
21 lets] prevents.

And by strong hand achieve eternal glory
That may be talked of in all memory!
And see how fortune favors mine intent:
25 Heard you not, lordings, how Prince Selimus
Against our royal father armèd went?
And how the janissaries made him flee
To Ramir, emperor of Tartary?
This his rebellion greatly profits me;
30 For I shall sooner win my father's mind
To yield me up the Turkish empery;
Which if I have, I am sure I shall find
Strong enemies to pull me down again,
That fain would have prince Selimus to reign.
35 Then civil discord and contentious war
Will follow Acomat's coronation.
Selim, no doubt, will broach seditious jar,
And Corcut, too, will seek for alteration.
Now, to prevent all sudden perturbation,
40 We thought it good to muster up our power,
That danger may not take it unprovided.
VIZIER: I like your highness' resolution well;
For these should be the chief arts of a king:
To punish those that furiously rebel
45 And honor those that sacred counsel bring;
To make good laws, ill customs to expel,
To nourish peace, from whence your riches spring;
And when good quarrels call you to the field,
T'excel your men in handling spear and shield.
50 Thus shall the glory of your matchless name
Be registered up in immortal lines:
Whereas that prince that follows lustful game
And to fond toys his captive mind inclines,
Shall never pass the temple of true fame,
55 Whose worth is greater than the Indian mines.
But is your grace assurèd certainly
That Bajazet doth favor your request?
Perhaps you may make him your enemy.
You know how much your father doth detest

60   Stout disobedience and obstinacy.
        I speak not this as if I thought it best
        Your highness should your right in it neglect,
        But that you might be close and circumspect.
ACOMAT: We thank thee, Vizier, for thy loving care.
65   As for my father Bajazet's affection,
        Unless his holy vows forgotten are,
        I shall be sure of it by his election.
        But after Acomat's erection
        We must forecast what things be necessary,
70   Lest that our kingdom be too momentary.
REGAN: First let my Lord be seated in his throne,
        installed by great Bajazet's consent.
        As yet your harvest is not fully grown,
        But when you once have got the regiment,
75   Then may your lords more easily provide
        Against all accidents that may betide.
ACOMAT: Then set we forward to Byzantium,
        That we may know what Bajazet intends.
        Advise thee, Acomat, what's best to do.
80   The janissaries favor Selimus,
        And they are strong undaunted enemies,
        Which will in arms 'gainst thy election rise.
        Then wile them to thy will with precious gifts
        And store of gold: timely largition
85   The steadfast persons from their purpose lifts.
        But then beware lest Bajazet's affection
        Change into hatred by such premonition.
        For then he'll think that I am factious
        And imitate my brother Selimus.
90   Besides, a prince his honor doth debase
        That begs the common soldiers' suffrages;
        And if the bassas knew I sought their grace,

---

68   erection] promotion, advancement.
74   regiment] rule, power.
83   wile] entice.
84   largition] generous gift-giving.
87   premonition] forewarning.

It would the more increase their insolentness.
To resist them were overhardiness,
95 And worse it were to leave my enterprise.
Well, howsoe'er, resolve to venture it.
Fortune doth favor every bold essay,
And 'twere a trick of an unsettled wit
Because the bees have stings with them alway
100 To fear our mouths in honey to embay.
Then resolution for me leads the dance,
And thus resolved, I mean to try my chance.

Exeunt all.

SCENE 9.
THE IMPERIAL COURT AT BYZANTIUM.

Enter Bajazet, Mustaffa, Cali Bassa, Hali Bassa, and the janissaries.

BAJAZET: What prince soe'er trusts to his mighty pow'r,
Ruling the reins of many nations,
And feareth not lest fickle Fortune lour,
Or thinks his kingdom free from alterations;
5 If he were in the place of Bajazet,
He would but little by his scepter set.
For what hath rule that makes it acceptable?
Rather what hath it not worthy of hate?
First of all is our state still mutable
10 And our continuance at the people's rate;
So that it is a slender thread whereon
Depends the honor of a prince's throne.
Then do we fear, more than the child newborn,
Our friends, our lords, our subjects, and our sons.

---

94   overhardiness] overboldness.
99   alway] always.
100   embay] bathe.
3   lour] frown.
10   rate] judgement, estimation.

Thus is our mind in sundry pieces torn
15   By care, by fear, suspicion, and distrust.
In wine, in meat, we fear pernicious poison;
At home, abroad, we fear seditious treason.
Too true that tyrant Dionysus
Did picture out the image of a king
20   When Damocles was placèd in his throne
And o'er his head a threatening sword did hang,
Fastened up only by a horse's hair.°
Our chiefest trust is secretly distrust;
For whom have we whom we may safely trust,
25   If our own sons, neglecting awful duty,
Rise up in arms against their loving fathers?
Their heart is all of hardest marble wrought
That can lay wait to take away their breath
From whom they first sucked this vital air.
30   My heart is heavy, and I needs must sleep.
Bassas, withdraw yourselves from me awhile,
That I may rest my overburdened soul.

They stand aside while the curtains are drawn.

Eunuchs, play me some music while I sleep.

Music within.

MUSTAFFA: Good Bajazet, who would not pity thee,
35   Whom thine own son so vildly persecutes?
More mildly do th'unreasonablest beasts
Deal with their dams than Selimus with thee.
HALI BASSA: Mustaffa, we are princes of the land
And love our emperor as well as thou;
40   Yet will we not for pitying his estate
Suffer our foes our wealth to ruinate.
If Selim have played false with Bajazet
And overslipped the duty of a son,

---

35   **vildly**] in an abhorrent manner.

Why, he was moved by just occasion.
45 Did he not humbly send his messenger
To crave access unto his majesty?
And yet he could not get permission
To kiss his hands and speak his mind to him.
Perhaps he thought his agèd father's love
50 Was clean estranged from him, and Acomat
Should reap the fruit that he had labored for.
'Tis lawful for the father to take arms,
Aye, and by death chastise his rebel son.
Why should it be unlawful for the son
55 To levy arms 'gainst his injurious sire?
MUSTAFFA: You reason, Hali, like a sophister;
As if 'twere lawful for a subject prince
To rise in arms against his sovereign
Because he will not let him have his will:
60 Much less is't lawful for a man's own son!
If Bajazet had injured Selimus,
Or sought his death, or done him some abuse,
Then Selimus' cause had been more tolerable.
But Bajazet did never injure him,
65 Nor sought his death, nor once abusèd him;
Unless because he gives him not the crown,
  ⋅ Being the youngest of his highness' sons.
Gave he not him an empire for his part,
The mighty empire of great Trebizond?
70 So that if all things rightly be observed,
Selim had more then ever he deserved.
I speak not this because I hate the prince,
For by the heavens I love young Selimus,
Better than either of his brethren;
75 But for I owe allegiance to my king
And love him much that favors me so much.
Mustaffa, while old Bajazet doth live,
Will be as true to him as to himself.
CALI BASSA: Why brave Mustaffa, Hali and myself
80 Were never false unto his Majesty.
Our father Hali died in the field

Against the Sophy in his highness' wars,
And we will never be degenerate.
Nor do we take part with Prince Selimus
85   Because we would depose old Bajazet,
But for because we would not Acomat
(That leads his life still in lascivious pomp)
Nor Corcut (though he be a man of worth)
Should be commander of our empery.
90   For he that never saw his foeman's face
But always slept upon a lady's lap
Will scant endure to lead a soldier's life,
And he that never handled but his pen
Will be unskillful at the warlike lance.
95   Indeed his wisdom well may guide the crown
And keep that safe his predecessors got,
But being given to peace as Corcut is,
He never will enlarge the empery:
So that the rule and power over us
100   Is only fit for valiant Selimus.
MUSTAFFA: Princes, you know how mighty Bajazet
Hath honored Mustaffa with his love.
He gave his daughter, beauteous Solyma,
To be the sovereign mistress of my thoughts.
105   He made me captain of the janissaries,
And too unnatural should Mustaffa be
To rise against him in his dying age.
Yet know, you warlike peers, Mustaffa is
A loyal friend unto prince Selimus;
110   And ere his other brethren get the crown,
For his sake, I myself will pull them down.
I love, I love them dearly, but the love
Which I do bear unto my country's good
Makes me a friend to noble Selimus.
115   Only let Bajazet while he doth live
Enjoy in peace the Turkish diadem.
When he is dead and laid in quiet grave,
Then none but Selimus our help shall have.

Sound within. A Messenger enters. Bajazet awaketh.

BAJAZET: How now, Mustaffa, what news have we there?
120   Is Selim up in arms 'gainst me again?
        Or is the Sophy entered our confines?
        Hath the Egyptian snatched his crown again?
        Or have the uncontrollèd Christians
        Unsheathed their swords to make more war on us?
125   Such news, or none, will come to Bajazet.
MUSTAFFA: My gracious lord, here's an ambassador
        Come from your son the soldan Acomat.
BAJAZET: From Acomat? Oh, let him enter in.

Enter Regan.

        Ambassador, how fares our loving son?
130 REGAN: Mighty commander of the warlike Turks,
        Acomat, Soldan of Amasia,
        Greeteth your grace by me his messenger

He gives him a letter.

        And gratulates your highness' good success,
        Wishing good fortune may befall you still.
135 BAJAZET: Mustaffa, read.

He gives the letter to Mustaffa and speaks to himself [while Mustaffa reads].

        [*aside*] Acomat craves thy promise, Bajazet,
        To give the empire up into his hands
        And make it sure to him in thy lifetime.
        And thou shalt have it, lovely Acomat,
140   For I have been encumbered long enough
        And vexed with the cares of kingly rule.
        Now let the trouble of the empery
        Be buried in the bosom of thy son.
        Ah Acomat, if thou have such a reign,

145   So full of sorrow as thy father's was,
        Thou wilt accurse the time, the day, and hour,
        In which thou was established emperor.

Sound [trumpets]. A Messenger from Corcut [arrives].

        Yet more news?
MESSENGER: Long live the mighty emperor Bajazet!
150   Corcut, the soldan of Magnesia,
        Hearing of Selim's worthy overthrow
        And of the coming of young Acomat,
        Doth certify your Majesty by me
        How joyful he is of your victory;
155   And therewithal he humbly doth require
        Your Grace would do him justice in his cause.
        His brethren both, unworthy such a father,
        Do seek the empire while your Grace doth live,
        And that by undirect sinister means.
160   But Corcut's mind, free from ambitious thoughts,
        And trusting to the goodness of his cause,
        Joined unto your Highness' tender love,
        Only desires your Grace should not invest
        Selim nor Acomat in the diadem,
165   Which appertaineth unto him by right;
        But keep it to yourself the while you live
        And when it shall the great Creator please,
        Who hath the spirits of all men in his hands,
        Shall call your Highness to your latest home,
170   Then will he also sue to have his right.
BAJAZET: Like to a ship sailing without stars' sight,
        Whom waves do toss one way and winds another,
        Both without ceasing; even so my poor heart
        Endures a combat between love and right.
175   The love I bear to my dear Acomat
        Commands me give my suffrage unto him;
        But Corcut's title, being my eldest son,
        Bids me recall my hand and give it him.
        Acomat, he would have it in my life,

180 But gentle Corcut, like a loving son,
　　 Desires me live and die an emperor
　　 And at my death bequeath my crown to him.
　　 Ah Corcut! Thou, I see, lov'st me indeed!
　　 Selimus sought to thrust me down by force,
185 And Acomat seeks the kingdom in my life,
　　 And both of them are grieved thou liv'st so long.
　　 But Corcut numbreth not my days as they:
　　 O how much dearer loves he me then they!
　　 Bassas, how counsel you your emperor?
190 MUSTAFFA: My gracious lord, myself will speak for all;
　　 For all, I know, are minded as I am.
　　 Your Highness knows the janissaries' love,
　　 How firm they mean to cleave to your behest;
　　 As well you might perceive in that sad fight
195 When Selim set upon you in your flight.
　　 Then we do all desire you on our knees
　　 To keep the crown and scepter to yourself.
　　 How grievous will it be unto your thoughts
　　 If you should give the crown to Acomat,
200 To see the brethren disinherited,
　　 To flesh their anger one upon another
　　 And rend the bowels of this mighty realm.
　　 Suppose that Corcut would be well content,
　　 Yet thinks your Grace if Acomat were king
205 That Selim ere long would join league with him?
　　 Nay, he would break from forth his Trebizond
　　 And waste the empire all with fire and sword.
　　 Ah then, too weak would be poor Acomat
　　 To stand against his brothers' puissance
210 Or save himself from his enhancèd hand.
　　 While Ismael and the cruel Persians
　　 And the great soldan of th'Egyptians
　　 Would smile to see our force dismembered so;
　　 Aye, and perchance the neighbor Christians
215 Would take occasion to thrust out their heads.

---

210 enhancèd] lifted up, raised in power and degree.

All this may be prevented by your grace,
If you will yield to Corcut's just request
And keep the kingdom to you while you live.
Meantime we that your Grace's subjects are
220   May make us strong, to fortify the man
Whom at your death your Grace shall choose as king.
BAJAZET: O how thou speakest ever like thyself,
Loyal Mustaffa! Well were Bajazet
If all his sons did bear such love to him.
225   Though loath I am longer to wear the crown,
Yet for I see it is my subjects' will,
Once more will Bajazet be emperor.
But we must send to pacify our son
Or he will storm, as earst did Selimus.
230   Come, let us go unto our council, lords,
And there consider what is to be done.

Exeunt all.

SCENE 10.
SOMEWHERE IN ANATOLIA, BETWEEN
AMASIA AND BYZANTIUM.

*Enter Acomat, Regan, Vizier and his Soldiers. Acomat reads a letter and then
[tears it up].*

ACOMAT: Thus will I rend the crown from off thy head,
False-hearted and injurious Bajazet!
To mock thy son that loved thee so dear!
What for? Because the head-strong janissaries
5   Would not consent to honor Acomat,
And their base bassas, vowed to Selimus,
Thought me unworthy of the Turkish crown?
Should he be ruled and overruled by them,
Under pretense of keeping it himself,
10   To wipe me clean for ever being king?
Doth he esteem so much the bassas' words

And prize their favor at so high a rate
That for to gratify their stubborn minds
He casts away all care and all respects
15   Of duty, promise, and religious oaths?
Now by the holy Prophet Mahomet,
Chief president and patron of the Turks,
I mean to challenge now my right by arms
And win by sword that glorious dignity
20   Which he injuriously detains from me.
Haply he thinks because that Selimus,
Rebutted by his warlike janissaries,
Was fain to fly in haste from whence he came
That Acomat (by his example moved)
25   Will fear to manage arms against his sire;
Or that my life forepassed in pleasure's court
Promises weak resistance in the fight;
But he shall know that I can use my sword
And like a lion seize upon my prey.
30   If ever Selim moved him heretofore,
Acomat means to move him ten times more.
VIZIER: 'Twere good your Grace would to Amasia
And there increase your camp with fresh supply.
ACOMAT: Vizier, I am impatient of delay;
35   And since my father hath incensed me thus,
I'll quench those kindled flames with his heart blood.
Not like a son, but a most cruel foe,
Will Acomat be henceforth unto him.
March to Natolia! There we will begin
40   And make a preface to our massacres.
My nephew Mahomet, son to Alemshae,
Departed lately from Iconium,
Is lodged there, and he shall be the first
Whom I will sacrifice unto my wrath.

Exeunt all.

---

42   **Iconium**] ancient name for Konya, a city in southeastern Anatolia.

SCENE 11.
ICONIUM IN NATOLIA.

Enter the young Prince Mahomet, the Beylerbey of Natolia, and one or two
Soldiers.

MAHOMET: Lord governor, what think you best to do?
    If we receive the soldan Acomat,
    Who knoweth not but his bloodthirsty sword
    Shall be emboweled in our countrymen?
5   You know he is displeased with Bajazet
    And will rebel (as Selim did tofore)
    And would to God, with Selim's overthrow.
    You know his angry heart hath vowed revenge
    On all the subjects of his father's land.
10 BEYLERBEY: Young prince, thy uncle seeks to have thy life
    Because by right the Turkish crown is thine.
    Save thou thyself by flight or otherwise,
    And we will make resistance as we can.
    Like an Armenian tiger that hath lost
15   Her loved whelps, so raveth Acomat:
    And we must be subject onto his rage.
    But you may live to venge your citizens.
    Then fly, good prince, before your uncle come.
MAHOMET: Nay, good my lord, never shall it be said
20   That Mahomet, the son of Alemshae,
    Fled from his citizens for fear of death;
    But I will stay and help to fight for you,
    And if you needs must die, I'll die with you.
    And I among the rest with forward hand,
25   Will help to kill a common enemy.

Exeunt all.

---

6   **tofore**] before.

SCENE 12.

OUTSIDE THE WALLS OF ICONIUM.

Enter Acomat, Vizier, Regan, and the Soldiers.

ACOMAT: Now, fair Natolia, shall thy stately walls
    Be overthrown and beaten to the ground!
    My heart within me for revenge still calls.
    Why, Bajazet, thought'st thou that Acomat
5   Would put up such a monstrous injury?
    Then had I brought my chivalry in vain
    And to no purpose drawn my conquering blade;
    Which now unsheathed, shall not be sheathed again
    Till it a world of bleeding souls hath made.
10   Poor Mahomet, thou thought'st thyself too sure
    In thy strong city of Iconium,
    To plant thy forces in Natolia,
    Weakened so much before by Selim's sword.
    Summon a parley to the citizens,
15   That they may hear the dreadful words I speak
    And die in thought before they come to blows.

[They] all [hold] a parley. Mahomet, Beylerbey, and Soldiers [appear above] on
the walls [of the city].

MAHOMET: What craves our uncle Acomat of us?
ACOMAT: That thou and all the city yield themselves;
    Or by the holy rites of Mahomet,
20   His wondrous tomb and sacred Alcoran,
    You all shall die: and not a common death,
    But even as monstrous as I can devise.
MAHOMET: Uncle, if I may call you by that name,
    Which cruelly hunt for your nephew's blood;
25   You do us wrong thus to besiege our town
    That ne'er deserved such hatred at your hands,

---

20 Alcoran] the Koran.

Being your friends and kinsmen as we are.

ACOMAT: In that thou wrongst me that thou art my kinsman.

MAHOMET: Why, for I am thy nephew dost thou frown?

30 ACOMAT: Aye, that thou art so near unto the crown.

MAHOMET: Why, uncle, I resign my right to thee,
    And all my title—were it ne'er so good.

ACOMAT: Wilt thou? Then know assuredly from me,
    I'll seal the resignation with thy blood;

35   Though Alemshae, thy father, loved me well,
    Yet Mahomet, his son, shall down to hell.

MAHOMET: Why, uncle, doth my life put you in fear?

ACOMAT: It shall not, nephew, since I have you here.

MAHOMET: When I am dead, more hinderers shalt thou find.

40 ACOMAT: When one's cut off, the fewer are behind.

MAHOMET: Yet think the gods do bear an equal eye.

ACOMAT: Faith, if they all were squint-eyed, what care I?

MAHOMET: Then Acomat know we will rather die
    Than yield us up into a tyrant's hand.

45 ACOMAT: Beshrew me, but you are the wiser, Mahomet;
    For if I do but catch you, boy, alive,
    'Twere better for you run through Phlegethon.
    Sirs, scale the walls, and pull the caitiffs down!
    I give to you the spoil of all the town.

*Alarum. [They] scale the walls. Enter Acomat, Vizier, and Regan, with
    Mahomet.*

50 ACOMAT: Now youngster, you that brav'dst us on the walls,
    And shook your plumèd crest against our shield,
    What wouldst thou give, or what wouldst thou not give,
    That thou wert far enough from Acomat?

55   How like the villain is to Bajazet!
    Well, nephew, for thy father loved me well,

---

47 **Phlegethon**] a river of fire, one of the five rivers in the classical underworld.

48 **scale the walls**] Acomat and his soldiers climb to the upper stage area and fight their way offstage
through the upper stage exits as if they were entering the besieged city. Then they reenter the lower
stage area, having defeated and taken captive Mahomet.

I will not deal extremely with his son:
Then hear a brief compendium of thy death.
Regan, go cause a grove of steelhead spears
Be pitched thick under the castle wall
60   And on them let this youthful captive fall.
    MAHOMET: Thou shalt not fear me, Acomat, with death,
        Nor will I beg my pardon at thy hands.
        But as thou giv'st me such a monstrous death,
        So do I freely leave to thee my curse.

Exit Regan with Mahomet.

65 ACOMAT: Oh, that will serve to fill my father's purse!

Alarum. Enter a Soldier with Zonara, sister to Mahomet.

    ZONARA: Ah pardon me, dear uncle, pardon me!
    ACOMAT: No, minion, you are too near a kin to me.
    ZONARA: If ever pity entered thy breast,
        Or ever thou wast touched with woman's love,
70   Sweet uncle, spare wretched Zonara's life!
        Thou once wast noted for a quiet prince,
        Soft-hearted, mild, and gentle as a lamb.
        Ah, do not prove a lion unto me!
    ACOMAT: Why would'st thou live when Mahomet is dead?
75 ZONARA: Ah, who slew Mahomet? Uncle, did you?
    ACOMAT: He that's prepared to do as much for you.
    ZONARA: Dost thou not pity Alemshae in me?
    ACOMAT: Yes, that he wants so long thy company.
    ZONARA: Thou art not, false groom, son to Bajazet!
80   He would relent to hear a woman weep;
        But thou wast born in desert Caucasus,
        And the Hyrcanian tigers gave thee suck,

---

61 **fear me**] frighten me.
81 **desert Caucasus**] uninhabitable mountain range in Caucasia, between the Black and Caspian seas.
82 **Hyrcanian**] from an ancient province of the Persian empire southeast of the Caspian Sea, a proverbially harsh and desolate wilderness.

Knowing thou wert a monster like themselves.
ACOMAT: Let you her thus to rate us? Strangle her!

They strangle her.

85   Now scour the streets, and leave not one alive
To carry these sad news to Bajazet;
That all the citizens may dearly say,
This day was fatal to Natolia.

Exeunt all.

SCENE 13.
THE IMPERIAL COURT AT BYZANTIUM.

Enter Bajazet, Mustaffa, and the janissaries.

BAJAZET: Mustaffa, if my mind deceive me not,
Some strange misfortune is not far from me.
I was not wont to tremble in this sort.
Methinks I feel a cold run through my bones,
5   As if it hastened to surprise my heart.
Methinks some voice still whispereth in my ears
And bids me to take heed of Acomat.
MUSTAFFA: 'Tis but your Highness' overchargèd mind
Which feareth most the things it least desires.

*Enter two Soldiers with the Beylerbey of Natolia in a chair, and the bodies of
Mahomet and Zonara in two coffins.*

10 BAJAZET: Ah, sweet Mustaffa, thou art much deceived.
My mind presages me some future harm;
And lo, what doleful exequy is here!
Our chief commander of Natolia!
What caitiff hand is it hath wounded thee?
15   And who are these covered in tomb-black hearse?
BEYLERBEY: These are thy nephews, mighty Bajazet,

The son and daughter of good Alemshae,
Whom cruel Acomat hath murdered thus.
These eyes beheld, when from an airy tour,
20 They hurled the body of young Mahomet,
Whereas a band of armed soldiers
Received him falling on their spears' sharp points.
His sister, poor Zonara, luckless maid,
Entreating life and not obtaining it,
25 Was strangled by his barbarous soldiers.

Bajazet falls in a swound. [He recovers and then speaks.]

BAJAZET: Oh, you dispensers of our hapless breath,
Why do ye glut your eyes and take delight
To see sad pageants of men's miseries?
Wherefore have you prolonged my wretched life,
30 To see my son, my dearest Acomat,
To lift his hands against his father's life?
Ah, Selimus, now do I pardon thee,
For thou didst set upon me manfully
And moved by an occasion, though unjust.
35 But Acomat, injurious Acomat,
Is ten times more unnatural to me.
Hapless Zonara, hapless Mahomet,
The poor remainder of my Alemshae!
Which of you both shall Bajazet most wail?
40 Ah, both of you are worthy to be wailed.
Happily dealt the froward Fates with thee,
Good Alemshae, for thou didst die in field
And so preventedst this sad spectacle;
Pitiful spectacle of sad dreariment,
45 Pitiful spectacle of dismal death.
But I have lived to see thee, Alemshae,
By Tartar pirates all in pieces torn,

---

19 airy tour] high tower.
39 wail] bewail, mourn.
44 dreariment] sorrow, grief.

To see young Selim's disobedience,
To see the death of Alemshae's poor seed,
50   And last of all to see my Acomat
Prove a rebellious enemy to me.
BEYLERBEY: Ah, cease your tears, unhappy emperor,
And shed not all for your poor nephew's death.
Six thousand of true-hearted citizens
55   In fair Natolia, Acomat hath slain:
The channels run like riverets of blood,
And I escaped with this poor company,
Bemangled and dismembered as you see,
To be the messenger of these sad news.
60   And now mine eyes fast-swimming in pale death,
Bids me resign my breath unto the heavens.
Death stands before, ready for to strike.
Farewell, dear emperor, and revenge our loss,
As ever thou dost hope for happiness.   *He dies.*
65 BAJAZET: Avernus' jaws and loathsome Tartarus,
From whence the damnèd ghosts do often creep
Back to the world to punish wicked men;
Black Demogorgon, grandfather of night,
Send out thy furies from thy fiery hall,
70   The pitiless Erinyes armed with whips,
And all the damnèd monsters of black hell,
To pour their plagues on cursèd Acomat!
How shall I mourn, or which way shall I turn
To pour my tears upon my dearest friends?
75   Couldst thou endure, false-hearted Acomat,
To kill thy nephew and his sister thus
And wound to death so valiant a lord?
And will you not, you all-beholding heavens,
Dart down on him your piercing lightning brand,
80   Enrolled in sulfur and consuming flames?
Ah do not, Jove! Acomat is my son

---

65   **Avernus' jaws**] the entrance to hell.
65   **Tartarus**] a place in Hades for the punishment of the wicked.
68   **Demogorgon**] an infernal deity of ancient mythology.
70   **Erinyes**] the Furies.

And may perhaps by counsel be reclaimed
And brought to filial obedience.
Aga, thou art a man of piercant wit:
85   Go thou and talk with my son Acomat
And see if he will any way relent.
Speak him fair, Aga, lest he kill thee, too.
And we, my lords, will in and mourn a while
Over these princes' lamentable tombs.

Exeunt all.

SCENE 14.
ICONIUM.

Enter Acomat, Vizier, Regan, and their Soldiers.

ACOMAT: As Tityus in the country of the dead,
With restless cries doth call upon high Jove,
The while the vulture tireth on his heart;
So, Acomat, revenge still gnaws thy soul.
5   I think my soldiers' hands have been too slow
In shedding blood and murth'ring innocents.
I think my wrath hath been too patient,
Since civil blood quencheth not out the flames
Which Bajazet hath kindled in my heart.
10 VIZIER: My gracious lord, here is a messenger
Sent from your father the emperor.

Enter Aga and one with him.

ACOMAT: Let him come in. Aga, what news with you?
AGA: Great prince, thy father mighty Bajazet
Wonders your grace whom he did love so much

---

84   piercant] penetrative.
1   **Tityus**] in classical mythology, a giant who was thrown into Tartarus for attempting to rape Leto.
He lay chained there while a vulture fed on his perpetually renewed liver.
3   **tireth on**] tears the flesh of.

15   And thought to leave possessor of the crown
        Would thus requite his love with mortal hate,
        To kill thy nephews with revenging sword
        And massacre his subjects in such sort.

ACOMAT: Aga, my father, traitorous Bajazet,
20   Detains the crown injuriously from me,
        Which I will have if all the world say nay.
        I am not like the unmanured land,
        Which answers not his honor's greedy mind:
        I sow not seeds upon the barren sand.
25   A thousand ways can Acomat soon find
        To gain my will, which if I cannot gain,
        Then purple blood my angry hands shall stain.

AGA: Acomat, yet learn by Selimus
        That hasty purposes have hated ends.

30 ACOMAT: Tush, Aga, Selim was not wise enough
        To set upon the head at the first brunt.
        He should have done as I mean to do:
        Fill all the confines with fire, sword, and blood;
        Burn up the fields and overthrow whole towns,
35   And when he had endamaged that way,
        Then tear the old man piecemeal with my teeth
        And color my strong hands with his gore-blood.

AGA: Oh see, my lord, how fell ambition
        Deceives your senses and bewitches you!
40   Could you unkind perform so foul a deed
        As kill the man that first gave life to you?
        Do you not fear the people's adverse fame?

ACOMAT: It is the greatest glory of a king
        When, though his subjects hate his wicked deeds,
45   Yet are they forced to bear them all with praise.

AGA: Whom fear constrains to praise their prince's deeds,
        That fear eternal hatred in them feeds.

ACOMAT: He knows not how to sway the kingly mace
        That loves to be great in his people's grace:

---

20 **injuriously**] unjustly.
23 **greedy**] hungry.
35 **endamaged**] inflicted damage.

50   The surest ground for kings to build upon
      Is to be feared and cursed of everyone.
      What though the world of nations me hate?
      Hate is peculiar to a prince's state.
  AGA: Where there's no shame, no care of holy law,
55   No faith, no justice, no integrity,
      That state is full of mutability.
  ACOMAT: Bare faith, pure virtue, poor integrity
      Are ornaments fit for a private man.
      Beseems a prince for to do all he can.
60 AGA: Yet know, it is a sacrilegious will
      To slay thy father, were he ne'er so ill.
  ACOMAT: 'Tis lawful, graybeard, for to do to him
      What ought not to be done unto a father.
      Hath he not wiped me from the Turkish crown?
65   Preferred he not the stubborn janissaries
      And heard the bassas' stout petitions
      Before he would give ear to my request?
      As sure as day, mine eyes shall ne'er taste sleep
      Before my sword have riven his perjured breast.
70 AGA: Ah, let me never live to see that day!
  ACOMAT: Yes, thou shalt live—but never see that day,
      Wanting the tapers that should give thee light.

[Acomat] pulls out [Aga's] eyes.

      Thou shalt not see so great felicity
      When I shall rend out Bajazet's dim eyes
75   And by his death install myself a king.
  AGA: Ah, cruel tyrant and unmerciful!
      More bloody than the anthropophagi
      That fill their hungry stomachs with man's flesh!
      Thou shouldst have slain me, barbarous Acomat;
80   Not leave me in so comfortless a life,
      To live on earth and never see the sun.

---

59 **Beseems**] It is fitting for.
77 **anthropophagi**] man-eaters.

ACOMAT: Nay, let him die that liveth at his ease.
          Death would a wretched caitiff greatly please.
AGA: And thinkst thou then to scape unpunishèd?
85   No, Acomat, though both mine eyes be gone,
          Yet are my hands left on to murther thee.
ACOMAT: 'Twas well remembred: Regan, cut them off.

They cut off his hands and give them [to] Acomat.

          Now in that sort go tell thy emperor
          That if himself had but been in thy place,
90   I would have used him crueller then thee.
          Here, take thy hands. I know thou lov'st them well.

[Acomat] opens [Aga's] bosom and puts them in.

          Which hand is this? right? or left? Canst thou tell?
AGA: I know not which it is, but 'tis my hand.
          But oh, thou supreme architect of all,
95   First mover of those tenfold crystal orbs
          Where all those moving and unmoving eyes
          Behold thy goodness everlastingly;
          See, unto thee I lift these bloody arms
          (For hands I have not for to lift to thee);
100   And in thy justice, dart thy smoldering flame
          Upon the head of cursèd Acomat!
          Oh cruel heavens and injurious Fates!
          Even the last refuge of a wretched man
          Is took from me: for how can Aga weep?
105   Or rain a brinish show'r of pearlèd tears,
          Wanting the watery cisterns of his eyes?
          Come, lead me back again to Bajazet,
          The woefullest and sad'st ambassador
          That ever was dispatched to any king.
110 ACOMAT: Why so, this music pleases Acomat.
          And would I had my doting father here:
          I would rip up his breast and rend his heart,
          Into his bowels thrust my angry hands,

As willingly, and with as good a mind
115   As I could be the Turkish emperor.
And by the clear declining vault of heaven,
Whither the souls of dying men do flee,
Either I mean to die the death myself
Or make that old false faitour bleed his last.
120   For death no sorrow could unto me bring,
So Acomat might die the Turkish king.

Exeunt all.

SCENE 15.
THE IMPERIAL COURT IN BYZANTIUM.

Enter Bajazet, Mustaffa, Cali Bassa, Hali Bassa, and Aga (led by a Soldier)
who [kneels before Bajazet and embraces Bajazet's legs].

AGA: Is this the body of my sovereign?
Are these the sacred pillars that support
The image of true magnanimity?
Ah Bajazet, thy son false Acomat
5   Is full resolved to take thy life from thee!
'Tis true, 'tis true! Witness these handless arms;
Witness these empty lodges of mine eyes;
Witness the gods that from the highest heaven
Beheld the tyrant with remorseless heart
10   Pulled out mine eyes and cut off my weak hands;
Witness that sun whose golden-colored beams
Your eyes do see but mine can ne'er behold;
Witness the earth that sucked up my blood,
Streaming in rivers from my trunkèd arms;
15   Witness the present that he sends to thee!
Open my bosom: there you shall it see.

---

119   **faitour**] imposter.
14   **trunkèd**] lopped, mutilated.

[Mustaffa] opens his bosom and takes out his hands.

Those are the hands which Aga once did use
To toss the spear and in a warlike gyre
To hurtle my sharp sword about my head.
20   Those sends he to thee, woeful emperor,
With purpose so to cut thy hands from thee.
Why is my sovereign silent all this while?
BAJAZET: Ah Aga, Bajazet fain would speak to thee,
But sudden sorrow eateth up my words.
25   Bajazet, Aga, fain would weep for thee,
But cruel sorrow drieth up my tears.
Bajazet, Aga, fain would die for thee,
But grief hath weakened my poor agèd hands.
How can he speak, whose tongue sorrow hath tied?
30   How can he mourn, that cannot shed a tear?
How shall he live, that full of misery
Calleth for death, which will not let him die?
MUSTAFFA: Let women weep, let children pour forth tears,
And cowards spend the time in bootless moan.
35   We'll load the earth with such a mighty host
Of janissaries, stern-born sons of Mars,
That Phoeb shall fly and hide him in the clouds
For fear our javelins thrust him from his wain.
Old Aga was a prince among your lords.
40   His counsels always were true oracles,
And shall he thus unmanly be misused?
And he unpunishèd that did the deed?
Shall Mahomet and poor Zonara's ghosts
And the good governor of Natolia
45   Wander in Stygian meadows unrevenged?
Good emperor, stir up thy manly heart,
And send forth all thy warlike janissaries

---

37 **Phoeb**] Phoebus Apollo, god of the sun.
38 **his wain**] Apollo's chariot.
45 **Stygian meadows**] fields by the River Styx in the classical underworld.

To chastise that rebellious Acomat.
Thou know'st we cannot fight without a guide,
50   And he must be one of the royal blood,
Sprung from the loins of mighty Ottoman.
And who remains now, but young Selimus?
So please your Grace to pardon his offense
And make him captain of th'imperial host.
55 BAJAZET: Aye, good Mustaffa, send for Selimus.
So I may be revenged, I care not how.
The worst that can befall me is but death;
'Tis that would end my woeful misery.
Selimus—he must work me this good turn.
60   I cannot kill myself: he'll do't for me.
Come, Aga, thou and I will weep the while:
Thou for thy eyes and loss of both thy hands;
I for th'unkindness of my Acomat.

Exeunt all.

SCENE 16.
EXILE IN TARTARIA.

Enter Selimus and a Messenger with a letter from Bajazet.

SELIMUS: Will Fortune favor me yet once again?
And will she thrust the cards into my hands?
Well, if I chance but once to get the deck,
To deal about and shuffle as I would;
5   Let Selim never see the daylight spring
Unless I shuffle out myself a king.
Friend, let me see thy letter once again,
That I may read these reconciling lines.

---

63 **unkindness**] cruelty, unnatural behavior.

Reads the letter.

Thou hast a pardon, Selim, granted thee.
10   Mustaffa and the forward janissaries
Have sued to thy father Bajazet
That thou mayst be their captain-general
Against th'attempts of Soldan Acomat.
Why, that's the thing I requested most:
15   That I might once th'imperial army lead;
And since it's offered me so willingly,
Beshrew me, but I'll take their courtesy.
Soft, let me see. Is there no policy
T'entrap poor Selimus in this device?
20   It may be that my father fears me yet,
Lest I should once again rise up in arms,
And like Antaeus quelled by Hercules,
Gather new forces by my overthrow,
And therefore sends for me under pretense
25   Of this, and that; but when he hath me there,
He'll make me sure for putting him in fear.
Distrust is good when there's cause of distrust.
Read it again: perchance thou dost mistake.

Reads.

O here's Mustaffa's signet set thereto.
30   Then Selim, cast all foolish fear aside,
For he's a prince that favors thy estate
And hateth treason worse than death itself,
And hardly can I think he could be brought,
If there were treason, to subscribe his name.
35   Come friend, the cause requires we should be gone:
Now once again, have at the Turkish throne!

Exeunt both.

---

22   Antaeus quelled by Hercules] Antaeus, son of Mother Earth, was a giant who when touching the ground drew strength from his mother and was invulnerable. He was defeated by Hercules who lifted him up and crushed him.

SCENE 17.
THE IMPERIAL COURT AT BYZANTIUM.

Enter Bajazet leading Aga, Mustaffa, Hali Bassa, Cali Bassa, Selimus, and the
janissaries.

BAJAZET: Come, mournful Aga; come and sit by me.
    Thou hast been sorely grieved for Bajazet:
    Good reason, then, that he should grieve for thee.
    Give me thy arm. Though thou hast lost thy hands
5   And liv'st as a poor exile in this light,
    Yet hast thou won the heart of Bajazet.
AGA: Your Grace's words are very comfortable,
    And well can Aga bear his grievous loss
    Since it was for so good a prince's sake.
10 SELIMUS: Father—if I may call thee by that name,
    Whose life I aimed at with rebellious sword—
    In all humility thy reformed son
    Offers himself into your Grace's hands
    And at your feet layeth his bloody sword,
15   Which he advanced against your majesty.
    If my offense do seem so odious
    That I deserve not longer time to live,
    Behold, I open unto you my breast,
    Ready prepared to die at your command.
20   But if repentance in unfeignèd heart
    And sorrow for my grievous crime forepassed
    May merit pardon at your princely hands,
    Behold where poor inglorious Selimus
    Upon his knees begs pardon of your grace.
25 BAJAZET: Stand up, my son. I joy to hear thee speak;
    But more to hear thou art so well reclaimed.
    Thy crime were ne'er so odious unto me,
    But thy reformèd life and humble thoughts
    Are thrice as pleasing to my aged spirit.
30   Selim, we here pronounce thee by our will,
    Chief general of the warlike janissaries.
    Go lead them out against false Acomat,

Which hath so grievously rebelled 'gainst me.
Spare him not, Selim; though he be my son
35   Yet do I now clean disinherit him
As common enemy to me and mine.
SELIMUS: May Selim live to show how dutiful
And loving he will be to Bajazet.
[*aside*] So now doth fortune smile on me again
40   And in regard of former injuries
Offers me millions of diadems!
I smile to see how that the good old man
Thinks Selim's thoughts are brought to such an ebb
As he hath cast off all ambitious hope.
45   But soon shall that opinion be removed;
For if I once get 'mongst the janizars,
Then on my head the golden crown shall sit.
Well, Bajazet, I fear me thou wilt grieve
That e'er thou didst thy feigning son believe.

Exit Selimus, with all the rest, save Bajazet and Aga.

50   BAJAZET: Now, Aga, all the thoughts that troubled me
Do rest within the center of my heart,
And thou shalt shortly joy as much with me
When Acomat by Selim's consuming sword
Shall leese that ghost which made thee lose thy sight.
55   AGA: Ah, Bajazet, Aga looks not for revenge,
But will pour out his prayers to the heavens
That Acomat may learn by Selimus
To yield himself up to his father's grace.

Sound within: Long live Selimus, Emperor of Turks!

BAJAZET: How now, what sudden triumph have we here?
60   MUSTAFFA: Ah, gracious lord, the captains of the host
With one assent have crowned Prince Selimus,

---

46   **janizars**] janissaries.
54   **leese**] set free.

And here he comes with all the janissaries
To crave his confirmation at thy hands.

Enter Cali Bassa, Selimus, Hali Bassa, Sinam Bassa, and the janissaries.

SINAM BASSA: Bajazet, we the captains of thy host,
65   Knowing thy weak and too unwieldy age
Unable is longer to govern us,
Have chosen Selimus, thy younger son,
That he may be our leader and our guide
Against the Sophy and his Persians,
70   'Gainst the victorious Soldan Tonombey.
There wants but thy consent, which we will have,
Or hew thy body piecemeal with our swords.
BAJAZET: Needs must I give what is already gone.

He takes off his crown.

Here, Selimus, thy father Bajazet,
75   Wearied with cares that wait upon a king,
Resigns the crown as willingly to thee
As e'er my father gave it unto me.

Sets it on his head.

ALL: Long live Selimus, Emperor of Turks!
BAJAZET: Live thou a long and a victorious reign
80   And be triumpher of thine enemies.
Aga and I will to Dimoticum
And live in peace the remnant of our days.

Exit Bajazet and Aga.

SELIMUS: Now sit I like the arm-strong son of Jove
When, after he had all his monsters quelled,

---

81   **Dimoticum]** Demitoka, city in Turkey and birthplace of Bajazet II.
83   **son of Jove]** Hercules.

85   He was received in heaven 'mongst the gods
      And had fair Hebe for his lovely bride.
      As many labors Selimus hath had
      And now at length attainèd to the crown.
      This is my Hebe, and this is my heaven.
90   Bajazet goeth to Dimoticum,
      And there he purposes to live at ease;
      But Selimus, as long as he is on earth,
      Thou shall not sleep in rest without some broil;
      For Bajazet is unconstant as the wind.
95   To make that sure I have a platform laid:
      Bajazet hath with him a cunning Jew,
      Professing physic; and so skilled therein,
      As if he had pow'r over life and death.
      Withal, a man so stout and resolute
100   That he will venture anything for gold.
      This Jew with some intoxicated drink
      Shall poison Bajazet and that blind lord:
      Then one of Hydra's heads is clean cut off.
      Go some and fetch here Abraham the Jew.

Exit one for Abraham.

105   Corcut, thy pageant next is to be played;
      For though he be a grave philosopher,
      Given to read Mahomet's dread laws,
      And Razius' toys, and Avicenna's drugs;
      Yet he may have a longing for the crown.
110   Besides, he may by devilish negromancy
      Procure my death or work my overthrow:
      The devil still is ready to do harm.
      Hali, you and your brother presently

---

86   **Hebe**] goddess of youth and cupbearer to the Olympian gods.
99   **Withal**] nevertheless.
108 **Razius**] Razius (or Rhazes) was the author of a Greek medical treatise on smallpox and measles.
108 **toys**] trifles.
108 **Avicenna**] Ibn Sina, Arab physician and philosopher.
110 **negromancy**] black magic.

Shall with an army to Magnesia.
115   There you shall find the scholar at his book.
And hear'st thou, Hali? Strangle him.

Exeunt Hali Bassa and Cali Bassa.

Corcut once dead, then Acomat remains,
Whose death will make me certain of the crown.
These heads of Hydra are the principal;
120   When these are off, some other will arise,
As Amurath and Aladin, sons to Acomat;
My sister Solyma, Mustaffa's wife;
All these shall suffer shipwrack on a shelf,
Rather than Selim will be drowned himself.

Enter Abraham the Jew.

125   Jew, thou art welcome unto Selimus.
I have a piece of service for you, sir,
But on your life be secret in the deed.
Get a strong poison whose envenomed taste
May take away the life of Bajazet
130   Before he pass forth of Byzantium.
ABRAHAM: I warrant you, my gracious sovereign,
He shall be quickly sent unto his grave;
For I have potions of so strong a force
That whosoever touches them shall die.
135   [*aside*] And would your grace would once but taste of them,
I could as willingly afford them you,
As your agèd father Bajazet.
[*To Selimus*] My Lord, I am resolved to do the deed.

Exit Abraham.

SELIMUS: So this is well: for I am none of those
140   That make a conscience for to kill a man.
For nothing is more hurtful to a prince
Than to be scrupulous and religious.

I like Lysander's counsel passing well:
If that I cannot speed with lion's force,
145   To clothe my complots in a fox's skin.
For th'only things that wrought our empery
Were open wrongs and hidden treachery.
Oh, th'are two wings wherewith I use to fly
And soar above the common sort.
150   If any seek our wrongs to remedy,
With these I take his meditation short;
And one of these shall still maintain my cause:
Or fox's skin, or lion's rending paws.

Exeunt all.

SCENE 18.
DIMOTICUM.

Enter Bajazet and Aga in mourning cloaks, Abraham the Jew with a cup.

BAJAZET: Come, Aga, let us sit and mourn a while,
For fortune never showed herself so cross
To any prince as to poor Bajazet.
That woeful emperor, first of my name,
5   Whom the Tartarians locked in a cage,
To be a spectacle to all the world,
Was ten times happier then I am now.
For Tamburlaine, the scourge of nations,
Was he that pulled him from his kingdom so,°
10   But mine own sons expel me from the throne.
Ah, where shall I begin to make my moan?
Or what shall I first reckon in my plaint?
From my youth up I have been drowned in woe,
And to my latest hour I shall be so.
15   You swelling seas of never-ceasing care,

---

143   **Lysander**] Spartan naval commander and statesman (died 395 B.C.).
148   **th'are**] they are.

Whose waves my weatherbeaten ship do toss,
Your boisterous billows too unruly are
And threaten still my ruin and my loss.
Like hugie mountains do your waters rear
20   Their lofty tops and my weak vessel cross.
Alas, at length allay your stormy strife,
And cruel wrath within me raging rise;
Or else my feeble bark cannot endure
Your slashing buffets and outrageous blows;
25   But while thy foamy flood doth it immure,
Shall soon be wracked upon the sandy shallows.
Grief, my lewd boatswain, steereth nothing sure,
But without stars 'gainst tide and wind he rows
And cares not though upon some rock we split,
30   A restless pilot for the charge unfit.
But out, alas, the god that vails the seas,
And can alone this raging tempest stent,
will never blow a gentle gale of ease
But suffer my poor vessel to be rent.
35   Then, O thou blind procurer of mischance
That stay'st thyself upon a turning wheel,
Thy cruel hand, even when thou wilt, enhance
And pierce my poor heart with thy thrillant steel.
AGA: Cease, Bajazet—now it is Aga's turn.
40   Rest thou awhile and gather up more tears,
The while poor Aga tell his tragedy.
When first my mother brought me to the world,
Some blazing comet ruled in the sky,
Portending miserable chance to me.
45   My parents were but men of poor estate,
And happy yet had wretched Aga been,
If Bajazet had not exalted him.
Poor Aga! Had it not been much more fair

---

27   lewd] unskilled, foolish.
31   vails] causes or allows to descend or sink (*O.E.D.*).
32   stent] cause to desist.
37   enhance] strike.
38   thrillant] piercing.

T'have died among the cruel Persians
50   Than thus at home by barbarous tyranny
To live and never see the cheerful day
And to want hands wherewith to feel the way?
BAJAZET: Leave weeping, Aga: we have wept enough.
Now Bajazet will ban another while
55   And utter curses to the concave sky,
Which may infect the regions of the air
And bring a general plague on all the world.
Night, thou most ancient grandmother of all,
First made by Jove for rest and quiet sleep
60   When cheerful day is gone from th'earth's wide hall,
Henceforth thy mantle in black Lethe steep
And clothe the world in darkness infernal.
Suffer not once the joyful daylight peep,
But let thy pitchy steeds, aye, draw thy wain,
65   And coal-black silence in the world still reign.
Curse on my parents that first brought me up
And on the cradle wherein I was rocked;
Curse on the day when first I was created
The chief commander of all Asia;
70   Curse on my sons that drive me to this grief;
Curse on myself that can find no relief;
And curse on him, an everlasting curse,
That quenched those lamps of ever burning light
And took away my Aga's warlike hands;
75   And curse on all things under the wide sky!
Ah, Aga, I have cursed my stomach dry.
ABRAHAM: I have a drink, my lords of noble worth,
Which soon will calm your stormy passions
And glad your hearts if so you please to taste it.
80 BAJAZET: And who art thou that thus dost pity us?
ABRAHAM: Your Highness' humble servant, Abraham.
BAJAZET: Abraham, sit down and drink to Bajazet.
ABRAHAM: [*aside*] Faith, I am old as well as Bajazet

---

54 ban] curse.
61 **Lethe**] one of the rivers of Hades. Its water caused forgetfulness in those who drank from it.

And have not many months to live on earth.

85   I care not much to end my life with him.

[*To Bajazet and Aga*] Here's to you, lordings, with a full carouse.

He drinks.

BAJAZET: Here, Aga, woeful Bajazet drinks to thee.

Abraham, hold the cup to him while he drinks.

ABRAHAM: Now know, old lords, that you have drank your last.

90   This was a potion which I did prepare

To poison you, by Selimus' instigation,

And now it is dispersèd through my bones,

And glad I am that such companions

Shall go with me down to Prosperpina.

He dies.

95 BAJAZET: Ah, wicked Jew! Ah, cursèd Selimus!

How have the destins dealt with Bajazet,

That none should cause my death but my own son!

Had Ismael and his warlike Persians

Pierced my body with their iron spears,

100   Or had the strong unconquered Tonombey

With his Egyptians took me prisoner

And sent me with his valiant mamelukes

To be prey unto the crocodilus;

It never would have grieved me half so much.

115   But welcome death, into whose calmy port

My sorrow-beaten soul joys to arrive.

And now, farewell, my disobedient sons;

Unnatural sons, unworthy of that name.

Farewell, sweet life, and Aga now, farewell,

120   Till we shall meet in the Elysian fields.

---

94   **Prosperpina**] classical goddess of the underworld.

96   **destins**] the Fates.

102   **mamelukes**] a military caste, initially composed of slaves who seized control of the Egyptian sultanate in 1250. They ruled in Egypt until defeated by the army of Selim I in 1517.

He dies.

AGA: What greater grief had mournful Priamus
       Than that he lived to see his Hector die,
       His city burnt down by revenging flames,
       And poor Polites slain before his face?°
125   Aga, thy grief is matchable to his,
       For I have lived to see my sovereign's death;
       Yet glad that I may breath my last with him.
       And now, farewell sweet light which my poor eyes
       These twice six months never did behold.
130   Aga will follow noble Bajazet
       And beg a boon of lovely Prosperine,
       That he and I may in the mournful fields
       Still weep and wail our strange calamities.

He dies.

SCENE 19.
NEAR SMYRNA ON THE TURKISH COAST.

Enter Bullithrumble the shepherd, running in haste and laughing to himself.

BULLITHRUMBLE: Ha, ha, ha! "Married," quoth you? Marry, and
       Bullithrumble were to begin the world again, I would set a tap abroach
       and not live in daily fear of the breach of my wife's ten
       commandments. I'll tell you what: I thought myself as proper a fellow
5   at wasters as any in all our village, and yet when my wife begins to play
       clubs trump with me, I am fain to sing:
       What hap had I to marry a shrew,

---

1   **Marry**] a mild oath.
5   **wasters**] mock combat conducted with a wooden sword or staff.
5–6   **to play club's trump with me**] to beat me with a club (punning on the image of playing trump with the suit of clubs in a card game).
6   **fain**] obliged.

For she hath given me many a blow,
And how to please her, alas, I do not know.
10   From morn to even her tongue ne'er lies.
Sometime she laughs, sometime she cries;
And I can scarce keep her talents from my eyes.
When from abroad I do come in,
"Sir knave," she cries, "where have you been?"
15   Thus please or displease, she lays it on my skin.
Then do I crouch, then do I kneel,
And wish my cap were furred with steel
To bear the blows that my poor head doth feel.
But out, Sir John, beshrew thy heart;
20   For thou hast joined us, we cannot part;
And I, poor fool, must ever bear the smart.
I'll tell you what: this morning while I was making me ready, she came
with a holly wand and so blessed my shoulders that I was fain to run
through a whole alphabet of faces. Now at the last seeing she was
25   so crammock with me, I began to swear all the criss-cross row over,
beginning at great "A," little "a," till I came to "w, x, y." And snatching
up my sheephook, and my bottle and my bag, like a desperate fellow
ran away, and here now I'll sit down and eat my meat.

While he is eating, enter Corcut and his Page, disguised like mourners.

CORCUT: O hateful hellish snake of Tartary
30   That feedest on the soul of noblest men,
Damned Ambition, cause of all misery!
Why dost thou creep from out thy loathsome fen
And with thy poison animatest friends
To gape and long, one for the other's ends?
35   Selimus, could'st thou not content thy mind

---

12   **talents**] sharp fingernails.
23   **holly wand**] a branch from a holly bush, punning on "holly/holy."
23   **blessed**] punning on the older sense of "to bless" as "to wound."
25   **crammock**] a crooked stick or club, such as the stick used to drive a ball in a game of hockey.
25   **criss-cross row**] a phonetic reduction of "Christ-cross row," referring to "The alphabet; so called from the figure of a cross prefixed to it in hornbooks" (*O.E.D.*).

With the possession of the sacred throne,
Which thou didst get by father's death unkind,
Whose poisoned ghost before high God doth groan?
But thou must seek poor Corcut's overthrow,
40   That never injured thee—so, nor so?
Old Hali's sons, with two great company
Of barded horse, were sent from Selimus
To take me prisoner in Magnesia;
And death I am sure should have befell to me,
45   If they had once but set their eyes on me.
So thus disguisèd, my poor page and I
Fled fast to Smyrna; where in a dark cave
We meant t'await th'arrival of some ship
That might transfreight us safely unto Rhodes.
50   But see how fortune crossed my enterprise.
Bostangi Bassa, Selimus' son-in-law,
Kept all the sea coasts with his brigandines,
That if we had but ventured on the sea,
I presently had been his prisoner.°
55   These two days have we kept us in the cave,
Eating such herbs as the ground did afford;
And now through hunger are we both constrained
Like fearful snakes to creep out step by step
And see if we may get us any food.
60   And in good time! See, yonder sits a man,
Spreading a hungry dinner on the grass.

Bullithrumble spies them and puts up his meat.

BULLITHRUMBLE: These are some felonians, that seek to rob me! Well, I'll
make myself a good deal valianter then I am indeed, and if they will
needs creep into kindred with me, I'll betake me to my old
65   occupation and run away.

---

41   **Old Hali's sons**] Hali Bassa and Cali Bassa.
42   **barded**] armored.
49   **transfreight**] transport.
62   **felonians**] wicked people.

CORCUT: Hail, groom.

BULLITHRUMBLE: Good lord sir, you are deceived. My name's Master
     Bullithrumble. [*aside*] This is some cozening, cony-catching crossbiter
     that would fain persuade me he knows me, and so under a
70   tense of familiarity and acquaintance, uncle me of victuals.

CORCUT: Then Bullithrumble, if that be thy name—

BULLITHRUMBLE: My name, sir—O Lord, yes—and if you will not
     believe me, I will bring my godfathers and godmothers, and they shall
     swear it upon the font-stone, and upon the church book, too, where it
75   is written. [*aside*] Mass, I think he be some justice of peace, *ad*
     quorum, and *omnium populorum*. How he 'samines me! [*To Corcut*] A
     Christian—yes, marry am I, sir. Yes, verily and do believe: and it
     please you I'll go forward in my catechism.

CORCUT: Then, Bullithrumble, by that blessèd Christ,
80   And by the tomb where he was burièd,
     By sovereign hope which thou conceiv'st in him,
     Whom dead, as everliving thou adorest.

BULLITHRUMBLE: O Lord help me, I shall be torn in pieces with devils
     and goblins!

85 CORCUT: By all the joys thou hop'st to have in heaven,
     Give some meat to poor hunger-starvèd men.

BULLITHRUMBLE: [*aside*] Oh, these are, as a man should say, beggars! Now
     will I be as stately to them as if I were Master Pigwiggen our
     constable. [*To Corcut and Page*] Well, sirs, come before me. Tell me, if
90   I should entertain you, would you not steal?

PAGE: If we did mean so, sir, we would not make your worship acquainted
     with it.

BULLITHRUMBLE: A good, well nutrimented lad. Well, if you will keep my
     sheep truly and honestly, keeping your hands from lying and

---

68   cozening, cony-catching crossbiter] swindling con artist.
70   tense] pretense.
70   uncle] a parallel pun to "cousin/cozen," "uncle" being a form of the verb "unclead," meaning to
strip or remove.
76   ad quorum, and ommum populorum] Latin phrases that traditionally appeared in formal com-
missions giving a magistrate or a justice of the peace the authority to investigate a case.
76   'samines] shortened form of "examines."
85   thou hop'st] you hope.
93   nutrimented] nourished.

95   slandering, and your tongues from picking and stealing, you shall be
      Master Bullithrumble's servitures.

CORCUT: With all our hearts.

BULLITHRUMBLE:. Then come on and follow me: we will have a hog's
      cheek, and a dish of tripes, and a society of puddings, and to field. "A
100   society of puddings"—did you mark that well used metaphor?
      Another would have said, "a company of puddings." If you dwell with
      me long, sirs, I shall make you as eloquent as our parson himself.

Exeunt Corcut and Bullithrumble.

PAGE: Now is the time when I may be enriched.
      The brethren that were sent by Selimus
105   To take my lord, Prince Corcut, prisoner,
      Finding him fled, proposed large rewards
      To them that could declare where he remains.
      Faith, I'll to them and get the portagues,
      Though by the bargain Corcut lose his head.

Exit Page.

SCENE 20.
BYZANTIUM.

*Enter Selimus, Sinam Bassa, the corses of Bajazet and Aga with funeral pomp,
Mustaffa and the janissaries.*

SELIMUS: [*aside*] Why, thus must Selim blind his subjects' eyes
      And strain his own to weep for Bajazet.
      They will not dream that I made him away
      When thus they see me with religious pomp
5   To celebrate his tomb-black mortuary.
      And though my heart, cast in an iron mould,

---

96   **servitures**] servants (Bullithrumble commits a series of comic malapropisms and verbal mix-ups).
108   **portagues**] Portuguese gold coins, also called "crusadoes."
s.d. **corses**] corpses, bodies.

Cannot admit the smallest dram of grief,
Yet that I may be thought to love him well,
I'll mourn in show, though I rejoice indeed.

[Selimus speaks] to the corses:

10   Thus after he has five long ages lived,
The sacred phoenix of Arabia
Loadeth his wings with precious perfumes
And on the altar of the golden sun
Offers himself a grateful sacrifice.
15   Long didst thou live triumphant, Bajazet,
A fear unto thy greatest enemies;
And now that Death, the conqueror of kings,
Dislodgèd hath thy never-dying soul,
To flee unto the heavens from whence she came
20   And leave her frail, earthly pavilion,
Thy body, in this ancient monument
Where our great predecessors sleep in rest,

Suppose the Temple of Mahomet.°

Thy woeful son Selimus thus doth place.
Thou wert the phoenix of this age of ours
25   And diedst wrapped in the sweet perfumes
Of thy magnific deeds, whose lasting praise
Mounteth to highest heaven with golden wings.
Princes, come bear your emperor company
In, till the days of mourning be o'erpassed,
30   And then we mean to rouse false Acomat
And cast him forth of Macedonia.

Exeunt all.

---

24 **phoenix**] a mythical bird, proverbial for uniqueness and immortality because it was believed that only one such creature existed. It never died, but renewed itself by plunging into a fire and then rising, reborn, from the ashes.
26 **magnific**] great, glorious.

SCENE 21.

A PASTORAL SCENE NEAR SMYRNA.

Enter Hali Bassa, Cali Bassa, Corcut's Page, and one or two Soldiers.

PAGE: My lords, if I bring you not where Corcut is, then let me be hanged;
 but if I deliver him upon into your hands, then let me have the reward
 to so good a deed.

HALI BASSA: Page, if thou show us where thy master is,
5 Be sure thou shalt be honored for the deed
 And high exalted above other men.

Enter Corcut and Bullithrumble.

PAGE: That same is he, that in disguisèd robes
 Accompanies yon shepherd to the fields.

CORCUT: The sweet content that country life affords
10 Passeth the royal pleasures of a king;
 For there our joys are interlaced with fears,
 But here no fear nor care is harborèd
 But a sweet calm of a most quiet state.
 Ah, Corcut, would thy brother Selimus
15 But let thee live, here should'st thou spend thy life,
 Feeding thy sheep among these grassy lands.
 But sure I wonder where my page is gone.

HALI BASSA: Corcut.

CORCUT: Ay me! Who nameth me?

20 HALI BASSA: Hali, the governor of Magnesia.
 Poor prince, thou thought'st in these disguisèd weeds
 To make unseen; and happily thou might'st,
 But that thy page betrayèd thee to us.
 And be not wrath with us, unhappy prince,
25 If we do what our sovereign commands:
 'Tis for thy death that Selim sends for thee.

CORCUT: Thus I, like poor Amphiaraus, sought
 By hiding my estate in shepherd's coat

---

21 **weeds**] clothes.

T'escape the angry wrath of Selimus,
30   But as his wife false Eriphyle did
Betray his safety for a chain of gold,
So my false page hath vilely dealt with me.
Pray God that thou mayst prosper so as she.°
Hali, I know thou sorrowest for my case,
35   But it is bootless; come and let us go.
Corcut is ready, since it must be so.

CALI BASSA: Shepherd.

BULLITHRUMBLE: That's my profession, sir.

CALI BASSA: Come, you must go with us.

40 BULLITHRUMBLE: Who, I? Alas sir, I have a wife and seventeen cradles rocking, two ploughs going, two barns filling, and a great herd of beasts feeding, and you should utterly undo me to take me to such a great charge.

CALI BASSA: Well, there is no remedy.

Exeunt all but Bullithrumble, stealing from them closely away.

45 BULLITHRUMBLE: The more's the pity. "Go with you," quoth he! Marry, that had been the way to preferment—down Holborn, up tribune!° Well, I'll keep my best joint from the strappado as well as I can. Hereafter, I'll have no more servants!

Exit, running away.

SCENE 22.
THE IMPERIAL COURT IN BYZANTIUM.

Enter Selimus, Sinam Bassa, Mustaffa, and the janissaries.

SELIMUS: Sinam, we hear our brother Acomat
Is fled away from Macedonia,

---

s.d.   closely] secretly.

47   strappado] instrument of torture whereby the victim, with arms bound behind, was raised up by a rope attached to the wrists.

To ask for aid of Persian Ismael
And the Egyptian soldan, our chief foes.
5 SINAM BASHA: Herein, my lord, I like his enterprise,
    For if they give him aid (as sure they will,
    Being your Highness' vowed enemies),
    You shall have just cause for to war on them
    For giving succor 'gainst you to your foe.
10   You know they are two mighty potentates
    And may be hurtful neighbors to your grace.
    And to enrich the Turkish diadem
    With two so worthy kingdoms as they are
    Would be eternal glory to your name.
15 SELIMUS: By heavens, Sinam, th'art a warrior
    And worthy counselor unto a king.

Sound [trumpet] within. Enter Cali Bassa and Hali Bassa, with Corcut
and his Page.

    How now, what news?
    CALI BASSA: My gracious lord, we here present to you
        Your brother Corcut, whom in Smyrna coasts,
20   Feeding a stock of sheep upon a down,
        His traitorous page betrayed to our hands.
    SELIMUS: Thanks, ye bold brethren; but for that false part,
        Let the vile page be famishèd to death.
    CORCUT: Selim, in this I see thou art a prince,
25   To punish treason with condign reward.
    SELIMUS: O sir, I love the fruit that treason brings,
        But those that are the traitors, them I hate.
        But Corcut, could not your philosophy
        Keep you safe from my janissaries' hands?
30   We thought you had old Gyges' wondrous ring,
        That so you were invisible to us.
    CORCUT: Selim, thou dealst unkindly with thy brother,

---

30 **Gyges' wondrous ring**] a magical golden ring, conferring invisibility upon the wearer. It was discovered by Gyges, a humble shepherd living in Lydia, who used it to assassinate King Candaulus. He then married the queen and became king himself.

To seek my death and make a jest of me.
Upbraid'st thou me with my philosophy?
35 Why, this I learned by studying learnèd arts:
That I can bear my fortune as it falls
And that I fear no whit thy cruelty;
Since thou wilt deal no otherwise with me
Than thou hast dealt with agèd Bajazet.
40 SELIMUS: By heavens, Corcut, thou shalt surely die
For slandering Selim with my father's death.
CORCUT: Then let me freely speak my mind this once,
For thou shalt never hear me speak again.
SELIMUS: Nay, we can give such losers leave to speak.
45 CORCUT: Then, Selim, hear thy brother's dying words
And mark them well, for ere thou die thyself,
Thou shalt perceive all things will come to pass
That Corcut doth divine before his death.
Since my vain flight from fair Magnesia,
50 Selim, I have conversed with Christians
And learned of them the way to save my soul
And 'pease the anger of the highest God.
'Tis he that made this pure crystalline vault
Which hangeth over our unhappy heads.
55 From thence he doth behold each sinner's fault,
And though our sins under our feet he treads
And for a while seems for to wink at us,
It is but to recall us from our ways.
But if we do, like headstrong sons, neglect
60 To hearken to our loving father's voice;
Then in his anger will he us reject
And give us over to our wicked choice.
Selim, before his dreadful majesty
There lies a book written with bloody lines
65 Where our offenses all are registered;
Which if we do not hastily repent,
We are reserved to lasting punishment.
Thou, wretched Selimus, hast greatest need

---

52   'pease] shortened from of the word "appease."

To ponder these things in thy secret thoughts;
70   If thou consider what strange massacres
And cruel murthers thou hast caused be done.
Think on the death of woeful Bazajet:
Doth not his ghost still haunt thee for revenge?
Selim, in Chiurlu didst thou set upon
75   Our agèd father in his sudden flight;
In Chiurlu shalt thou die a grievous death.
And if thou wilt not change thy greedy mind,
Thy soul shall be tormented in dark hell;
Where woe, and woe, and never-ceasing woe
80   Shall sound about thy ever-damnèd soul.
Now Selim, I have spoken; let me die.
I never will entreat thee for my life.
Selim, farewell. Thou God of Christians,
Receive my dying soul into thy hands.

                    [They] strangle him.

85 SELIMUS: What, is he dead? Then Selimus is safe
And hath no more corrivals in the crown.
For as for Acomat he soon shall see
His Persian aid cannot save him from me.
Now Sinam, march to fair Amasia walls,
90   Where Acomat's stout queen immures herself,
And girt the city with a warlike siege.
For since her husband is my enemy,
I see no cause why she should be my friend.
They say young Amurath and Aladin,
95   Her bastard brood, are come to succor her.
But I'll prevent this their officiousness,
And send their souls down to their grandfather.
Mustaffa, you shall keep Byzantium,
While I and Sinam girt Amasia.

          Exit Selimus, Sinam, and all the janissaries save one.

———————
91   **girt**] encircle.

100 MUSTAFFA: It grieves my soul that Bajazet's fair line
    Should be eclipsèd thus by Selimus,
    Whose cruel soul will never be at rest
    Till none remain of Ottoman's fair race
    But he himself. Yet for old Bajazet
105   Loved Mustaffa dear unto his death,
    I will show mercy to his family.
    Go, sirrah! Post to Acomat's young sons
    And bid them, as they mean to save their lives,
    To fly in haste from fair Amasia,
110   Lest cruel Selim put them to the sword.

Exit one [janissary, going] to Amurath and Aladin.

    And now Mustaffa, prepare thou thy neck,
    For thou art next to die by Selim's hands.
    Stern Sinam Bassa grudgeth still at thee
    And crabbèd Hali stormeth at thy life.
115   All repine that thou art honored so,
    To be the brother of their emperor.

Enter Solyma.

    But wherefore comes my lovely Solyma?
  SOLYMA: Mustaffa, I am come to seek thee out.
    If ever thy distressèd Solyma
120   Found grace and favor in thy manly heart,
    Fly hence with me unto some desert land;
    For if we tarry here, we are but dead.
    This night when fair Lucina's shining wain
    Was past the chair of bright Cassiopei,
125   A fearful vision appeared to me.

---

107 Post] ride at top speed.
112 for] because.
114 crabbèd] ill-tempered.
123 Lucina's shining wain] the chariot of the moon, here driven by the Roman goddess Lucina, who was sometimes identified with Diana.
124 the chair of Bright Cassiopei] the constellation known as Cassiopeia's Chair.

Methought, Mustaffa, I beheld thy neck
(So often folded in my loving arms)
In foul disgrace of bassa's fair degree,
With a vile halter basely compassèd;
130   And while I poured my tears on thy dead corpse,
A greedy lion with wide gaping throat
Seized on my trembling body with his feet
And in a moment rent me all to nought!
Fly, sweet Mustaffa, or we be but dead!
135   MUSTAFFA: Why should we fly, beauteous Solyma,
Moved by a vain and a fantastic dream?
Or if we did fly, whither should we fly?
If to the farthest part of Asia,
Know'st thou not, Solyma, kings have long hands?
140   Come, come, my joy; return again with me
And banish hence these melancholy thoughts.

Exeunt.

SCENE 23.
AMASIA.

Enter Aladin, Amurath, Messenger.

ALADIN: Messenger, is it true that Selimus
Is not far hence encampèd with his host?
And means he to disjoin the hapless sons
From helping our distressèd mother's town?
5   MESSENGER: 'Tis true, my lord, and if you love your lives,
Fly from the bounds of his dominions;
For he, you know, is most unmerciful.
AMURATH: Here, messenger, take this for thy reward.

Exit Messenger.

---

128   **In foul disgrace of bassa's fair degree**] in disgraceful violation of the rights and privileges of a
Turkish "bassa" (the execution of a Turkish nobleman was traditionally by strangulation with a silken
cord, not hanging.
129   **halter**] noose.

But we, sweet Aladin, let us depart
10   Now in the quiet silence of the night;
That ere the windows of the morn be ope,
We may be far enough from Selimus.
I'll to Aegyptus.
ALADIN: I to Persia.

Exeunt.

SCENE 24.
OUTSIDE THE CITY WALLS OF AMASIA.

Enter Selimus, Sinam Bassa, Hali Bassa, Cali Bassa, janissaries.

SELIMUS: But is it certain, Hali, they are gone?
    And that Mustaffa moved them to fly?
HALI BASSA: Certain, my lord. I met the messenger
    As he returned from young Aladin
5   And learned of him Mustaffa was the man
    That certified the princes of your will.
SELIMUS: It is enough: Mustaffa shall abuy
    At a dear price his pitiful intent.
    Hali, go fetch Mustaffa and his wife;

Exit Hali Bassa.

10   For though she be sister to Selimus,
    Yet loves she him better than Selimus,
    So that if he do die at our command
    And she should live, soon would she work a mean
    To work revenge for her Mustaffa's death.

Enter Hali Bassa, Mustaffa, and Solyma.

---

13   **Aegyptus**] Egypt.
6   **certified**] informed.
7   **abuy / At a dear price**] pay dearly for.
8   **pitiful intent**] attempt, moved by pity (to save the princes' lives).

15   False of thy faith, and traitor to thy king,
        Did we so highly alway honor thee?
        And dost thou thus requite our love with treason?
        For why should'st thou send to young Aladin
        And Amurath, the sons of Acomat,
20   To give them notice of our secrecies,
        Knowing they were my vowèd enemies?
    MUSTAFFA: I do not seek to lessen my offense,
        Great Selimus, but truly do protest
        I did it not for hatred of your Grace
25   (So help me God and holy Mahomet),
        But for I grieved to see the famous stock
        Of worthy Bajazet fall to decay.
        Therefore I sent the princes both away.
        Your highness knows Mustaffa was the man
30   That saved you in the battle of Chiurlu
        When I and all the warlike janissaries
        Had hedged your person in a dangerous ring.
        Yet I took pity on your daunger there
        And made a way for you to scape by flight.
35   But those your bassas have incensed you,
        Repining at Mustaffa's dignity.
        Stern Sinam grinds his angry teeth at me;
        Old Hali's sons do bend their brows at me
        And are aggrievèd that Mustaffa hath
40   Showed himself a better man then they.
        And yet the janissaries mourn for me;
        They know Mustaffa never provèd false.
        Aye, I have been as true to Selimus
        As ever subject to his sovereign,
45   So help me God and holy Mahomet.
    SELIMUS: You did it not because you hated us,
        But for you loved the sons of Acomat.
        Sinam, I charge thee quickly strangle him.
        He loves not me that loves mine enemies.
50   As for your holy protestation,

---

33   daunger] danger.
34   scape] escape.

It cannot enter into Selim's ears.
For why, Mustaffa? Every merchantman
Will praise his own ware, be it ne'er so bad.
SOLYMA: For Solyma's sake, mighty Selimus,
55 Spare my Mustaffa's life and let me die;
Or if thou wilt not be so gracious,
Yet let me die before I see his death.
SELIMUS: Nay Solyma, yourself shall also die
Because you may be in the selfsame fault.
60 Why stay'st thou, Sinam? Strangle him, I say!

Sinam strangles [Mustaffa].

SOLYMA: Ah, Selimus, he made thee emperor!
And wilt thou thus requite his benefits?
Thou art a cruel tiger and no man,
That could'st endure to see before thy face
65 So brave a man as my Mustaffa was
Cruelly strangled for so small a fault.
SELIMUS: Thou shalt not after-live him, Solyma.
'Twere pity thou should'st want the company
Of thy dear husband. Sinam, strangle her.
70 And now to fair Amasia let us march.
Acomat's wife, and her unmanly host,
Will not be able to endure our sight,
Much less make strong resistance in hard fight.

Exeunt.

SCENE 25.
AT THE OTTOMAN-EGYPTIAN BORDER.

Enter Acomat, Tonombey, Vizier, Regan, and their Soldiers.

ACOMAT: Welcome, my lords, in my native soil;
The crown whereof by right is due to me,
Though Selim by the janissaries' choice,
Through usurpation, keep the same from me.

5   You know contrary to my father's mind
       He was enthronized by the bassas' will
       And, after his installing, wickedly
       By poison made good Bajazet to die,
       And strangled Corcut and exiled me.
10   These injuries we come to revenge
       And raise his siege from fair Amasia walls.
TONOMBEY: Prince of Amasia, and the rightful heir
       Unto the mighty Turkish diadem,
       With willing heart great Tonombey hath left
15   Egyptian Nilus and my father's court
       To aid thee in thy undertaken war.
       And by the great Usan-Cassano's ghost,
       Companion unto mighty Tamburlaine,
       From whom my father lineally descends;°
20   Fortune shall show herself too cross to me,
       But we will thrust Selimus from his throne
       And revest Acomat in the empery.
ACOMAT: Thanks to thee, uncontrollèd Tonombey!
       But let us haste us to Amasia,
25   To succor my besiegèd citizens.
       None but my queen is overseer there,
       And too, too weak is all her policy
       Against so great a foe as Selimus.

                    Exeunt all.

                  SCENE 26.
       OUTSIDE THE CITY WALLS OF AMASIA.

   Enter Selimus, Sinam Bassa, Hali Bassa, Cali Bassa, and the janissaries.

SELIMUS: Summon a parley, sirs, that we may know
       Whether these mushrooms here will yield or no.

---

20   **too cross**] unfairly opposed.
27   **policy**] strategy, wiles.
2   **mushrooms**] upstarts.

[Selimus' men sound] a parley. The queen of Amasia and her Soldiers [appear] on the walls.

QUEEN: What cravest thou, bloodthirsty parricide?
        Is't not enough that thou hast foully slain
5   Thy loving father, noble Bajazet?
        And strangled Corcut, thine unhappy brother?
        Slain brave Mustaffa and fair Solyma
        Because they favored my unhappy sons?
        But thou must yet seek for more massacres?
10   Go, wash thy guilty hands in lukewarm blood!
        Enrich thy soldiers with robberies!
        Yet do the heavens still bear an equal eye,
        And vengeance follows thee even at the heels.
SELIMUS: Queen of Amasia, wilt thou yield thyself?
15 QUEEN: First shall the over-flowing Euripus
        Of swift Euboea stop his restless course,
        And Phoeb's bright globe bring the day from the West
        And quench his hot flames in the Eastern sea.
        Thy bloody sword, ungracious Selimus,
20   Sheathed in the bowels of thy dearest friend!
        Thy wicked guard which still attends on thee,
        Fleshing themselves in murther, lust, and rape!
        What hope of favor? What security?
        Rather, what death do they not promise me?
25   Then think not, Selimus, that we will yield,
        But look for strong resistance at our hands.
SELIMUS: Why, then, you never-daunted janissaries,
        Advance your shields and uncontrollèd spears!
        Your conquering hands in foemen's blood embay,
30   For Selimus himself will lead the way.

Alarum. [Selimus] beats them off the walls.
[Exeunt.] Alarum.

---

s.d.   parley] request for a parley made by sounding a drum and/or trumpet.
15 Euripus / Of swift Euboea] the strait between the Greek island of Euboea and Boeotia on the Mainland, known for the violent flow of its waters.
29 embay] bathe.

SCENE 27.
AMASIA.

Enter Selimus, Sinam Bassa, Hali Bassa, Cali Bassa, janissaries with Acomat's
Queen [as] prisoner.

SELIMUS: Now, sturdy dame, where are your men of war
      To guard your person from my angry sword?
      What though you braved us on your city walls,
      Like to that Amazonian Menalip,
5   Leaving the banks of swift-streamed Thermodon
      To challenge combat with great Hercules,°
      Yet Selimus hath plucked your haughty plumes.
      Nor can your spouse, rebellious Acomat,
      Nor Aladin or Amurath, your sons,
10   Deliver you from our victorious hands.
QUEEN: Selim, I scorn thy threat'nings as thyself;
      And though ill hap hath given me to thy hands,
      Yet will I never beg my life of thee.
      Fortune may chance to frown as much on thee;
15   And Acomat whom thou dost scorn so much
      May take thy base Tartarian concubine
      As well as thou hast took his loyal queen.
      Thou hast not fortune tied in a chain,
      Nor dost thou like a wary pilot sit
20   And wisely steer this all-containing barge.
      Thou art a man as those whom thou hast slain,
      And some of them were better far then thou.
SELIMUS: Strangle her, Hali. Let her scold no more.
      Now let us march to meet with Acomat.
25   He brings with him that great Egyptian bug,
      Strong Tonombey, Usan-Cassano's son.
      But we shall soon with our fine tempered swords
      Engrave our prowess on their burgonets.
      Were they as mighty and as fell of force
30   As those old earth-bred brethren, which once

---

25 **bug**] bugbear, bogey.

Heaped hill on hill to scale the starry sky,
When Briareus, armed with a hundreth hands,
Flung forth a hundreth mountains at great Jove;
And when the monstrous giant Monichus
35 Hurled mount Olympus at great Mars his targe
And darted cedars at Minerva's shield.°

Exeunt all.

SCENE 28.
FIELD OF BATTLE NEAR AMASIA.

Alarum. Enter Selimus, Sinam Bassa, Cali Bassa, Hali Bassa, and the janissaries
at one door, and Acomat, Tonombey, Regan, Vizier, and their Soldiers at another.

SELIMUS: What, are the urchins crept out of their dens
Under the conduct of this porcupine?
Dost thou not tremble, Acomat, at us,
To see how courage masketh in our looks,
5   And white-winged Victory sits on our swords?
Captain of Egypt, thou that vaunt'st thyself
Sprung from great Tamburlaine the Scythian thief,
Who bad thee enterprise this bold attempt
To set thy feet within the Turkish confines
10   Or lift thy hands against our majesty?
ACOMAT: Brother of Trebizond, your squarèd words
And broad-mouthed terms can never conquer us.
We come resolved to pull the Turkish crown,
Which thou does wrongfully detain from me,
15   By conquering sword from off thy coward crest.

---

35 **great Mars his targe**] the shield of Mars, Roman god of war.
1   **urchins**] hedgehogs.
8   **bad thee enterprise**] asked you to undertake (here, "bad" is a past tense from of "to bid," meaning "to ask").
11 **squarèd**] ready to fight (from the image of an army drown up in a square formation before battle).
15 **crest**] top of the head or helmet.

SELIMUS: Acomat, sith the quarrel toucheth none
          But thee and me, I dare, and challenge thee.
TONOMBEY: Should he accept the combat of a boy
          Whose unripe years and far unriper wit,
20   Like to the bold, foolhardy Phaëthon
          That fought to rule the chariot of the sun,
          Hath moved thee t'undertake an empery?
SELIMUS: Thou that resolvest in peremptory terms
          To call him "boy" that scorns to cope with thee;
25   But thou canst better use thy bragging blade
          Than thou canst rule thy overflowing tongue.
          Soon shalt thou know that Selim's mighty arm
          Is able to overthrow poor Tonombey.

Alarum. They fight. Tonombey beats Hali Bassa and Cali Bassa in. Selimus beats
Tonombey in. Alarum. [Enter] Tonombey.°

TONOMBEY: The field is lost, and Acomat is taken!
30   Ah Tonombey, how canst thou show thy face
          To thy victorious sire, thus conquerèd?
          A matchless knight is warlike Selimus,
          And like a shepherd 'mongst a swarm of gnats,
          Dings down the flying Persians with their swords.
35   Twice I encountered with him hand to hand,
          And twice returnèd foilèd and ashamed.
          For never yet since I could manage arms
          Could any match with mighty Tonombey
          But this heroic emperor Selimus.
40   Why stand I still and rather do not fly
          The great occasion which the victors make?

Exit Tonombey.

---

20 **Phaëthon**] son of Apollo who tried to drive the chariot of the sun by himself but could not control the solar horses and brought the sun so dangerously close to the earth that Zeus was forced to
strike him down with a thunderbolt.
24 **cope with**] encounter (in combat).

SCENE 29.
AMASIA.

Alarum. Enter Selimus, Sinam Bassa with Acomat [held] prisoner, Hali Bassa,
Cali Bassa, janissaries.

SELIMUS: Thus when the coward Greeks fled to their ships,
　　　　The noble Hector, all besmeared in blood,
　　　　Returned in triumph to the walls of Troy.°
　　　　A gallant trophy, bassas, have we won,
5　　　Beating the never-foilèd Tonombey
　　　　And hewing passage through the Persians.
　　　　As when a lion, raving for his prey,
　　　　Falleth upon a drove of hornèd bulls
　　　　And rends them strongly in his kingly paws;
10　　Or Mars armed in his adamantine coat,
　　　　Mounted upon his fiery-shining wain,
　　　　Scatters the troops of warlike Thracians
　　　　And warms cold Hebrus with hot streams of blood.
　　　　Brave Sinam, for thy noble prisoner,
15　　Thou shalt be general of my janissaries
　　　　And beylerbey of fair Natolia.
　　　　Now, Acomat, thou monster of the world,
　　　　Why stoop'st thou not with reverence to thy king?
ACOMAT: Selim, if thou have gotten victory,
20　　Then use it to thy contention.
　　　　If I had conquered, know assuredly
　　　　I would have said as much and more to thee.
　　　　Know I disdain them as I do thyself
　　　　And scorn to stoop or bend my lordly knee
25　　To such a tyrant as is Selimus.
　　　　Thou slew'st my queen without regard or care

7　**raving for**] wandering in search of.
13　**Hebrus**] principal river of Thrace.
20　**contention**] contentment, satisfaction.
23　**I disdain them**] Acomat refers here to the onlooking "bassas" who fought with Selimus.

Of love or duty, or thine own good name.
Then, Selim, take that which thy hap doth give.
Disgraced, displaced, I longer loath to live.
30 SELIMUS: Then, Sinam, strangle him. Now he is dead,
Who doth remain to trouble Selimus?
Now am I king alone, and none but I.
For since my father's death until this time,
I never wanted some competitors.
35   Now as the weary, wandering traveler
That hath his steps guided through many lands,
Through boiling soil of Africa and Ind,
When he returns unto his native home
Sits down among his friends and with delight
40   Declares the travels he hath overpassed,
So mayst thou Selimus; for thou hast trode
The monster-guarded paths that lead to crowns.
Ha, ha! I smile to think how Selimus,
Like the Egyptian ibis, hath expelled
45   Those swarming armies of swift-wingèd snakes
That sought to overrun my territories.
When soultring heat the earth's green children spoils;
From forth the fens of venomous Africa,
The generation of those flying snakes
50   Do band themselves in troops and take their way
To Nilus' bounds; but those industrious birds,
Those ibises, meet them in set array
And eat them up like to a swarm of gnats,
Preventing such a mischief from the land.
55   But see how unkind nature deals with them:
From out their eggs rises the basilisk,
Whose only sight kills millions of men.°
When Acomat lifted his ungracious hands
Against my agèd father Bajazet,
60   They sent for me, and I (like Egypt's bird)
Have rid that monster and his fellow mates.

---

37 Ind] the Indies.
47 **soultring**] sweltering, sultry.

But as from ibis springs the basilisk,
Whose only touch burneth up stones and trees,
So Selimus hath proved a cockatrice
65 And clean consumed all the family
Of noble Ottoman, except himself.
And now to you, my neighbor emperors,
That durst lend aid to Selim's enemies:
Sinam, those soldans of the Orient,
70 Egypt and Persia, Selimus will quell;
Or he himself will sink to lowest hell.
This winter will we rest and breathe ourselves,
But soon as Zephyrus' sweet-smelling blast
Shall gently creep over the flow'ry meads,
75 We'll have a fling at the Egyptian crown,
And join unto ours, or lose our own.

Exeunt.

CONCLUSION

Thus have we brought victorious Selimus
Unto the crown of great Arabia.
Next shall you see him with triumphant sword
Dividing kingdoms into equal shares
5 And give them to his warlike followers.
If this first part, gentles, do like you well,
The second part shall greater murthers tell.

FINIS.

---

64 cockatrice] like the basilisk, a monstrous creature with a deadly glance. According to legend it was hatched by a serpent from a chicken's egg and had the head, legs, and wings of a cock with the body and tail of a serpent.

73 Zephyrus' sweet-smelling blast] the west wind, harbinger of the spring.

6 gentles] literally, persons belonging to the upper classes or polite society, but here a euphemism for the spectators at the theater.

Notes

~

No list of characters is included in the original printed text. This list is my own, based on the play itself.

SCENE I.

40–46. **The Persian Sophy . . . in the field**   The reign of Bajazet II was a relatively nonaggressive period in Ottoman imperial history, coming between the expansionism of Bajazet's father, Mehmet II, and that of his son, Selim I. This passage refers to various defensive campaigns fought by Bajazet against Persian, Mameluke, and Turkoman attacks. "Sophy" was the term commonly used in early modern English to designate the Persian emperor. The title is derived from the Arabic epithet "safi-ud-din" ("purity of the faith") and was used by the first Savafid shah of Persia, Ismail Safi (ruled 1502–24), who is referred to here as "mighty Ismael." Shiite forces loyal to the Savafids posed a religious and military threat to the Sunni Ottoman regime. In Anatolia, Shiites rebelled against Sunni Ottoman rule and joined a Persian-sponsored attack on Ottoman territory in a series of campaigns beginning in 1508. These Shiite rebels were defeated at Kayseri in June 1511 by an Ottoman army led by Prince Ahmet (Acomat) and the Turkish Grand Vizier Hadim Ali Pasha ("Hali Bassa"), who was killed in the battle. This passage probably refers to the defeat of the Turkish Anatolian army by Shiites at the battle of Alashehir in the spring of 1511. Greene's text seems to confuse that event with a defeat suffered by the Ottoman commander and governor of Karaman, Karagöz Pasha ("Caraguis Bassa") during a campaign waged in 1485 against a Mameluke-Turcoman alliance.

48–53. **Ramirchan the Tartarian . . . my sad distress.**   An earlier editor (Hopkinson) identifies Ramirchan as "Ramir Chan Khan." In 1511, while his father was still on the throne, Selimus did in fact form an alliance with Mengli Girai, the khan of the Crimean Tatars (who were Ottoman vassals after 1475), and they fought for him against Bajazet at Tchorlu (Chiurlu) on 3 August 1511. Perhaps the name "Ramirchan" refers to Ramazan-oghlu, a contemporary Turkoman leader. In either case, Ottrante and the "Tartars" in the play represent a force of nomadic horsemen-warriors who were allied with Selim. Bajezet's son, Alemshae (or Alemshah), died in 1512.

98. **run gate** In early modern texts, "renegade" is frequently spelled "run(n)-agate." This spelling stresses the notion of a deserter, a vagabond or runaway—one who has "run out of the gate"—a masterless man who refuses to be confined in servitude and becomes a fugitive from justice and a transgressor of the social order. The *O.E.D.* cites Nashe's *Unfortunate Traveler* (1594): "The first traveler was Cain, and he was called a vagabond runnagate on the face of the earth" (*Works,* 5.141). In R. Sanders, *Physiogn., Moles* 25 (1653), we have this usage: "he is a runnagate fugitive, and wanders out of his native country." Cf. Marlowe, *1 Tamburlaine:* ". . . the cruel pirates of Argier, / That damned train, the scum of Africa, / Inhabited with straggling runagates" (3.3.55–57).

SCENE 2.

75–94. **When first this . . . govern bloody fights.** Here Selimus offers his own version of the Golden Age myth found in Hesiod's *Works and Days* and Ovid's *Metamorphoses.* According to Classical tradition, Ninus, the son of Belus and husband of Semiramus, was the mythical founder of Ninevah.

SCENE 3.

64–67. **all great Samandria . . . given our states.** Samandria, the fortress capital of Serbia (modern-day Smederevo), is located on the Danube near Belgrade, in an area that for several centuries was the site of intermittent warfare between the Turks and their Christian foes.

SCENE 4.

4–6. **Samandria/From whence . . . back with shame.** Bajazet's father was the "mighty Emperor Mahomet," or Mehmet II (ruled 1451–81), called "the Conqueror" because his armies besieged and captured Constantinople. Though he conquered extensive territory in Europe, Mehmet's army was not always victorious. This passage refers to the victory of John Hunyadi, a famous hero for the Christian-Hungarian cause who defeated a large Ottoman army at the Battle of Belgrade in July 1456, forcing Mehmet to abandon his siege and withdraw to his capital.

11–19. **Here the Polonian . . . else take all!** This passage mentions various Christian powers to the north of the Ottoman empire that tried to oppose Ottoman expansion during this time but also frequently fought with each other. "Basilius" is Basil IV, czar of Russia (1505–1533).

SCENE 9.

18–22. **Too true that . . . a horse's hair.** Damocles was a court flatterer who, having extolled the happiness of Dionysus, tyrant of Syracuse, was forced by Dionysus to sit at a banquet with a sword suspended over his head by a single hair to demonstrate the perilous and delicate nature of a ruler's worldly happiness.

SCENE 18.

4–9. **That woeful emperor . . . his kingdom so.** The deposed emperor alludes to the fate of Bajazet I, an Ottoman emperor who was defeated and humiliated by the Tartar conqueror, Timur the Lame (1336–1405). These events are staged in Marlowe's play, *Tamburlaine the Great, Part I* (see, especially, act 4, scene 2).

121–24. **What greater grief . . . before his face?** Priam, king of Troy, survived the death of his eldest son, Hector (who was killed by the Greek hero Achilles). Later, when the Greeks sacked and burned the city of Troy, Priam witnessed the death of his last surviving son, Polites. While Priam was kneeling before the altar of Zeus, Polites, pursued by Achilles' son Pyrrhus, rushed into the temple and died at his father's feet. Priam was then killed by Pyrrhus. See Virgil, The *Aeneid,* Book II, 665–704, where Aeneas' description of this event is an archetypal instance of narrative pathos.

SCENE 19.

51–54. **Bostangi Bassa, Selimus' . . . been his prisoner.** This probably refers to the Ottoman naval commander under Bajazet, Iskender Beg, who was reported to have been Selim's son-in-law, and who supported Selim against his brother Acomat (Ahmet).

SCENE 20.

22–23. s.d. **Suppose the Temple of Mahomet.** It was common in English texts describing Islamic culture to represent a mosque as a pagan temple, imagined as a shrine dedicated to the worship of the idol, Mahomet. The stage direction, "Suppose," indicates that the actors should be placed before a backdrop depicting such a "temple," or that the audience should imagine such a setting—perhaps both.

SCENE 21.

27–31. **Thus I, like . . . so as she.** According to Greek mythology, Amphiaraus was a heroic, pious king of Argos, a great athlete, warrior, and soothsayer. After Polynices of Thebes bribed Amphiaraus's wife Eriphyle with the necklace of Harmonia, Eriphyle forced her husband to join the expedition of the Epigoni against Thebes, though Amphiaraus knew they would be defeated. During the rout that ensued, Amphiaraus escaped and fled to the banks of the river Ismenus, but Zeus caused the earth to open beneath him and swallow him. Eriphyle was later murdered in vengeance by the sons of Amphiaraus.

46. **down Holborn, up tribune!** This cheer expresses Bullithrumble's joy and relief when he escapes the Turkish courtiers, abandoning his ambition to gain preferment and become an aristocratic master. Holborn was a fashionable district in London known for its aristocratic residences. A "tribune" is a defender of the people's rights (alluding to the ancient Roman tribunes who represented the interests of the plebian class). Thus Bullithrumble reasserts his freedom and solidarity with the common people.

SCENE 25.

17–19. **And by the . . . father lineally descends**   Greene's Tonombey claims descent from Usumcasane, one of Tamburlaine's original followers in Marlowe's *Tamburlaine, Part I and II*. Usumcasane is made king of Morocco in Marlowe's play, but the link between Usumcasane and Tonombey is based on literary influence, not historical fact, since the real Usumcasane was a Persian king who lived and reigned after the time of Tamburlaine. Tonombey (or Tuman Bey) was a Mamluke sultan who was defeated by Selim's army and killed in the Mamluke-Ottoman war of 1516–17 (what would have been the crowning scene of triumph in Greene's planned sequel). By having his hero, Selimus, defeat Tonombey (presented as the heir of Marlowe's Usumcasane), Greene expresses his ambition to outdo his predecessor, Marlowe, and supercede the Tamburlaine plays with his (projected) Selimus plays.

SCENE 27.

4–6. **Like to that . . . with great Hercules**   Menalip was queen of the Amazons and sister to Hippolyta. One of the twelve labors assigned to Hercules was to go to the bank of the river Thermodon, in Cappadocia, and take the girdle of Hippolyta.

29–36. **Were they as . . . at Minerva's shield.**   Selimus compares himself and his army to Jove and the Olympian gods who defeated the Titans, a race of giant, "earthbred" deities who reigned over the world before the coming of Jove, Mars, and Minerva.

SCENE 28,

28–36. s.d. **Tonombey beats Hali Bassa . . . [Enter] Tonombey.**   a stage direction indicating that first Tonombey drives Hali and Cali Bassa offstage with his sword, then encounters Selimus, who chases Tonombey offstage and pursues him through the door at the back of the stage. Presumably some of the other actors would also move offstage because after the battle is over, Tonombey enters alone and, before fleeing, delivers the lines that follow immediately in a speech to the audience.

SCENE 29.

1–3. **Thus when the . . . walls of Troy.**   See book 12 of Homer's *Iliad*, where Hector and the Trojans drive the Greeks back to the sea and begin to burn their ships.

44–57. **Like the Egyptian . . . millions of men.**   Selimus refers to popular legends about the ibis, a bird that was believed to eat up venomous snakes but then lay eggs from which basilisks would hatch. He compares himself first to the ibis who removes the vipers (his ridding Bajazet of the threat of Acomat) and then declares that he has now taken the form of the murderous basilisk. Sir Thomas Browne discusses "the Aegyptian tradition concerning the bird ibis" in his *Pseudodoxia Epidemica*, book 3, chapter 7 ("Of the Basilisk"). According to Browne, "the ibis feeding upon serpents, that venomous food so inquinated their oval conceptions, or eggs within their bodies, that they sometimes came forth in serpentine shapes."

A
Chriſtian turn'd Turke:

OR,

The Tragicall Liues and Deaths of the two Famous Pyrates,

WARD and DANSIKER.

As it hath beene publickly Acted.

VVRITTEN

By ROBERT DABORN, Gentleman.

Nemo ſapiens, Miſer eſt.

LONDON,
Printed by for *William Barrenger*, and are to be ſold
at the great North-doore of *Pauls.* 1612.

A Christian Turned Turk

or
The Tragical Lives and Deaths of
the Two Famous Pirates,
Ward and Dansiker.

As it hath been publicly acted.

Written
By Robert Daborne, Gentleman.

Nemo Sapiens, Miser est.

LONDON
PRINTED BY WILLIAM BARRENGER, AND ARE TO BE SOLD
AT THE GREAT NORTH DOOR OF PAUL'S. 1612.

Nemo Sapiens, Miser est] L., no one who is wise is miserable.

To the Knowing Reader

As no argument more proveth the excellency of poesy° than the contempt [that] is thrown upon it by silken gulls and ignorant citizens, so there is no blemish [that] taketh from the beauty of this only all-comprehending art so much as the same wherewith her own professors brand her; for I may truly vary that of the tragedian, *Quemcunq; poëtam vides, miserum dicas.* I speak it especially in regard of that free title better times allowed this heavenly science, now made captive by each unworthy hand; in recovery whereof I have, so far as my weak power extended, procured the publishing [of] this oppressed and much martyred tragedy.° Not that I promise to myself any reputation hereby or affect to see my name in print, ushered with new praises, for fear the reader should call in question their indulgements that give applause in the action. For had this wind moved me, I had prevented others' shame in subscribing some of my former labors, or let them gone out in [the] Devil's name alone: which since impudence will not suffer, I am content they pass together. It is then to publish my innocence concerning the wrong of worthy personages, together with doing some right to the much-suffering actors that hath caused my name to cast itself in the common rank of censure, accompanied with so weak comforts, as this trivial work can give it, and that my gratitude may be in the first place, I must (in despite of any justly neglected cynic) confess to have received so much worthy respect, and approved so much generous honesty in them, that with any indifferent hazard, I will study to make good their loss and my gratitude. I write this, led by no mercenary hopes to share in their fortunes, which hath so put out some's eyes, that measuring others' sight by their own weaknesses gave her out for blind; but led by that spirit [that] knoweth no sin equal to ingratitude. As for the former imputation, granting

---

Quemcunq; poëtam vides, miserum dicas] L., "Whatsoever poet you see, think of him as miserable."

all objections, I clear myself by these two positions: no man can feign any ill of a parricide, the greater always including the less; this being so tolerable, especially in oratory, which is an unseparable branch of poesy, that it subsists not without aggravation; the second is, no man can entitle another to his crimes, for *Alia est cognatio culpae, alia sanguinis,* from which I so far abhor, as my own descent is not obscure but generous. If this will not give satisfaction, know I live under too safe a law to fear the stab of a roving boy, and for any wrong, *Aequo marte,* I forgive it, daring thus far to boast my knowledge that I cannot be a coward. I write succinctly, knowing the bounds of an epistle, the rather because I wish no other perusers than those to whom I dedicate myself. Though herein I speak against the printer's profit, if these accept my impolished labors, I promise the next shall be cooked for the stomachs of the critical mess itself. *Sanabimur si separemur a coetu.*

Alia est cognatio culpae, alia sanguinis] L., "It's one thing to be connected to a fault; it's another to be connected by blood."

Aequo marte] L., "fairly contested; with equal advantage."

the critical mess itself] the most discerning diners, i.e., educated readers and critics.

Sanabimur si separemur a coetu] L., "We will be cured if separated from the throng."

Dramatis Personae

~

Ward	*English pirate captain, in love with Voada.*
Dansiker	*Dutch pirate captain.*
Francisco	*Pirate captain.*
Gismund	*Ward's officer.*
Gallop	*Ward's officer.*
Sares	*Dansiker's captain.*
Lieutenant	*Dansiker's officer.*
Monsieur Davy	*Master of a French merchant ship.*
Ferdinand	*French merchant.*
Albert	*French merchant.*
Lemot	*French gentleman, Alizia's brother.*
Carolo	*French gentleman, friend of Lemot.*
Frederick	*French gentleman.*
Raymond	*French gentleman.*
First Son	*Son to Raymond.*
Second Son	*Later Raymond, eponymous son of Raymond.*
Governor	*Viceroy of Tunis.*
Crosman	*Captain of the janissaries in Tunis, Voada's brother.*
Mufti	*Religious leader to the Muslim community of Tunis.*
Mulli	*A Turk of Tunis.*
Benwash	*A wealthy Jewish merchant.*
Ruben Rabshake	*Servant to Benwash.*

Dramatis Personae] This is a full list of characters' names with brief descriptions that should help clarify their identities and relationships. The list of dramatis personae printed in the 1612 quarto is incomplete and inaccurate. I have revised the list, adding missing characters' names, removing "ghost characters," correcting inconsistencies, and eliminating confusion.

Alizia	*Sister to Lemot, disguised as a sailor's boy, then as the page*
	Fidelio. Betrothed to Raymond the younger.
Agar	*Turkish wife of Benwash.*
Voada	*Sister of Crosman, married to Ward after his conversion.*

Turks, Janissaries, Sailors, Guards, Knights, Priests of Mahomet, Surgeon, Actors in the dumb shows, Dansiker's wife, children, and followers, Governor of Provence, Merchants, Chorus.

The Prologue

~

[Enter Chorus.]

CHORUS: All fair content dwell here, and may our strains
Give you that choice delight which crowns our pains.
Our subject's low, yet to your eyes presents
Deeds high in blood, in blood of innocents:
5   Transcends them low, and your invention calls
To name the sin beyond this black deed falls.
What heretofore set others' pens awork,
Was Ward turned pirate; ours is Ward turned Turk.°
Their trivial scenes might best afford to show
10   The baseness of his birth, how from below
Ambition oft takes root, makes men forsake
The good they enjoy, yet know not. Our Muse doth take
A higher pitch, leaving his piracy
To reach the heart itself of villainy.
15   What to that period makes the nearest way,
Our scene pursues. You must suppose his stay
Hath lately been upon the Irish shore,
Where wanting men he invites some strangers o'er
Into his bark. In height of wine and game,
20   He slips his anchor, and reveals his name.
There fate succeeds, and to your gentle view
We give not what we could, but what know true.
Our ship's afloat; we fear nor rocks nor sands,
Knowing we are environed with your helping hands.

---

8 **turned Turk**] converted to Islam.

SCENE 1.
A CABIN INSIDE WARD'S PIRATE SHIP.

Enter Ward, Gismund, Albert, Ferdinand, Sailors. [They play at cards and dice.]
[They] rise from a table.

WARD: I'll play no more.

FERDINAND: Set but my hand out. Here's four hundred crowns unlost yet.
Fortune may make them yours.

GISMUND: Fortune's a bitch, a mere strumpet. She hath turned up the ace
5   so long, I have ne'er an eye to see with—she hath soaked me!°

ALBERT: We came aboard to venture with you: deal merchant-like, put it
upon one main and throw at all.°

FERDINAND: One cast, and we will leave you.

GISMUND: Leave us yet? We have a cast worth two of the rest.

[The cards are dealt.]

10 ALBERT: 'Tis set. Throw at it gently, sir.

[Ferdinand prepares to throw the dice. Ward stops him.]

---

2 **Set but my hand out**] deal just one more hand of cards.

8 **One cast**] throw of the dice.

9 **a cast**] contrivance or trick, with a pun on the sense of "cast" expressed by Ferdinand in the previous line.

10 **'Tis set**] cards have been dealt and bets have been placed.

WARD: We shall have time enough hereafter: you are too violent.

GISMUND: I fear you'll not be half so forward anon when we should use you.

SAILOR: A sail, a sail, a sail!

All shout.

15 WARD: Why stand you so amazed? Conceive you not the language of
the sea?

GISMUND: Now you may show yourselves gamesters: you shall have your
bellies full of hazard.

FERDINAND: We are betrayed.

20 ALBERT: Are you not merchantmen?

GISMUND: How else? And deal by wholesale, take up much at a long day.
Do you know this honorable shape? Heroic Captain Ward, lord of the
ocean, terror of kings, landlord to merchants, rewarder of
manhood, conqueror of the Western world, to whose followers the
25 lands and seas pay tribute; and they to none but once in their lives to
the manor of Wapping and then free ever after. This is he, my noble
mummers.

ALBERT: We are forever lost.

FERDINAND: If't be our moneys that you covet, willingly we give it up.

30 Only deprive us not of our fair home, our country: do but land us.

WARD: Know we have other use for you,
Have not enticed you hither for your gold:
It is the man we want. Is't not a shame
Men of your qualities and personage
35 Should live as cankers, eating up the soil
That gave you being (like beasts that ne'er look further
Than where they first took food)? That men call "home"
Which gives them means equal unto their minds,
Puts them in action.

40 GISMUND: True, who is't would not smile
To hear a soldier that hath nothing left
But misery to speak him man, can show
More marks then pence, upon whose back contempt

---

25 *they to none*] "they" refers to Ward's "followers."

26 *Wapping*] wharf district of London where condemned pirates were hanged.

27 *mummers*] actors in a dumb show (Albert and Ferdinand are momentarily "dumbstruck" by the
sudden revelation of Ward's identity).

Heaps on the weight of poverty—who would not smile
45　To hear this piece of wretchedness boast his wounds?
How far he went to purchase them? With what honor
He put them on? And now for sustenance,
Want of a little bread, being giving up
His empty soul, should joy yet that his country
50　Shall see him breathe his last when that air he terms his
Ungratefully doth stifle him?

FERDINAND: You tell us of a gulf, which to eschew,
You dash us 'gainst a rock more full of fear
Of danger: for we should call that action
55　Which gives unto posterity our name
Writ in the golden lines of honor; where this brands
Our foreheads with the hateful name of thieves, of robbers.
Piracy, its theft most hateful, swallows up
The estates of orphans, widows, who—born free—
60　Are thus made slaves, enthralled to misery
By those that should defend them at the best.
You rob the venting merchants, whose manly breast
(Scorning base gain at home) puts to the main
With hazard of his life and state, from other lands
65　To enrich his own, whilst with ungrateful hands
He thus is overwhelmed.

GISMUND: These children have been at Saint Antholin's.°
They'll persuade's out of our profession.
A plague upon this scholarship!
70　One man that savors of an university
Is able to infect a whole navy with cowardice.

FERDINAND: Cowardice? Thou liest! There's not a man here dares less than
thyself.

GISMUND: Zounds, I'll try that!

75　WARD: Hold, or by all my hopes, who makes next proffer
Falls on my sword. If you will try your valors,
The enemy is at hand. As for your virtuous lectures,
We are mariners and soldiers, not tattered yet

62　**venting**] selling commodities.
74　**Zounds**] an oath, from "God's wounds." Cf. other oaths such as "Sheart," "Sfoot," "Sblood," etc.

Enough to hear them, though in time we might
80   Be apt for such tongue-comfort, being swayed
By your directions.

[Shout from] within: A sail, a sail, a sail!
Enter Sailor.

WARD: How? More sails yet?

SAILOR: The first that we descried doth bear ahead,
85   And as it seems pursued by a man-of-war;
They make with us for succor.°

GISMUND: Yes, we'll succor her, and suck her, too—as dry as a usurer's
palm!

ALBERT: Nay, then we are put from shore!

90   GISMUND: Without ken. Boys, more sails—the least delay!
Oh, let's turn servingmen, the trencher hold
Whilst others eat the meat.

WARD: Away! Make ready for the fight.

GISMUND: Courage, brave sparks! Now to gain wealth—or graves:
95   To die in peace fits beasts and abject slaves.

FERDINAND: Thou needst not fear the curse, bloodthirsty monster.
O that our better part should thus be captived
By sense and will! Who, like a ship unmanned,
That's borne by motion of the violent waves
100   And giddy winds, doth seem to make a course
Direct and punctive, till we see it dash
Against some prouder Scylla, and display
How much she inward wanted to her sway.

---

84 **bear ahead**] "bear" in the nautical sense, "to sail in a certain direction"; "ahead" meaning "forward
or onward at a rapid pace" (*O.E.D.*).

90 **Without ken**] out of sight (of the shore).

90 **the least delay**] do it quickly, with the least delay possible.

91 **trencher**] wooden serving platter.

94 **sparks**] high-spirited men.

97–98 **our better part . . . sense and will**] our powers of reason and conscience should be dominated
and controlled by our sensual appetites and selfish desires.

101 **punctive**] "making straight for a point" (*O.E.D.*107–8).

103 **she inward wanted to her sway**] the unmanned ship (i.e., the mind controlled by the irrational
will) lacked an internal power to direct its outward course safely.

ALBERT: You have well described him—but to our own fortunes.

105 FERDINAND: We must obey necessity, since 'tis our fates
      To be surprised thus by this monster beast.
      We must, as did that captain, so much famed,
      Lick the fierce lion's feet till happier times
      Do give us freedom in his punished crimes.

110 ALBERT: You have well advised. Fortune, in spite of thee,
      Howe'er my body's thralled, my mind rests free.

   FERDINAND: This stand our comfort: we may happen to be
      The chorus only to their tragedy.   [*Exeunt.*]

SCENE 2.
ON BOARD MONSIEUR DAVY'S SHIP.

Enter Lemot, his sister Alizia (putting on the weed of a sailor's boy),
Monsieur Davy, and Sailors.

LEMOT: Unfortunate sister, my heart dissolves to blood
      And pays sad tribute to thy sadder griefs.
      Nay, make no period: our woes are not at full;
      Hymen did ne'er behold so black a nuptial.

5   Alas! With our delay we hasten misery.
      See how they bear up to us. Dear sister, hide
      At least thy sex, though not thy sorrow.

ALIZIA: Wretched Alizia, little thinks young Raymond
      His bride's so near unto captivity.

10   Be gentle yet, you seas, and swallow me.
      Since I am denied his arms, let my virginity
      Be offered unto him in sacrifice.
      'Twill be some comfort his love a maiden dies.

LEMOT: Nay then, thou cleav'st my soul! Do not distrust:

15   Chaste thoughts are guided by a power that's just.

107–8 that captain . . . lion's feet] perhaps an allusion to Daniel in the lion's den?
s.d. weed] clothes.
4 Hymen] classical god of marriage.

My worthy friends, yet what persuasion needs
To stir up valor where necessity
And justice of our cause, in basest spirits
Would strike a fire to kindle cowardice?
20   Three days we have been pursued by a Dutch pirate,
And now we are fallen upon no less a monster.
Methinks I see your eyes darting forth flames
Like lions in their chase, the greedy hunter
Seeming to warm that blood whose heat and rage
25   Proves his destruction.

Enter Ward, Gismund, Sailors above.

GISMUND: Hoy!
LEMOT: [*To Alizia*] Not ready yet? Alas, thou wilt betray
Thyself unto their lust.
ALIZIA: Rather to death. Nature this comfort gave:
30   No place too miserable but yields a grave
To wretchedness.
GISMUND: Hoy! Of whence your ship? And whither are you bound?
DAVY: We are of Marcelles, bound for Normandy.
Of which are you?
35 GISMUND: We are of the Sea!
SAILOR: The Devil land you!
GISMUND: Bring your master aboard, or we'll give you a broad.
LEMOT: As you are men, I do conjure your valors.
ALIZIA: As you are virtuous, keep from slavery
40   A hapless, hapless maid.
DAVY: Misdoubt it not, fair maid.
There's not a man here but well knows how much
He hath advantage of his enemy;
A race of thieves, bankrupts that have lain
45   Upon their country's stomach like a surfeit;

---

33 **Marcelles**] Marseilles, French port on the Mediterranean.
37 **broad**] broadside.
38 **conjure your valors**] call upon your honor and courage.

Whence, being vomited, they strive with poisonous breath
To infect the general air. Creatures that stand
So far from what is man they know no good,
But in their prey, not for necessity
50   But for mere hate to virtue, pursuing vice,
And being down themselves, would have none rise.
GISMUND: The curs are sure asleep. We'll waken 'em.
Gunner, give fire.

[Sound of cannonfire is heard.]

LEMOT: In their own language answer them.

[More cannonfire heard.]

55 GISMUND: Zounds, do they begin to prate? Have with you! Lace the
netting! Let down the fights! Make ready the small shot!° Gunner,
give them a broadside—we'll prate with 'em. A starboard there!
LEMOT: Brave countrymen,
Think through how many dangers, with what sweat, what care,
60   How long expense of time, we have been getting
Those goods these robbers fight for, that should make good to us
The sweat of just endeavors. Look on this maid;
Think with what honorable welcomings
You shall deliver her to her betrothed husband,
65   How much you shall engage him. Lastly, think that you see
Even all the miseries despised poverty
Can throw on men, that by this one hour's valor
We only can redeem ourselves from death.
O think how happy 'tis to innocence,
70   Where unto guilty souls it looks black and fearful.
At least let this all thoughts of fear dispel:
Truth fights 'gainst theft, and heaven opposes hell.
ALL: We are resolved! St. Dennis! Victory!
LEMOT: A constant breast may fall, but cannot die.   *Exeunt.*

---

73 St. Dennis] patron saint of France. His name is the traditional battle cry of French soldiers.

SCENE 3.
ON BOARD WARD'S SHIP.

Enter Ward with a slain friend and Ferdinand.

WARD: Recall thy spirit, brave friend! A while yet stay—
       At least bear thy revenge hence with thee.
FERDINAND: He hath lost all motion.
WARD: Injurious heaven, that with so excellent matter
5   As is our soul, didst mingle this base mould,
         So frail a substance earth, as if thou hadst framed man
         The subject of thy laughter, gav'st him a spirit
         Free, unbounded, whose fiery temper breaks
         Through all the clouds of danger, dares even heaven,
10   Swells and bears high, when with one little prick
         This bubble breaks, displays a vanity—
         Ridiculous vanity—this building
         That hath been twenty and odd years a-rearing,
         One blast thus lays it flat. I could e'en tremble
15   To think that such a coward I bear about me
         As is this flesh that for so small a wound
         Betrays our life.
FERDINAND: This shows, sir, Nature ne'er intended man
         Other than as she sent him to the world,
20   All unoffensive, unarmed. When unto beasts
         She gave the means to hurt as to defense,
         The armor she gave man was innocence.
WARD: True, there was some other end in our creation
         Than to be that which men term valiant.
25 FERDINAND: There was.

Enter Gismund.

GISMUND: Courage, brave sparks! The slaves begin to faint.
FERDINAND: It is his evil spirit sure that in this likeness haunts him.
WARD: See where he lies.
GISMUND: 'Sfoot, we shall share the more, sir. I always thought
30   Fortune had marked him out to die by the French;
         He had so much of the English spirit in him.

WARD: Fortune! True, the fate of man is fixed,
Unmoveable as the pole: how idle then were he
Should strive to cross unvoided destiny
35 And think to stay his course, seeing we are swayed
As are the motionary engines of a clock
By the dull weight that still doth downward tend
Till it strike earth, and so there motion end.
FERDINAND: Give me the hearing, sir.
40 WARD: Persuade no more. We have no will to act—
Or not to act—more than those orbs we see
And planetary bodies, which in their offices
Observe the will of fate. The difference is:
They are confined; we are not. They are stars fixed,
45 We wandering. Run on, thou purple line
That draw'st my life's fate out. Thou that dost frown
Upon the births of men—now Saturn smile!
Those under milder planets born live servile, good.
Mars called our birth; my race shall be through blood.

Exit [Ward and Gismund].

50 FERDINAND: Abused knowledge, that first werst given to man
As light, now helpst to dazzle him; and whate'er want
Befall through our own imperfect judgment,
Unbridled will then throws on fortune, chance.
I see man's happiness were his ignorance.   *Exit.*

SCENE 4.
ON BOARD MONSIEUR DAVY'S SHIP.

GALLOP: [*Shouting from*] *within.* Aboard, aboard, aboard!

[*Enter Alizia, Frederick, French Sailors, Lemot (blinded by his wounds)
and Carolo, guiding him.*]

[CAROLO]: Dear sir, withdraw. You are deprived of sight.

---
34 **unvoided**] unavoidable.
45 **purple**] bloody.

LEMOT: So much the better: I see no fear in fight.
Courage, brave countrymen! What's nature's part
5   May fall; what's heaven's can never. It is the odds
That just men have of bad. Still to the gods
They stand or fall.
GALLOP: [*Boarding the ship, followed by Sailors.*] Enter, enter, enter!

Enter Ward, Gismund, Ferdinand.

WARD: Zounds, the slave winks and fights!

[Ward's pirates take the French crew prisoner.]

10 [WARD'S FOLLOWERS] SHOUT: A Ward, a Ward, a Ward!
WARD: Down with them, down with them! Away! Let him go overboard!
Were he a second Alexander, there's not a man of them lives but shall
go overboard. We'll offer them to our deceased friends in sacrifice.

[They seize Lemot and take him away to throw him overboard.]

ALIZIA: My brother, my dear, dear brother!
15 [FREDERICK]: There were no conscience, no religion in't.
GALLOP: How? Conscience? Were it but to banish those two words, they
shall go overboard.
WARD: They shall go overboard? Suppose I speak the contrary?
GALLOP: My captain, my man-of-war, speak the contrary; they are as safe
20   as the Great Turk.
WARD: Now they shall overboard.
GALLOP: Outswaggered?
WARD: How many French are left?
GISMUND: There's only five of four-and-twenty living.
25   Never did men with equal spirit stand
A day so black and stormy. Rob not yourself, then,
Of so brave witnesses of this day's valor.
WARD: How dare you, sir, give us directions?

---

9 **winks**] has his eyes closed.

GISMUND: How dare I, sir? I am a gentleman
30   Equal unto your self.
WARD: Take that now! I am before you.   [*Ward strikes Gismund.*]
GISMUND: You are, I'll not be long behind you.
WARD: Know that our word shall be a law.
GALLOP: [*aside*] That may be, for he hath had conscience by the ears
35   already.
WARD: Hoist me a vessel up of Maligo.
    We'll drink a health unto the wandering ghosts
    Of our slain followers, and every draught
    The cannon makes report of, a Frenchman
40   Shall overboard, who to our friends may tell,
    We drank a rouse to them.
FERDINAND: [*aside*] As low as hell.   *Enter Sailor.*
SAILOR: Francisco, captain of the man-of-war pursued our prize, hath set
    a pinnace forth, who (according to the custom of the sea) demands
45   half of the spoil. To your demand he threatens instant fight, force
    against force; or if you dare to accept it, he makes you offer of single
    opposition.
WARD: Accept it? He could not name that honor
    We covet more. Reward the messenger:
50   They two shall be the hostages
    For the equal trial. What's his weapon?
    Where the place of fight?
SAILOR: His weapons are sword and dagger, the place
    Here on our hatches, both our ships being grappled.
55   The oath on each side given, who conquers the other
    Shares the whole booty.
WARD: Agreed—we seal to his condition.
    "Francisco," call you him? I emulate
    His daring spirit.
60 GALLOP: [*aside, to Gismund*] Fortune shapes our revenge, you see.
FERDINAND: What need you give yourself unto this danger,
    When in our general strength we have advantage?

---

34 **had conscience by the ears**] had overcome his sense of right and wrong.
36 **Maligo**] wine from Malaga, in Spain.

WARD: I prithee, do not move my patience. I scorn to take
     From others to my rising. He's only worthy state
65   From Fortune's wheel plucks boldly his own fate,
     And here's an arm shall do't.
[GISMUND]: [*aside, to Gallop*] You see his insolence, how he
     contemns us.
FERDINAND: [*To Ward*] No more, we are agreed.

[Gismund and Gallop speak aside while the other mutineers listen.]

70 GISMUND: How shall we hinder their pursuit?
   GALLOP: When both the ships are grappled, privately
        We'll cut their hawsers. The wind blows fair
        To give our lesser bark advantage. 'Tis not ten leagues
        To Tunis, where entered, we are as safe
75   As in a tower of brass.
   GISMUND: How if we shoot him, as we make away?
   GALLOP: By no means—'t shall be Francisco's task
        To cut his throat. This makes our revenge full:
        We share the prize he fights for.
80 GISMUND: Rare gull! We are all firm and secret.

All: All!

GALLOP: So that I rise, let the world sink, heaven fall.

[Exit Gismund and Gallop.]

WARD: My merit—shall I thrall them? The sway of things
     Belongs to him dares most. Such should be kings,
85   And such am I. What Nature in my birth
     Denied me, Fortune supplies. This maxim I hold:
     He lives a slave that lives to be controlled.

---

64 **worthy state**] deserving of power and dignity.
68 **contemns**] shows contempt for.
83 **thrall**] take captive, enslave.

But see the man whose ruin crowns me. *Enter Francisco.*

FRANCISCO: Art thou the chief and guide of this bark?

90 WARD: The same, sir.

FRANCISCO: May I impute it to your ignorance

In marine actions, or the daring spirit,

That bars my right in thy achieved prize?

WARD: This makes you answer: what do you see in me

95 Doth promise I should be the sutler, sir,

Fetch you provision in?

FRANCISCO: A little calmer, sir! You are not in Kent,

Crying, "Herrings, seven a penny!" Nay, we have heard of you:

You can bawl well; you have served apprenticeship

100 Unto the trade, affrighting of whole streets

With your full oyster voice.°

WARD: Damnation!

FRANCISCO: Poor fisher's brat, that never didst aspire

Above a mussel boat; that were not born

105 Unto a fortune 'bove two cades of sprats

(And those smoked in thy father's bedchamber);

That by a beggar in mere charity

(Being made drunk) 'stead of a mariner

Wert stole aboard, and being awake didst smell

110 Worse then thy shell commodity at midsummer;

That desperate through fear wert made a captain,

When to have been ashore again, thou wouldst have turned

Swabber unto a Peter-man.

WARD: By all my hopes, thou hadst been better digged

115 Thy grandsire's urn up and have swallowed it.

FRANCISCO: Thou bark'st too much to bite.

WARD: Clear the deck there; each man bestow himself.

[Gismond and Gallop enter above.]

---

95 **sutler**] a soldier's servant or petty tradesman supplying an army.

105 **cades**] barrels.

105 **sprats**] a small, thin sea fish, often dried like herring.

113 **Swabber**] a sailor of low rank who swabs the deck.

113 **Peter-man**] fisherman.

GISMUND: [*aside to Gallop*] It's done: their hawsers cut without descry.
GALLOP: Away! [*To Ward*] Farewell, brave captain. Conquest sits on
120   thy brow.
WARD: Leave me, I say.
GALLOP: [*aside*] Th'wert never gulled till now.

Exit [Gallop and Gismund].

FRANCISCO: Give a charge there. Say your prayers, knight!
        Doomsday is nigh.   *[They] fight.*
125 WARD: True, it sinks thee to hell, whilst thus it bears me high.
        Stand'st thou so long? Thou hast some enchantment sure,
        Or have I lost my wonted vigor?
FRANCISCO: Flatter no more thyself. Wilt thou deliver
        A moiety of thy prize up?
130 WARD: Yes, thus thou shar'st it. Damnation!   *His sword falls.*
        Oh that my gall could spout out through mine eyes
        A poisonous vapor to put out your lights
        And in a vale of darkness leave the world.
FRANCISCO: Wilt thou yet yield me right?
135 WARD: Know, Francisco,
        Wert thou an army that encompassed me,
        I would breathe defiance to thee, and with this arm,
        As shot from out a cannon's mouth, thus would I make
        A way through death and danger.
140 FRANCISCO: I do applaud thee, and that thou well mayest know
        All valor's not confined within thy breast
        I thus oppose thee. Fortune shall have no share
        In what I conquer. *He flings away his sword and after looseth his dagger.*
WARD: Why, now I envy thee—thy life is mine!
145 FRANCISCO: Take it! I dare thy let.
WARD: Not for the world! Thus I return thy debt:
        Not only in the prize, but in myself
        Thou hast an equal share. Henceforth, I vow thee brotherhood.

---

122 Th'wert] you were.
131 gall] bitter bile secreted by the liver; thus, a malevolent and bitter spirit.
145 I dare thy let] I dare you to hold back.

FRANCISCO: Your love—I ask no more.   *Enter Ferdinand.*

150 FERDINAND: You need not: there's one gone before
    Takes order for your share.

WARD: Whither makes the slaves? Where's Gallop?

FERDINAND: Posting as fast as his sails will bear him.

WARD: Incarnate devil! Forthwith give them chase!

155   Why mov'st not?

SAILOR: They have cut our hawsers. We cannot budge a foot.

WARD: The death of slaves pursue him!

FRANCISCO: You are too violent.

WARD: To be baffled by a cur, a foisting hound!

160   My zani—A creature without a soul
    Made to mock man with!

FRANCISCO: Forbear, I say, and let us turn our anger
    On the next passenger.

WARD: Might I but live to see the dog-fish once again.

165 FRANCISCO: Ne'er doubt it, sir—next prize we take, forthwith
    We'll make to Tunis. Meantime, let revenge sleep.
    Those tides most violent are, which winds back keep.

WARD: For this alone I vow, whom next I meet
    Shall feel my fury. Nation nor quality

170   Shall be their privilege. My sword now vengeance craves,
    And who escape this do worse—I'll sell for slaves!   *Exeunt.*

SCENE 5.
DANSIKER'S LODGINGS IN TUNIS.

Enter Dansiker, three or four Sailors, Lieutenant. Dansiker reads a letter.

LIEUTENANT: What news, brave captain?

DANSIKER: Good. These letters from my wife bring certainty
    Of our obtained pardons, on condition

---

159 **foisting**] cheating.

160 **zani**] a clown or fool; a stock character in commedia dell' arte who clownishly aped the leading actors.

169 **quality**] social rank.

171 **And who escape this do worse—I'll sell for slaves!**] And those who avoid death on my sword will fare even worse—I'll sell them as slaves!

We henceforth for the state of France employ

5   Our lives and service.

ALL SHOUT: Long live King Henry of France!°

DANSIKER: My valiant friends, this four years Dansiker

Hath led you proudly through a sea of terror,

Through deeds so full of prowess they might have graced

10   The brow of worthiness, had justice to our cause

Given life and action. But since the breach of laws

Of nations, civil society, justly entitles us

With the hateful style of robbers, let's redeem our honor

And not return into our country with the names

15   Of pardoned thieves, but by some worthy deed,

Daring attempt, make good unto the world.

Want of employment, not of virtue, forced

Our former act of spoil and rapine.

LIEUTENANT: Set the design down may regain us credit.

20   Deserve this grace so freely offered us,

We'll or accomplish it, or with our lives;

Seal the attempt.

ALL: Brave captain, through death we'll follow thee!

DANSIKER: Then, thus—that with the same weapon we may

25   Our country cure, with which we wounded her;

My purpose is to ruin all the pirates

Lie in the harbor here.

LIEUTENANT: Rare! It may be easy done. Observe the wind

And firing but of one, consume the rest.

30 DANSIKER: We must not trust to such uncertainties.

Thus I have plotted it: we first will set afire

Some house i'th'town, to which when each man makes,

As they will be enforced from the haven

To yield their helps, with much facility

35   We may perform our purpose.

---

21 **We'll or accomplish it**] Either we'll accomplish it.

LIEUTENANT: How, undescried, shall we attempt the town?

DANSIKER: That charge be mine. The renegado Jew,°

    You know, gives free and open entertain

    To all of our profession. In some out-house of his

40   I will convey a pot of wildfire to it.

    I'll make a train of match, that at three hours

    Shall give it fire.

SAILORS: Excellent! The time, sir?

DANSIKER: Tomorrow night. Meantime make ready

45   For our departure, but with such secrecy

    Suspicion's self may not descry it. Provide the balls

    We must bestow upon the ships.

LIEUTENANT: That care be ours.

DANSIKER: The rest leave unto me.

50   We'll return nobly, or else nobly die.

Exeunt, [except Dansiker]. Enter Ruben [Rabshake].

DANSIKER: Ruben, what news?

RABSHAKE: My master, sir, desires your company.

    There's a new pirate landed: his name is Gallop.

DANSIKER: More yet? Do they come on so fat?

55   Your master would engross his prize.

RABSHAKE: He would, and for your courtesy herein,

    He will forbear three months the crowns you owe him.

DANSIKER: I'll use my art, sir, to his benefit.

    And for the crowns, no longer I'll delay him.

60   Here is my hand. Tomorrow night I'll pay him.   *Exeunt.*

---

39 **out-house**] a building belonging to and adjoining the main house.

40 **wildfire**] "A composition of highly inflammable substances, readily ignited and very difficult to extinguish, used in warfare" (*O.E.D.*).

41 **train**] "A line of gunpowder or other combustible substance laid so as to convey fire to a mine or charge for the purpose of exploding it" (*O.E.D.*).

41 **match**] rope prepared for use as a fuse.

41 **three hours**] three in the morning.

46 **balls**] bullets or cannonballs.

55 **engross**] to buy all, so as to monopolize.

SCENE 6.
AT THE HOUSE OF BENWASH THE JEW.

Enter Rabshake, Agar, Voada.

AGAR: Speak freely—what think you of the newcome captain, Voada?

VOADA: He looks as if his father and mother had got him in fear: his eyes
go like a city catchpole, several ways at once. There's no stuff in him.
Give me the Dutch cavalier Dansiker.

5 AGAR: Out upon him, puff-paste! He was spoiled in his infancy, ill-bred.

RABSHAKE: How? Spoiled with ill bread? It was ill drink spoiled him. I am
of my master's mind: the newcome pirate is a reasonable handsome
man of a Christian.

AGAR: Why? Doth religion move anything in the shapes of men?

10 RABSHAKE: Altogether! What's the reason else that the Turk and Jew is
troubled (for the most part) with gouty legs and fiery nose? To express
their heart-burning. Whereas the puritan is a man of upright calf and
clean nostril.

VOADA: Setting aside your nose, you should turn Christian. Then your calf
15 swells upward mightily.

RABSHAKE: How? I turn Christian? They have Jew enough already
amongst 'em. Were it but three qualities they have, I'll be none of their
society.

AGAR: Three qualities? I prithee tell 'em us, Rabshake.

20 RABSHAKE: First, they suffer their wives to be their masters. Secondly, they
make men thieves for want of maintenance and then hang them up for
stealing. Lastly, they are mad four times a year, and those they call
term-times, and then they are so purged by their physicians (which
they name lawyers), some of 'em are never their own men after it. I
25 turn Christian? They shall have more charity amongst 'em first! They
will devour one another as familiarly as pikes do gudgeons and with as
much facility as Dutchmen do flapdragons.

---

3 catchpole] a term of contempt referring to a small-time officer of the law who specializes in making
arrests.
5 puff-paste] literally, a light, flaky kind of flour paste. Here it refers to someone of light or insubstan-
tial character.
23 term-times] those times of the year when the London law courts were in session.
26 gudgeons] small, easily caught baitfish.
27 flapdragons] burning raisins, soaked in brandy, that were caught and extinguished in the mouth.

AGAR: How? Eat up one another?

RABSHAKE: Aye, eat up one another! You have an innocent Christian called
30   a gallant—your city Christian will feed upon no other meat, by his
good will.

VOADA: But their wives will not feed on 'em, too.

RABSHAKE: The truth is, they are not altogether so great devourers;
marry, they will be sucking at the bones. But see my master, the great
35   thief and the little thieves, the robbers and the receiver.

Enter Gallop [Dansiker, Sares].

AGAR: He's come. Thou powerful god of love, strike through mine eyes
Those awful darts of thine, whose burning heads
Pierce thorough hearts of ice, melt frostiest breasts,
Make all stoop to thy deity! Now, give thy art!
40   No god but Cupid pities mortal's smart.

Enter Benwash, Gismund, Frederick, Carolo, Alizia disguised.

GISMUND: Five ducats a tun! 'Sheart, the cask is worth more!

BENWASH: You must remember at what rate you bought 'em.

DANSIKER: And at what price you may have more.

GISMUND: You speak like men that know how the market goes.
45   Your ear, Jew.

ALIZIA: [*aside*] What misery remains to add to mine?
My brother lost his life in my defense;
And with his life, my sex and liberty,
I stand deprived of. Are not these wounds sufficient
50   To let out my weak breath? Thou flinty breast,
Art thou impenetrable? Or is that thing called death
Too great a good for such wretch as I am? It is, it is,
And that's the cause so many miseries
Do stop the way to't.

55 BENWASH: I am your merchant. Ruben Rabshake! My wife! Here, sister!
Fetch me three hundred ducats for this gentleman.

---

34 **sucking at the bones**] sucking out the marrow after their husbands have eaten the meat, with a
bawdy reference to fellatio or vaginal suction, where "bone" is an erect penis.

RABSHAKE: This newcome thief, sir?

BENWASH: "Gentleman," slave!

RABSHAKE: Why, your thief is a gentleman: he scorns to do anything, and
60   he lives upon his comings in.

BENWASH: Peace, dog! You see, gallants, we are not Italianate to lock our
        women up: we set 'em free, give open entertainment.

GALLOP: [aside] It seemes this Jew keeps a bawdy house. I like his wife well.
        I could find in my heart to cast away half a ducat on her.

65 SARES: [To Benwash] You are of a noble mind, sir, courtly and high.
        It's want of merit that breeds jealousy,
        From which I know you clear.

BENWASH: [paying Gallop] Captain, your gold.

AGAR: He saw our eyes meet. No matter—may I cool my heat,
70   Let the world burn! Thy counsel, Voada.

[Voada and Agar walk aside and examine the captives.]

BENWASH: I do not like this fellow's looks, Rabshake.

RABSHAKE: He hath a hanging countenance indeed, sir.

BENWASH: Tush, my wise man! Thou hast forgot how dear
        I bought my liberty, renounced my law
75   (The law of Moses), turned Turk—all to keep
        My bed free from these Mahometan dogs.
        I would not be a monster, Rabshake—a man-beast,
        A cuckold.

RABSHAKE: I have not forgotten, sir, that you damned yourself because you
80   would not be a cornuto. If every man should sign so dear for his horns,
        we should have but a few Christians left. But seeing you fear your
        vessel hath a leak, wherefore do you put her to sea, man her thus?

BENWASH: For commodity: thou seest rich shopkeepers set their wives
        at sale to draw in custom, utter their wares, yet keep that gem
85   untouched—all for profit, man.

---

60 **comings in**] revenues, especially from rent.
63 **bawdy house**] brothel.
80 **cornuto**] cuckold.
83 **commodity**] profit, selfish interest.
84 **utter**] offer for sale publicly.

RABSHAKE: I am not of your mind, sir. There is no profit without
   some pain.

BENWASH: No more, villain! Should I suspect myself to have that disease,
   I would run mad; first fury of my horns should light on thee: look
90   to't—thou art no longer living than my wife is honest.

RABSHAKE: I fear my days are but short then, if my life lasts no longer then
   I can keep a woman honest against her will.

VOADA: [*admiring Alizia*] It is a lovely boy, rare featured! Would he
   were mine!

95 AGAR: It is so, Voada. He hath made the slave my jailor.

VOADA: I have not seen so much of beauty in a man.

AGAR: You lose yourself. What man? What beauty? I tell thee, I am
   undone: Rabshake is made my overseer.

VOADA: I would use him like an overseer then. He should stand by whilst
100   the executioner opened the bags.° I must enjoy his love, though
   quenching of my lust did burn the world besides.

BENWASH: It's right, captain.

[Gallop finishes counting the gold and puts it away in his purse.]

[GALLOP]: Yes, 'tis right.

[GISMUND]: But that's the wrong way, sir. Your fellows expect their equal
105   shares.

BENWASH: The fellow raves: talk to a captain of equal sharing! I'll take
   order for landing the goods and be with you presently. Rabshake, thou
   knowest thy doom, slave—look to't. Thine eyes, villain, thine eyes!

RABSHAKE: I'll warrant you, sir, I'll look to't.

Exit Benwash [with Frederick, Carolo, Alizia].

110 GALLOP: Here, carry 'em these two ducats to drink upon receipt of the
   whole. I'll deal like a commander with 'em, as men do with their
   followers. That is, as you have followed me to earn means, so now you
   shall follow me as long to get your earnings. You shall be followers
   still: I will discharge none of you.

115 SARES: [*aside*] We took him for a gull, but now I see he hath had
   command, he can cheat his soldiers.

GISMUND: I hope, sir, you will make better respect of your credit. You
know your oaths and promise.

GALLOP: My promise? If a citizen had bought a company, he could but
120   keep day with 'em: you must pardon him, gentlemen, a fresh soldier
wants seasoning.

GISMUND: Salt us! Look to't—we shall hardly relish you, sir.

GALLOP: How? Threatens and braves?

DANSIKER: [*To Gallop*] Forbear! Give the poor fellow leave to prate—he
125   pays for't.

GISMUND: Good. You are now upon your guard. We shall meet you upon
discharge of the watch and knock you down with a bill of accounts.
We shall skeld.

Exit Gismund.

GALLOP: Out, gull! Talk to a commander, a man of war, of equal sharing!
130   We have other use for our money than to pay followers. Shall we
accost these ladies, gallants?

RABSHAKE: 'Tis the custom of the whole world: the greater thief preys
upon the less still. How's this?

DANSIKER: The happiness of the day befall you, ladies.

135 SARES: The night equal the day's happiness, say I.

GALLOP: All content, both night and day stand to your desires.

AGAR: Our desires equal your wishes, sir.

GALLOP: Your desires are above my performance then.

RABSHAKE: I am drawing on. If my life lie upon her honesty, I am upon
140   the point of giving up already.

AGAR: That gentleman is very moving.

RABSHAKE: [*To Agar*] Could you not entreat him stay his pace?

SARES: And trot in your ring, lady, if you please.

AGAR: I purpose not to take a courser of your choosing, lest I be jaded, sir.

---

122 relish] please.
123 braves] defies.
127 bill of accounts] a document listing what is owed, but punning on the sense of "bill" as a weapon
(a hook-shaped blade with a spike on the back, mounted on a staff).
128 skeld] obtain money by force, by fraud, or by begging in the guise of a disbanded soldier.
136 stand] attend, serve; but also, maintain an erection.
139 drawing on] approaching the end (of life).

145 SARES: You presume the more of your own horsemanship.

RABSHAKE: Hoyday, they are riding already. 'Sfoot, I am like to go post to the Devil° for this.

DANSIKER: Next night, time of my project, if I prove not as hot a shot as come in your quarters since the loss of your virginity, let me

150 suffer the pains of St. Anthony's purgatory.°

AGAR: He must necessarily be a man of deeds, he is of so few words.

SARES: You shall do well to put him to the trial.

AGAR: [*To Gallop*] Without immodesty, may I question the reason you're so heavy, sir?

155 RABSHAKE: Nay, then, it rings out for me! Should the Jew see this, I were as good as speechless: there were but a little gasping between me and the grave.

[Exit Rabshake.]

GALLOP: The reason of my heaviness is that you and I might agree the better. For women love contraries, and you are light, I see.

160 AGAR: How's this? You see me light, true, to be in love with one so far disdainful.

VOADA: What success, woman? The Dutchman and I have bartered wares.

AGAR: I have made exchange, too, sold my liberty to purchase base ingratitude. I am rejected, Voada.

[Re-]Enter Rabshake.

165 RABSHAKE: My mistress, gentlemen, did you see my mistress?

AGAR: Your business, sirrah?

RABSHAKE: You must make provision to entertain two of the richest pirates ever landed here, one Captain Ward and Franciscus. They have brought a prize in worth three thousand ducats: besides, they sell their

170 prisoners as slaves. My master hath engrossed them all.

AGAR: Vengeance seize him and them! Back, sirrah—say we will expect

---

149 **in your quarters**] between your lower limbs; in the middle section of the ship.

154 **heavy**] heavy-hearted, sad in demeanor.

155 **it rings out**] referring to the church bells rung for a funeral, with a pun on "wrings" meaning to squeeze (the neck in hanging).

159 **light**] wanton, morally loose.

them. You sir, attend your master his coming; see you give us
notice on't.

RABSHAKE: Nay, I hold it the best course, too, for mine own safety. My
175   charge is charged; my watch must be now, lest my master know it.
If all the world were eyes, women (I see) would to it.

Exit Rabshake.

GALLOP: I do but dream, sure! Ward and Franciscus?

DANSIKER: What moves this passion?

SARES: Why look you pale?

180 GALLOP: Pale? I have a cause: I have less color by six hundred ducats
than I had.

SARES: As how, sir?

GALLOP: I'll tell you. I took an adventure to pay this Ward six hundred
ducats at our two meetings at Tunis, and see how the Devil hath
185   brought it about! I must leave you gallants.

DANSIKER: By no means: we will compound the business.

AGAR: I can conceal it no longer.

VOADA: You will betray yourself to their contempt, by your own
forwardness.

190 AGAR: I ne'er shall have so fair occasion to speak my love again. You know
my husband's watchful jealousy.

VOADA: Now by my sex I am ashamed of you. Were the Jew mine,
I would have no other pander. Be ruled by me.
It's he shall hire the captain to thy love
195   And his own horning. What cannot we persuade?
Man was asleep when woman's brain was made.

AGAR: Thou giv'st me a new life. I am thy scholar.

VOADA: I'll prick thee forth a lesson whose choicer strain
Shall tell men that all art 'gainst lust and women's vain.

Exit Voada and Agar.

---

183 **took an adventure**] took a risk (hoping to make a profit); made a deal.
186 **compound the business**] settle the dispute by a cash payment; come to terms and pay for an offense or injury.
195 **horning**] being made a cuckold.
198 **prick thee forth**] write or set down (music) for you (with a bawdy pun on "prick").

[Enter Rabshake.]

200 RABSHAKE: As you are men, conceal your weapons! Here are
women in the room.

Enter three Sailors with Gismund.

GALLOP: Gismund.
GISMUND: We are come to give you thanks for the two ducats, sir.
GALLOP: As you are men of the sword, draw!
205 GISMUND: We are fresh men. We'll powder you.   *[They] fight.*
GALLOP: Murder, murder! I shall be torn in pieces, by my hands!

Enter Ward, Francisco, Ferdinand, Alizia [disguised as a] page.

GISMUND: Ward! Franciscus! We are betrayed! Away!

Exit Gismund and Sailors.

WARD: Gallop.
GALLOP: My noble general alive, come to my rescue! My loyalty to the
210   brave knight did thus engage me: the slaves could not be content to
stow me underboard and force me from thee, but would have shared
the prize, too: but I have shared with 'em. See, here's three hundred
ducats. Thou shalt have them all, brave spark. *[aside]* The Devil to
boot with 'em.
215 WARD: Then you think this gold shall purchase your pardon?
GALLOP: 'Sfoot, I am overjoyed with the sight of thee. See the heroic
Dansiker, his Captain Sares.
WARD: Your loves, gentlemen.
DANSIKER: This is no slave. He pays six hundred ducats at their meeting—
220   true, we are witness on't.
WARD: I will be gulled for once thus, I will. These ducats shall stop
my mouth.
GALLOP: 'Sheart, there are many more in bank. You shall have 'em all.

---

205 **powder**] pulverize.

I prize thy countenance above a second Indies. [*aside*] Were they
225   molten in your garbage! The world runs round with me: *sicut erat in*
principio. Naked I came in, and penniless I shall go out. What stays
the Jew so long?

WARD: See, he is come.

     Enter Benwash, Raymond and his two Sons (bound), Rabshake.

You'll give my price, sir?

230 BENWASH: Yes, for these slaves, I will.

RAYMOND: Forever be he servile that so makes 'em.
    Hard-hearted! "Man" I cannot term thee. It's
    A name that bears too much of pity in't,
    Compared with so inhumane. Creature, wert thou a father,
235   These tears would move thee, that bemoan a son's,
    Nay all my children's, worse than funeral,
    Their ever thralldom. But Nature well denied
    Issue to thee, lest in thy barbarous guilt
    She had been a party when thy affectioned soul
240   Had felt how much the name of child moves, with what care,
    How many jealous fears, we view their infancy;
    Lest having felt all this, thy accursed hand
    Should yet have dared to make men childless.

FIRST SON: Can then your marble heart endure these drops?

245 SECOND SON: The soil that bred you, sir, doth not bring forth
    Such hideous monsters that we should imagine
    You can be so cruel to betray
    So many innocent lives, for in us bleed
    An agèd father, a mother, to whose grief
250   No other misery can be added.
    Myself contracted to a virtuous maid,
    Who ere this hath left Marcel
    And in Normandy expects the consummation of our happiness.

---

224 **countenance**] favor, good opinion.
225 **garbage**] guts.
225 **sicut erat in principio**] L., "just as it was in the beginning."
230 **these slaves**] Raymond's two sons, but not their father.
252 **Marcel**] Marseilles.

You have our goods, our ship, all the substance
255   Should succor our old parents. You have only left
These arms to earn them bread, and can your eyes
Relentless see these chained?

FERDINAND: Do not they move you, sir?

WARD: Yes, as the Jew. Art not thou moved, Benwash?

260 BENWASH: As a hangman at an execution makes no other holiday in
the year.

RAYMOND: Inhuman dog! Oh I could tear thee, villain!

BENWASH: I'll give thirty crowns for this old beast to be revenged on him.

RAYMOND: [*To Ward*] Be gentle—take his money. Forgive me, sir.
265   I see you are kind, would not now part us
That twenty and odd years have grown together.
Will you not take it? Give him so, Jew,
I will deserve 'em. See, I am not old.
No wrinkle is on my brow; these are but frowns,
270   Raised by his unkind refusal of my offer.
See what plump veins I have, no sinews shrunk.
These are not gray hairs: they are only white
To show the lightness of my spirit. Come
Manacle these arms. You shall see us three
275   Tug the day's eye out. There's not a father
And his two boys shall dare to undertake us.
The sun outvied, we'll set us down together
and with our sadder cheer outmourn the night,
And speak the happiness we might have lived, too:
280   How by mine own hearth in cold winter eves
I might have told my sons some ancient tales,
Which they might one day from their grandsire speak.
We'll add unto our woes thus by compare
Of what our joys might have been. Then we'll curse,
285   And when we want a plague, we'll think upon
This bloody murtherer—we shall have store then,
Be eloquent in bitter execrations.
Our choler vented, then again we'll weep,
Till tears glue up our eyes to mock sad sleep.

---

264 gentle] noble and virtuous.

290 WARD: Ha, ha, ha.

FIRST SON: Dost laugh at agèd sorrow? Be just, ye powers:
    As ye judge innocent causes, revenge ours.

WARD: My money for 'em, Jew. So, away with 'em.

ALBERT: FERDINAND: We will redeem them, pay their ransom.

295 WARD: You redeem them? Your means?

FERDINAND: All that we have aboard.

WARD: Such another syllable, I'll make a sale of you, too.

BENWASH: I am your first man: I'll give you four hundred crowns for 'em.

ALBERT: A sale of us?

300 FERDINAND: Know that if all our fortunes will set them free, 'tis theirs.

WARD: I'll try that—give me four hundred crowns.

BENWASH: Here.

WARD: They are yours. I'll justify the sale.

SARES: Of your own fellows? Countrymen? Do they not stand
305   conditioned as yourself?

GALLOP: Who gave you patent to examine him?

WARD: Forbear. Because you're men of action, I'll descend
    To give you notice they are my lawful prize,
    Such as denied my party, would willingly
310   Betray me, yea, all of us, into the hands
    Of our vowed enemies.

SARES: Are you not men of war then?

FERDINAND: We are no pirates, sir. Our country yields us
    more honest means of living.

315 SARES: Away with 'em! More honest means of living!
    Make 'em sure.

ALBERT: Give us the hearing.

WARD: Away with 'em! Zounds, I'll set them free else!

SECOND SON: Let's take our father's blessing with us yet.

320 WARD: All curses under heaven go with you.

[Exit Benwash and Rabshake with Ferdinand, Albert and Raymond's sons.]

RAYMOND: Is there no ear for misery to beat at?
    My sons—Ferdinand! Albert! They are gone, sent
    To perpetual vassalage. I loved you boys

---

323 **vassalage**] servitude.

A little better than to outlive your slaveries.

325   I will not curse thee, monster. I know my thoughts

Cannot arrive unto so black revenge

As shall attend thee. Crack, crack, you o'erloaden strings,

And set a miserable old man free.

So, so. I will appeal for you, my sons, to yon high court.

330   Here none but beasts of prey, tigers, resort.   *Dies.*

DANSIKER: [*aside*] I hate this villain. He's all blood.

But that instead of words, my eyes thus speak.

WARD: How is't, my noble spirits? Dulled with one tragedy?

Let us digest it with a jig, a catch!

335   Some wine there! Shall we to hazard?

DANSIKER: I willingly would stake my life to thine at that just

game. There wants but an occasion.

SARES: What's your sport?

GALLOP: Adam's game at one whole—every male to his female.

340 WARD: How should we be furnished?

GALLOP: I'll fit you with an Eve, sir, a temptress.

WARD: What is she?

GALLOP: Your peer, a beauty that would take you

From out your self to gaze at her,

345   The Jew's wife's sister.

Enter Benwash, Crosman, Agar, Voada.

WARD: First sight of her yields thee a hundred ducats.

GALLOP: I'll be a conjunction copulative to join you together for the money.

It is a fate follows us soldiers when we are down: the reason is, we

hold it no shame to live upon spoil of the enemy, and a greater foe

350   to man than a whore is impossible. 'Sheart, I am prevented: the Jew

panders them himself. That's she, sir. That Turk's her brother. His

name is Crosman.

BENWASH: Is it possible?

GALLOP: The slave hath a goat in his looks.

355 CROSMAN: That's he in the Judas beard. Use but thy art, he's thine.

---

334   catch] song.

335   Shall we to hazard?] Shall we play the game of hazard?

339   Adam's game at one whole] meaning sexual intercourse, with a pun on "whole/hole."

354   goat] associated with lechery.

AGAR: If I liked not his thirty thousand ducats better than's person, I would
     never strain my complexion for him.

WARD: She equals thy commends indeed! So true a fair
     I ne'er beheld till now.

360 AGAR: Nay, more to entice me, this well stuffed purse
     He did enforce upon me. But 'tis your sin:
     So you have profit, all religious laws
     Must suffer violence, your wife be exposed
     Unto all undergoers.

365 BENWASH: Forgiveness, honest wife—my chaste, chaste wife.

AGAR: Nay, use your pleasure: you had best keep the gold
     To gild your shame with. I trow I would give it him.
     Tell him he must not think I am the woman
     He takes me for. If he will not believe you,
370   Let him make trial with the ladder of ropes
     He vowed to climb my chamber with this night,
     When, as it seems, he learnt you were enforced
     To be in the synagogue.

BENWASH: Better and better! I cannot but admire thy chastity.
375   A ladder of ropes! Would he make that the beginning
     Lechery should be the end of? I'll hamper him!
     If he have any grace, thy honesty overthrows him.

AGAR: If he have any wit it will, I hope.

BENWASH: My dull-eyed villain Rabshake saw none of this. He's all for
380   *rem in re.* He would have me a cuckold by law forsooth, by statute law.
     I shall put you a book case, for he shall moot I'll prize him but
     to the present business.° Noble captain, to express how much you
     are welcome, my wife and sister, laying all rites aside, and customary
     observes, come to invite you to a mean banquet, sir.

385 WARD: Best thanks, sir. Your welcome's prodigal. I am already feasted in
     this bounteous dish, sir.

---

357 **complexion**] natural disposition or temperament.
358 **commends**] praise, recommendation.
364 **all undergoers**] all interested parties.
367 **trow**] believe.
372 **enforced**] required.
380 **rem in re**] L., the thing in the thing.
384 **observes**] observances.

DANSIKER: But you are not likely to surfeit on it. I'll have a finger in the
platter with you, were you the Great Turk's self.

WARD: With me? I tell thee, Dansiker,

390   Thou dost not merit it thy lips to touch
So choice a rarity. What darest thou for her?

DANSIKER: What thou dar'st not!   [*Draws his sword.*]

WARD: I'll put that to the trial.   [*Draws his sword.*]

Sares [and] Dansiker [fight] against Francisco, Gallop [and Ward].
Benwash hides himself [under a table].

VOADA: As you come of women!

395 AGAR: By all the rites you owe our sex, as you are men, enforce them part.

Crosman parts them.

CROSMAN: Respect the place! You are in danger of law!

WARD: [*To Voada*] You shall o'ersway me, lady.

[*To Dansiker*] We shall meet again, sir.

CROSMAN: So you are men!

Exit Ward, Francisco, Sares, Dansiker, [pursued by Crosman].

400 BENWASH: Are they gone? What hard fortune attends me that none of
their throats were cut? I might have seized their goods. Not so much
as the flesh-biter, but is come off.

GALLOP: S'hart, this poverty makes a man valiant. When I had my ducats, I
had no more heart than a Jew.

405 BENWASH: And that was the reason you so willingly parted with 'em, sir.

GALLOP: Old Benwash, where hidst thou thy head in this day of battle, man?

BENWASH: Here under this table. Did you think I am so branched no roof
would give me covering? I am but a pricket, a mere sorrel, my head's
not hardened yet; though, thanks unto your mastership, your fire was

410   not wanting.

---

388 **the Great Turk's self**] the Ottoman emperor in Istanbul.

397 **o'ersway**] overrule.

401-2 **Not so much . . . come off**] sense uncertain. Possibly a lacuna in the text.

402 **flesh-biter**] a sword or dagger?

408 **a pricket, a mere sorrel**] a young deer. A pricket is a young male deer with small, unbranched
antlers; a sorrel is a buck in its third year.

GALLOP: You speak in Hebrew: I understand you not.

BENWASH: Yet you can speak the whoremaster's language passing well.
    What made you, sir, take my wife for a flesh-seller, a whore?

GALLOP: You are abused, sir.

415 BENWASH: By thee, lecher. You know not this purse, this gold?
    You have your tricks to climb up cuckold's haven—
    Your ladder of ropes! You had best keep that hour:
    My wife this night expects you. My absence
    Will be enforced, she bid me tell you so.

420   Insatiate goat, thou thinkst our wives are such,
    As are your holy sisters, religious votaries,
    Your spittle nuns. Here, take your ill-got trash!
    May I but know thou once more temp'st my wife,
    You shall not need a ladder. I'll mount you, sir!

425   I will, you oxgall,° I will.

GALLOP: [aside] Ha, this is gold.

BENWASH: Do you hear, sir?
    Hereafter know a Turk's wife from a Christian's.
    You are one of those hold all women bound

430   Under the domination of the moon,
    All wavering. Now you have seen one of the sun, sir.
    Constant, you slave, and as she is, with us are millions more.

[Enter Crosman.]

CROSMAN: Benwash, brother! S'foot, I have sought each nook
    of the house for you.

435 GALLOP: [aside] It is beyond my thoughts; imagination's drowned in't.

BENWASH: Rare! Doth she plead chastity?

CROSMAN: Like a bawd that would put off a virginity. The knight is as
    good as ours already. Besides, I have procured the Governor in person
    to regreet him.

440   All that art can by ambition, lust, or, flattery do,
    Assure yourself this brain shall work him to.

---

422 **spittle nuns**] lit., nuns employed in a hospital; slang for diseased prostitutes.
424 **mount**] raise up; get up on, for the purpose of copulation (a term suggesting animal breeding).
437 **put off**] to dispose of; to sell.
439 **regreet**] greet; receive.

BENWASH: Nay, if the flesh take hold of him, he's past redemption.
He's half a Turk already; it's as good as done.
Woman is hell, out; in we ne'er return.

Exit Benwash and Crosman.

445 GALLOP: Were not I confident of my good parts, this gold would buy me
out of my five senses. A full purse, a ladder of ropes, and his wife in
the tail on't able to overcome any man breathing! Yet what should I
fear that have so many good angels about me? Sure she's in love with
me—it is no other—and out of her honesty it seems she hath vowed
450 to do nothing but what she dares acquaint her husband with. If she
have made him usher his own crest,° I'll swear she is a woman of the
sun. She hath dazzled his eyes well! This night makes the trial. I'll take
your instructions, Jew, climb the matter of preferment.
It may be 'twas my destiny gave me this crown:
455 Woman and ropes should raise me, that put others down. *Exit.*

SCENE 7.
AT WARD'S HOUSE IN TUNIS.

Enter Governor, Ward, Crosman, Benwash.

WARD: I am o'ercharged, sir, with so high a favor
As your descending thus to visit me.
GOVERNOR: You are the man we covet, whose valor
Hath spoke out, so impartial worthy,
5 We should do wrong to merit, not gracing you.
Believe me, sir, you have injured much your self,
Vouchsafing familiarity with those
Men of so common rank as Dansiker.
Your hopes should fly a pitch above them.
10 CROSMAN: It may be that our clime stands not to give
That full content, the air you drew at home,
And therefore purpose shortly a return.

---

447 **in the tail on't**] included in the total (or tally), with a quibble on "tail" as female sexual part.
9 **fly a pitch**] reach a high point in flight (from falconry).

WARD: I know no country I can call home.
    What by your courtesy I might, my desert stands
15   Not to make promise of.
    GOVERNOR: Detract not from yourself; call this your own.
    I see there speaks a fortune in your brow
    Will make us proud to have acknowledged you.
BENWASH: I'll gage a thousand ducats on equal terms,
20   I live to see him the sultan's admiral.
CROSMAN: Why not as well as the great customer,
    My allied kinsman governor—neither born Turks?
WARD: I dare not look so high! Yet were I employed,
    What a poor Christian could, I durst make promise of.
25 BENWASH: Christian or Turk, you are more wise, I know,
    Than with religion to confine your hopes.
    GOVERNOR: He's too well read in poesy to be tied
    In the slave's fetters of religion.
    What difference in me as I am a Turk
30   And was a Christian? Life, liberty,
    Wealth, honor—they are common unto all!
    If any odds be, 'tis on Mahomet's side:
    His servitors thrive best, I am sure.
WARD: Is this the hook your golden bait doth cover?
35 BENWASH: I have oft with laughter thought how innocent
    My thoughts when first I turned were, how scrupulous
    I was, when with one argument I was confirmed—as thus:
    If this religion were so damnable
    As others make it, that God which owes the right,
40   Profaned by this, would soon destroy it quite.
WARD: That's easily answered: heaven is merciful.
    By their destruction it should take all means
    From giving possibility to their change,
    And so unjustly damn 'em. But for my part,
45   Is it not divinity but nature moves me,
    Which doth in beasts force them to keep their kind.
CROSMAN: But men that have two ends, safety and profit,

---

19 gage] wager.
21 customer] official in charge of customs.
37 confirmed] convinced.
39 owes] owns.

Where beasts no farther are transported
Than with the present object, must make their actions
50   Turn to those points.
GOVERNOR: Both which are in some sort proposed to you.
WARD: As how?
GOVERNOR: As thus, for profit, you cannot with yourself
Imagine that your virtue can be smothered,
55   Might there but be assurance of your trust.
WARD: How should I give you that?
GOVERNOR: As we did—turn Turk.
WARD: That were the way to more uncertainty.
Men sooner open foes then feigned friends try,
60   And where men's acts from their own ends proceed,
More look unto those ends than like the deed.
BENWASH: [*aside*] This gudgeon will not bite.
GOVERNOR: But when there are examples plentiful
To instance 'gainst your words, you need not fear.
65   Men what they see oppose 'gainst what they hear.
WARD: The cunning fowler to beguile the birds
Brings up some tame, and lets them fly abroad
To draw in others, that their liberty
May be the bait to others' misery.
70   Such is state policies, sometimes to advance an ill,
When others for less crimes it oft doth kill.
But to cut off your further argument:
What's mine of prowess, or art, shall rest by you
To be disposed of; but to abjure
75   My name—and the belief my ancestors
Left to my being! I do not love so well
The earth that bore me, to lessen my contempt
And hatred to her, by so much advantage,
So oblique act as this should give to her.
80 CROSMAN: [*aside to Benwash*] Work in my sister presently.
GOVERNOR: You are yourself free, nor will I further
Dissuade your resolution, nor less esteem
Your merit and fair worth.
WARD: You engage me to you, sir.

---

73 art] skill.

85 CROSMAN: [*aside*] He enjoys too much by promise to be won.
         T'must be a woman's act, to whom there's nought
         That is impossible. What devils dare not move
         Men to accomplish, women work them to.   [*Enter Voada.*]
         And see, in happy time she's come—we'll single them.
90 WARD: Here comes an argument that would persuade
         A god turn mortal. Until I saw her face,
         I never knew what men term beauty was;
         Besides whose fair, she hath a mind so chaste
         A man may sooner melt the Alps than her.
95 GOVERNOR: We will along with you. When makes she hence?
    BENWASH: The wind sits fair. The slaves are sending down
         Whom the next morn bears hence.
    GOVERNOR: We will aboard with you, fair sir. We'll leave
         Our love exchanged with you. Some happier time
100   May perfect that good work I wish were mine.

                    Exit Governor, Benwash, Crosman.

    WARD: My truest services. Nay lady, stay!
         Though hitherto I have been a hapless orator,
         Your milder measure, or my love-taught tongue,
         May find more fortunate hours. For by that guide,
105   Which rules and knows our thoughts—
    VOADA: Reserve your oaths, sir, to more easy ears.
         I understand myself too well to credit 'em.
    WARD: Ungentle maid, to triumph in my torment!
         If ever breast did feel the power of love,
110   Or beauty make a conquest of poor man,
         I am thy captive, by heaven, by my religion.
    VOADA: As my belief's in that, my faith gives trust
         To your protests.
    WARD: Then by thy god, by the great Mahomet.
115 VOADA: Too weak a bond to tie a Christian in.
    WARD: What shall I swear by? Propose an oath to me

---

86 T'must] It must.
89 single them] leave them alone.

The breach whereof would at once sink me lower
Than hell knows being—I'll take it willingly.

VOADA: I'll be concealed no longer. Know then I love,
120   But not the man whose daily orisons
Invoke confusion on me, whose religion
Speaks me an infidel.

WARD: 'Sheart, I am of none—only to feed discourse,
And fill up argument.

125 VOADA: But you must be of one if you'll enjoy me.
If then your thoughts answer to what you speak,
Turn Turk—I am yours.

WARD: Turn Turk?

VOADA: Do you demur already? How prodigal your words
130   Spoke your affection, and with one simple trial
Are you struck mute?

WARD: With patience hear me, lady!

VOADA: False knight, I have given too calm an ear already
To thy enchanted notes.

135 WARD: Should I forever sell my liberty?

VOADA: You need not: it is sufficient glory
You have betrayed a maiden's liberty.
But I'll do penance for my so black a sin,
Doting on thee. I'll henceforth hate thy whole sex.
140   The name of man to me shall (as the rock
From which the shipwracked wretch hath lately 'scaped)
Bring fear in the name of 't. Keep off, false siren!
Heaven well ordained man should the woman woe;
Should we their hard hearts prove, we all ill should know.

145 WARD: Stay, I will enforce thee else.

VOADA: Do these my tears delight thee then? Cruel,
Hardhearted man, glut thy relentless sight
With full-eyed sorrow.

WARD: [*aside*] She is all amorous, all fair! That she doth love,
150   Behold those tears, whose drops would pierce the hearts
Of tigers, make them pitiful.

---

143 **man should the woman woe**] that men should bring "woe" upon women.
144 **prove**] make trial of; know by experience.

They are witnesses she feigns not. [*To Voada*] Leave, leave to weep,
Lest putting out those lights the world should mourn,
Put on a veil of black. I am thine own.
155   If there be any divinity, it hath
His seat in beauty: th'art a god to me.
My country, friends, nay being—what wouldst thou have?

VOADA: To be no other than myself I crave.

WARD: I am no more mine own, rather than lose
160   So true a happiness as thy constant love.
There is no way so black I would not prove,
That lies from heaven to hell. Crosman, in vain
Thy arguments were spent: wouldst thou prevail?
Here is an orator can turn me easily.
165   Where beauty pleads, there needs no sophistry.
Thou hast o'ercome me, Voada.

VOADA: And I will raise thee, but thou dost name a good
I cannot call mine till I am professed of 't.

WARD: Call in thy friends, make preparation.
170   I'll take the orders instantly.
My speed shall give prevention to the prate
Of th'idle multitude. Away, the flame doth burn
Which sets the world on fire and makes me turn.

VOADA: Thou art all harmony! Best love, I fly;
175   [*aside*] I have my ends.
Howe'er thou sink, thy wealth shall bear me high.   *Exit Voada.*

WARD: So, the day leaves the world, chaste Voada.
Nothing can make him miserable enjoys thee.
What is 't I lose by this my change? My country?
180   Already 'tis to me impossible.
My name is scandalled? What is one island
Compared to the Eastern monarchy? This large,
Unbounded station shall speak my future fame;
Besides, they are slaves stand subject unto shame.
185   One good I enjoy outweighs all ills whatever
Can be objected. To sum my happiness:

---

170 **take the orders**] undergo the official rites (of conversion).
171 **prate**] prattle, talk.

That god on earth, to whom all men stand bare,
Gold, that doth usher greatness, lackeys me.
I have more than I can spend. What wants
190   Is in command, and that my valor makes
Due purchase of. I'll rather lead on slaves
Than be commanded by the power of kings.
Beauty, command, and riches—these are the three
The world pursues, and these follow me.

              Enter [Alizia, disguised as Fidelio].

195   Speak—what news, Fidelio?
    [ALIZIA]: The tongues of ravens are too mild to speak it,
      The very thought whereof methinks should turn
      Your hair to quills of porcupines. It's the denial
      Of your redeemer, religion, country,
200   Of him that gave you being.
    WARD: The slavery of man, how this religion rides us!
      Deprives us of our freedom from our cradles,
      Ties us in superstitious bondage.
    [ALIZIA]: Heaven stop mine ears from hearing thy dishonor!
205   Upon my knees, I do conjure you, sir:
      Sell not your soul for such a vanity
      As that which you term "beauty," eye-pleasing idol!
      Should you with the renouncing of your God,
      Taking the abhorred name of Turk upon you,
210   Purchase a little shameful being here, your case
      Might be compared to his, who adjudged to death
      By his head's loss, should crave (stead of one stroke)
      To die a lingering torment on the rack.
      Even such would be your life, whose guilt each hour
215   Would strike your conscious soul with terrors.
    WARD: No more, this boy's words trouble me.°
    [ALIZIA]: If none of these move, let the example
      Of that contempt is thrown on runagates,
      Even by these Turks themselves, at least move you
220   To fly this slavery.   *Enter Crosman.*

CROSMAN: Most worthy sir, now I dare call you "brother"!

[ALIZIA]: Too fair a name to cloak so great a foe.

This instant makes a trial of your virtue.

Think on Ulysses' constancy.°

225 CROSMAN: Why are you mute, sir?

WARD: I am not well.

[ALIZIA]: Alas! How can he, being so near to hell?

CROSMAN: Are you so weak to have a boy's words sway you?

[ALIZIA]: You have not mine: think 'tis heaven's hand doth stay you.

230 CROSMAN: Have you no other but my sister, sir,

To make a stale of? Did you not vow?

WARD: Whate'er, I do recant it. I am now

Myself. Her looks enchanted me.

[ALIZIA]: Against a man's own soul, no oath can tie.

235 CROSMAN: This thy disgrace revenged shall speak in blood.

Enter Voada.

VOADA: Where is my betrothed husband? All's ready.

CROSMAN: To publish infamy to thee and us!

The weathercock is turned. This boy's breath did it.

VOADA: Again turned?

240 [ALIZIA]: You cast your eyes too much upon the flame

Proves your destruction.

VOADA: Ungentle boy! Dost thou requite me thus?

How canst thou blushless view me? Have my tears

Procured me nought but scorn?

245 WARD: Forgiveness, Voada! Turn back thy comet-eyes!

Plagues, devils, poverty—may all ills fall

Man e'er was subject to, I will enjoy thee.

Force hence, I say, this boy.

[ALIZIA]: As I from hence, so thou art thrust from joy—eternal joys.

Exit Alizia.

250 CROSMAN: The Mufti's here. You know the custom, sir.

Some trivial ceremonies, they'll be soon o'er.

They once performed, you're ne'er unhappy more.

---

231 **stale**] low-class whore.

Besides, the captainship of our strong castle
Shall be my sister's portion—here's the key.
255 WARD: Do not delay them then.
CROSMAN: They are come, sir.

*Enter the Slaves, bound [including Ferdinand, Albert, and Raymond's Sons],
going to the port [escorted by guards].*

WARD: What means these slaves? Their sights like basilisks
Foretells my ruin. 'Sheart, make this way.
FERDINAND: Nay, do not shun our sight. Hear us but now,
260 We'll forgive all our wrongs, with patience row
At the unwieldy oar; we will forget
That we were sold by you, and think we set
Our bodies 'gainst your soul, the dearest purchase
Of your Redeemer, that we regained you so.
265 Leave but this path damnation guides you to.
SECOND SON: Our blood, our father's blood—all is forgiven,
The bond of all thy sins is cancelled.
Keep but thyself from this.
ALBERT: Let us redeem our country's shame by thee,
270 We willing will endure our slavery.
WARD: The words do rip my heart up—ha?
VOADA: Why stand you in this dilemma? Are you deprived
Of sense and being?
WARD: Thou tellst me true: with what brain can I think
275 Heaven would be glad of such a friend as I am?
A pirate? Murderer? Let those can hope a pardon care
To atone with heaven. I cannot; I despair.
FERDINAND: Will you yet hear me? Yet heaven hath mercy.
WARD: And hell damnation. On! Zounds, on I say!
280 The way that leads to love is no black way.

Exit Ward, Crosman, Voada, [others with a] shout.

FERDINAND: But thou wilt find it black: no hell I see's so low
Which lust and woman cannot lead us to.   *Exeunt.*

---

257 **basilisks**] legendary serpents or dragons whose glance was said to kill.

SCENE 8.

Enter Chorus.

CHORUS: Here could I wish that our period, or that our pen,
    Might speak the fictions, not the acts of men.°
    The deeds we have presented hitherto are white
    Compared unto those black ones we must write:
5   For now, no more at men, but giant-like
    The face of heaven itself he dares to strike.
    And with a blushless front he dares to do
    What we are dumb to think, much more to show.°
    Yet what may fall beyond uncertain guess
10   Your better favors bind us to express.

[A dumb show follows.]°
Enter two bearing half-moons, one with a Mahomet's head° following. After
them, the Mufti, or chief priest, two meaner priests bearing his train. The Mufti
seated, a confused noise of music, with a show. Enter two Turks, one bearing a
turban with a half-moon in it, the other a robe, a sword: a third with a globe in
one hand, an arrow in the other. Two knights follow. After them, Ward on an
ass, in his Christian habit, bare-headed. The two knights, with low reverence,
ascend, whisper the Mufti in the ear, draw their swords, and pull him off the ass.
He [is] laid on his belly, the tables (by two inferior priests) offered him, he lifts his
hand up, subscribes, is brought to his seat by the Mufti, who puts on his turban
and robe, girds his sword, then swears him on the Mahomet's head,° ungirts his
sword, offers him a cup of wine by the hands of a Christian. He spurns at him
and throws away the cup, is mounted on the ass, who is richly clad, and with a
shout, they exit.

---

1 **period**] time spent on stage; appointed end or goal.

7 **front**] face.

9 **Yet what may . . . bind us to express**] For your sake, what can only be guessed at, we must represent to you, the audience.

s.d. half-moons] the crescent moon, symbol of Turkish power and of Islam in general.

s.d. tables] a book for writing in; here, the book in which the convert officially enters his name.

subscribes] signifies his submission and allegiance by signing his name in the official book.

s.d. girds] fastens by means of a belt.

s.d. swears him on the Mahomet's head] swears allegiance to the pagan idol, Mahomet.

s.d. ungirts] unfastens and removes.

s.d. by the hands of a Christian] presumably one of the Christian captives in Tunis.

CHORUS: The accursed priests of Mahomet being set,
      Two knights present the wretch, who finds no let
      To his perdition: to whom nor shame, nor fear,
      Give any curb. Dismounted from that steed
15   Did best befit the rider: they then read
      The laws of their damned Prophet. He subscribes,
      Enrolls his name into their pagan tribes.°
      Now wears the habit of a free-born Turk,
      His sword excepted, which lest they should work
20   Just villainy to their seducers, is denied
      Unto all runagates, unless employed
      In wars 'gainst Christians.° Last, oh be he last,
      Forswears his name! With what, we blush to tell,
      But 'tis no wonder, black's the way to hell;
25   Who though he seems yet happy, his success
      Shows he exchanged with it, and wretchedness.
      Give patience to our scene, which hereto tends
      To show the world black deeds will have black ends.   *Exit Chorus.*

SCENE 9.
AT DANSIKER'S LODGINGS IN TUNIS.

Enter Dansiker, Sares, three Sailors.

DANSIKER: Ward turned Turk? It is not possible.
SARES: I saw him Turk to the circumcision.°
      Marry, therein I heard he played the Jew with 'em,
      Made 'em come to the cutting of an ape's tail.°
5 DANSIKER: I see the hand of heaven prevented mine.
      Death was too fair a guerdon for him. But to the present,

---

18 **the habit of a free-born Turk**] the turban and long robe traditionally worn by citizens of the Otto-man empire.
23 **Forswears his name**] Then, as today, converts to Islam customarily took a new, Arabic name at the time of their conversion.
25 **happy**] fortunate.
25 **his success**] what happens to him later.
26 **he exchanged with it, and wretchedness**] he exchanged his Christian name for a new Muslim one, and in doing so gave away true happiness and received wretchedness in return.
6 **guerdon**] reward.

Deserving sir. I now am to conjure you,
By all the offices of friendship past,
By what my future love and means may stead you,
10   To vow performance of one small request.
SARES: Whate'er it be, I'll be as just to you
As heaven to truth: by all that Ward denied,
I vow me yours.
DANSIKER: I accept your faith. Know then that I am bound
15   Unto a desperate attempt. How it may succeed,
Heaven and Fate only know. The circumstance
I do enjoin you further not to inquire.
What on your trust's imposed is the redeeming
Those two betrayed young men whom Ward did sell,
20   When to his barbarous cruelty they opposed,
And lost themselves and state. Their ransom's here. *Gives him a paper.*
As you prove just, from all mishaps rest clear.
SARES: And if I fail to accomplish your desires,
All my sins haunt me when my breath expires.
25 DANSIKER: I am most confident. Best sir, adieu.
If Dansiker do live, he lives to you.

Exit Sares. Enter Lieutenant.

Hast laid the train to my directions?
LIEUTENANT: It is done to the undoing of 'em all.
Time calls aboard which spends not half an hour
30   Before our train do take. It rests to be determined
What ships we fire, which bear along with us.
DANSIKER: Danville's makes with us; all the rest give fire to.
Sares' ship except. To him we are engaged;
Nor will we prove ungrateful. Are all things ready?
35 LIEUTENANT: To your own wishes.

---

7 conjure you] call upon you (in the name of something sacred); implore you.
27 train] "A line of gunpowder or other combustible substance laid so as to convey fire to a mine or charge for the purpose of exploding it" (*O.E.D.*).
29–30 Time calls aboard . . . our train do take] It is time to get on board our ship because less than a half hour remains before the fire we have started will catch and spread.
32 makes with us] leaves the harbor with us.

DANSIKER: Aboard then instantly. Tunis farewell!
    Dansiker bids all pirates now adieu.
    He'll show you what you might do, were you true!   *Exeunt.*

SCENE 10.
AT THE HOUSE OF BENWASH THE JEW.

Enter Agar above in the window.

AGAR: How dull a pace keeps time to lover's eyes,
    And yet to me how swift the night's black horse
    Makes way to raise the morn, whose least of light
    Takes all my hopes from me and damps me quite.   *Clock strikes.*
5   Eleven and yet not come! He was not capable
    Of my quaint stratagem, or being possessed
    Of what he wanted, gold, contemns my love.
    It is no other, Agar—he loathes thee.
    Man's curse is things forbid still to pursue;
10   What's freely offered not to hold worth their view.   *Enter Gallop.*
    Ha? Unless my credulous ears deceive me,
    I hear one make towards my window.

GALLOP: The coast is clear! Bawd night, I do salute thee! Thou that dost
    wink at all faults, that hug'st so many sins in thy black bosom, the
15   sun grows pale to view them. To thee, damnation's nurse, I make my
    prayer, conjure thee by all my lustful embraces thou hast been witness
    to, by all the cuckolds thou hast made twixt morn and twilight, to add
    one to the number. But one, thou black-eyed negro! Never did woman
    make such shift to dub her husband, though many thou dost
20   know have made most bare ones. O let this instrument that hath so
    many freed from the hell of usurers and from the jaws of their fear
    (bandogs!), hath paid so many's debts, relieve my wants. I'll never

---

4 **damps me quite**] extinguishes my fire; thoroughly discourages me.
19 **make such shift**] go to such lengths.
19 **dub**] cuckold.
20 **have made most bare ones**] have made their husbands poor, or perhaps have caused them to lose
their hair from venereal disease.
22 **bandogs**] dogs who are tied up on account of their ferocity.

blame thee, Fortune, henceforth if I lack. Put thyself but this once
on my back. No false light in the window, no bawdy landmark, no
25   handkerchief to waft me. I'll venture it. Agar, my lovely Agar!

AGAR: It's he who in this dead of night calls on my name.

GALLOP: Thy friend, thy understanding friend, with the ladder of ropes!
Here, make them sure above. Leave me to the lower parts.

AGAR: I hope you mean no wrong, sir, to me.

30   GALLOP: I'll do thee as much right as can be done to one of thy sex. Hast
made it fast?

AGAR: You may adventure, sir.

GALLOP: He that will not adventure for such a piece of flesh were worthy
to feed upon dumplings all days on's life. Nay, I will venture, thou
35   warden of the horned livery, omnipotent Vulcan.
Now set my shafts but right,   *He goes up the rope [ladder].*
I'll make one freeman more ere it be light.

Enter two Sailors.

FIRST SAILOR: There's no remedy: that which makes waiting-women
punks, and captains panders, that causeth decayed gentlemen
40   become solicitors, and bankrupt citizens sergeants, that makes us
thieves—necessity, that which hath no law on's side.

SECOND SAILOR: We shall have as little conscience anon in robbery.

FIRST SAILOR: Aye, should we rob hospitals, our betters have made that
a monopoly, but to steal from a rich Jew—it is no more sin then to
45   unload a weary ass.

SECOND SAILOR: By hook or crook, you will have it.

---

25 **waft**] beckon or signal.

34 **dumplings**] a doughy pudding, thought to be a sexual fortifier and fecundator.

34 **all days on's life**] all of his life.

35 **Vulcan**] classical god of fire and the forge; here, patron deity of cuckolds (since Mars slept with Vulcan's wife, Venus).

36 **set my shafts**] guide my shaft (with a glance at "shaft" as penis).

37 **freeman**] slang for married woman's lover.

39 **punks**] prostitutes.

39 **panders**] pimps.

39 **decayed**] reduced in wealth and prosperity.

40 **sergeants**] petty officers whose duty was to enforce legal judgments, make arrests, etc.

41 **on's**] on its.

42 **anon**] shortly.

FIRST SAILOR: We were bred in a country that had the charity to whip begging out of us when we were young, and for starving, manhood denies it. You know what must necessarily follow.

50 SECOND SAILOR: Nay, make your conclusion.

FIRST SAILOR: Press her in a dumb show!° Hereabouts should be the house, great windows and a little wicket, nobleman-like. What's here? A ladder of ropes! S'foot, we are prevented. St. Nicholas' clerks are stepped up before us.

55 SECOND SAILOR: Were they ten justices' clerks we would share with 'em.

FIRST SAILOR: Their masters would prevent us for that, yet since our case is desperate, we will put in with 'em.

[They climb up the rope ladder.]

SECOND SAILOR: Softly, for waking the maids.

FIRST SAILOR: S'hart, thou art the son of a Lapland-witch sure. This is
60 the maid's chamber. One of them is in a dream: she fetcheth her wind short, I am sure.

SECOND SAILOR: How long thou art poking at it! What is't, man?

FIRST SAILOR: Some light commodity or other.

SECOND SAILOR: A woman's lower part—it is altogether in fashion for
65 them to be light about the bum indeed.

FIRST SAILOR: I have the male part to't, the doublet. Your women will have it ever in request to have the man's part uppermost.°

SECOND SAILOR: *[holding up Gallop's trousers]* S'hart, a French slop! These are none of the Jew's trouses, and they should be no gallant's—for
70 he hath money in his purse.

[Discovers a purse full of money in Gallop's clothing.]

---

52 wicket] gate.

53 prevented] preceded, beaten to it.

53 St. Nicholas' clerks] thieves (St. Nicholas was their patron saint).

59 Lapland-witch] Lapland was thought to be inhabited by witches and magicians. Perhaps when he sees his accomplice fly nimbly up the rope-ladder, the Sailor refers to the witches' supposed ability to fly through the air.

60 fetcheth her wind short] breathes rapidly.

63 light commodity] meaning cheap trade goods (slang for whore) and referring here to Agar.

68 slop] wide, baggy trousers worn by sailors.

69 trouses] trousers.

FIRST SAILOR: Aye, marry sir, this fellow had good ware about him.
　　Indeed, upon my life we are little better than bawds get money by
　　others' venery. This Jew is a—

Enter Rabshake.

RABSHAKE: Fire, fire, fire!
75　SECOND SAILOR: Water, water, water!

Exit two Sailors.

RABSHAKE: Fire, fire, fire! The slaves lie on straw beds, and yet this cry will
　　take no hold on 'em. Fire, fire, fire!

[Enter Gallop and Agar above.]

GALLOP: Flames and brimstone, I am in hell! Zounds, my breeches! The
　　ladder! This Jew hath found us out and fired the house.
80　AGAR: Dear sir, contain yourself!
GALLOP: A plague on venery, a hot end comes on't still! Is the window
　　high enough that I may break my neck, die any death rather than be
　　roasted?
AGAR: Here's a vault leads to the common shower. It being low water, the
85　　sheets shall let you down to your escape.
GALLOP: Those sheets have brought me low enough already.

Shout from within: Fire, fire, fire!

GALLOP: Flames stop thy throat!
AGAR: Dear sir, adventure it and save your life.
90　GALLOP: Were it to hell, I must.
　　A plague on whores, I say, whose vast desires
　　Begins in watery tears and end in fires.　　　　　　*Exeunt.*

71　**good ware**] valuable merchandise; also refers to Gallop's sexual parts.
73　**venery**] sexual activity, lust.
84　**vault**] a privy; an underground, vaulted chamber through which a drain flows.
84　**shower**] sewer.

SCENE 11.
THE STREET IN FRONT OF BENWASH'S HOUSE.

Enter Rabshake at one door and Benwash at another.

RABSHAKE: Fire, fire!
BENWASH: An ocean overwhelm thee! Where is the fire, slave?
RABSHAKE: At the Jew's house! Benwash his house—your house, sir!

Exit Rabshake.

BENWASH: My bags, my obligations, my wife! Agar, I say! I shall run mad!
5   I will scale the windows, burn for company! My money and myself
will go together! What's here? A ladder of ropes! Gallop's breeches!
Burn on, burn on! Singe all the world! Consume it with thy flames,
thou best of elements! Burn on, I say!

Enter Ward, [Voada, Francisco, Alizia disguised,] Sailors.

WARD: As you are men, on this side heap to save our goods.
10 BENWASH: As you are ministers of Lucifer, let it burn on. It's mine own
house: come but on my ground, I'll have my action for't.
WARD: He is distracted. Help, as you are men!
BENWASH: Dogs, villains, thieves! Down with him that lays a hand to't! Be
just, you powers of heaven, and throw thy wildfire down upon the
15   heads of these adulterers. Room, room, room! I have it, I have it!
Room, room, room!
WARD: The Jew is mad indeed. His loss distracts him.

[Enter Rabshake.]

Speak, gentle friend—doth the fire slack?
RABSHAKE: The house is saved, but all the ships in the harbor
20   Unquenchable do burn.
WARD: The ships in the harbor!

---

5 **for company**] for company's sake.
9 **heap**] throw (dirt? water?) on top. .

RABSHAKE: [*To Ward*] Yours only excepted.

[ALIZIA]: My thoughts now have their ends.

VOADA: [*To Alizia*] Do not thou grieve, boy. Know I love thee.

25   Thy maintenance shall express it. I have friends

And jewels left for thee. [*To Ward*] But I hate thee more

Than all thy wealth made me love thee before.   *Exit.*

WARD: False woman, thou shall not shake me off thus!

Were all the impudence of thy whole sex—

30   All their blushless impieties—conjoined in thee,

I'll move thy flinty heart to sense and shame.

I will, thou sorceress. Now I do see too late

There is a hand o'errules our will and fate.   *Exit.*

FRANCISCO: This shows the greatest plague heaven keeps in store

35   Falls when a man is linked unto a whore.   *Exeunt.*

SCENE 12.
THE HOUSE OF BENWASH THE JEW.

Enter Benwash, Rabshake, Agar.

BENWASH: [*holding up Gallop's trousers*] I have it, I have it—here, here! Nay come on, you have come off, I am sure. Here's evidence looks pale to think but on't. You do not know the tenant to this cottage? He was an upright dealer; he paid me to a hair. [*To Rabshake*] Come forward

5   and be hanged! I shall advance you in a rope's name. You have made no cuckold of me—I made myself one, pandered my own horns. Now sirrah, you that go to't by art, put your cases one in the neck of another—your *rem in re*. What think you of this case?

RABSHAKE: I think the serpent crept into a narrow hole and left his case

10   behind him.

---

2 **come off**] been removed; achieved orgasm.

4 **to a hair**] exactly and fully; with a pun on "heir."

7 **by art**] professionally, with great skill.

7 **put your cases one in the neck of another**] a sexual innuendo (perhaps Benwash places Gallop's trousers over Rabshake's head?).

7 **your cases**] legal cases; articles of clothing.

8 **rem in re**] see long note referring to 6.378ff.

9 **his case**] skin.

BENWASH: Then I am a cornuto!

RABSHAKE: This makes the naked truth appear so.

BENWASH: The best is, the crest is mine own. I paid well for't.

AGAR: Dear husband, pardon me. I will confess.

15 BENWASH: What wilt thou confess? That thou hast made a mere ass of me,
    to pay thy journeyman wages beforehand?

RABSHAKE: It should seem he labored hard to earn it. He could keep no
    clothes about him.

BENWASH: This slave doth not think I'll cut his throat for this. You have
20   watched nearly, sirrah, you have!

RABSHAKE: Unless I should have been their bawd, I could watch no nearer.
    Methinks she hath done you a great pleasure, rid you of your disease,
    jealousy. Now you need fear no more: you are in possession on't; your
    doubts are at an end.

25 BENWASH: Good, very good, my doubts are at end. But I shall hang you
    in suspense for this. You manticora that plump upon raw flesh! Here,
    set your hand to this letter, that I may draw your captain on again
    upon the breach. I'll blow you up else. Why move you not?
    I am sure you laid your hand to the business when time was.

30 AGAR: Pardon me, sir. I know my life is forfeit
    To your just anger. Nor will I be the means
    To shed more blood. Mine shall suffice alone,
    Since only one is wronged, punish but one.

BENWASH: She loves him still, as I am a cuckold!
35   He has outgone me, do you hear? Subscribe!
    Move me no further.

AGAR: The worst can be but death—I will not.

BENWASH: I tell thee, I'll forgive thee. Give my revenge
    Scope but at him, thou art free.

40 AGAR: Swear it by Abraham's dust, the ashes of our forefathers.

---

13 **crest**] heraldic device (on a helmet); pair of horns.

16 **pay thy journeyman wages beforehand**] pay your lover in advance for cuckolding me.

20 **nearly**] carefully.

26 **manticora**] a monster having a human head with horns, the body of a beast, and the tail of a
dragon or serpent.

26 **plump**] feed excessively.

28 **upon the breach**] into the gap in defenses (a military phrase), but alluding to Gallop's "breeches" as
well as his penetration of Agar's vaginal "breach."

RABSHAKE: Dust and ashes—it's but a frail oath.

BENWASH: By that, and all that ties a virtuous mind,
　　　I vow and swear by written writ.

RABSHAKE: You'll swear as much to forgive me, I hope, too, sir.

45 BENWASH: Why, thou shalt be the messenger, nay, the actor
　　　In my just vengeance.

RABSHAKE: The hangman, you mean, sir. I am expert at it.   *Exeunt.*

SCENE 13.
TUNIS.

Enter Ward and Francisco.

WARD: Francisco. What news, man?

FRANCISCO: The worst your ears can hear. Our ships—

WARD: They are untouched: of all they are only safe.

FRANCISCO: You dazzle your own eyes. That villain Dansiker

5　　　Hath grappled them and fled.

WARD: Whirlwinds pursue him! Heaven, seas, earth—all at once
　　　Join to his confusion! Now I do see too late
　　　There is a hand o'errules our will and fate.

Enter Voada and Alizia.

VOADA: I shall then take your promise. Your brother being

10　　　Redeemed, this night I shall enjoy thee.°

ALIZIA: This diamond binds me to't—by this I swear.

VOADA: 'Tis thine. I will bestow it on thee. To tie thy faith
　　　Thou hast his ransom.

ALIZIA: 'Tis here.

15 VOADA: About it then.   *Exit Alizia.*
　　　Now fortune equal prove. I am happy:
　　　Yet her lust redeems my love.

WARD: Yet see, midst all my miseries I have a friend,
　　　My constant, loyal Voada. Could what we enjoy

20   Make a man happy, I am not miserable.

   Thou com'st to comfort me—I know thou dost.

 VOADA: This fellow raves sure. Do you know to whom you speak?

 WARD: Put not a further trial on me, thou best of women:

   Know, if this arm were barred all other means,

25   From hearts of Christians it should dig thee food.

 VOADA: We know you are a bloody murderer and are repaid

   By our just Prophet that hates false runagates.

 WARD: How couldst thou malice man so much, heaven,

   As to create a woman?

30   Thou hast forgot me sure! O look on him

   That hath denied his faith, sold all his hopes

   To purchase thee his bride.

 VOADA: To match with beggary! Know I contemn thee

   As a most abject slave, and hate thee more

35   Than all thy wealth could make me love before.   *Exit.*

 FRANCISCO: What mean you, sir? Could you expect a good,

   A happiness, from hell? She is a whore.

 WARD: Thou liest: this arm shall make it good.

   My soul for her I lost, and now my blood.   *Enter Rabshake.*

40 FRANCISCO: Your passion doth transport you. Here comes her pander,

   One that knows all her secrets. Examine him.

   If she stand clear, let my life answer it.

 WARD: I'll put you to the test.

 RABSHAKE: I have had a hot night of this—nothing but fire in my mouth

45   two hours together! Marry, the old Jew my master, I hear, hath

   stumbled on a cooler. I thought this captain would be coming so long

   on upon the breach he would break his neck at the last. This venery is

   a tempting dish: some ne'er lin licking at it till they burn their lips.

   Well, I must go comfort up old Benwash: he's heavy upon his

50   wife's lightness.

 WARD: You, Jew—a word with you!

 RABSHAKE: You, Turk, I have nothing to say to you. Ha, ha, ha! Poor

   fellow, how he looks since Mahomet had the handling of him! He

---

33 **contemn**] scorn.

46 **cooler**] a cooler of male sexual heat.

48 **lin**] cease.

hath had a sore night at "Who's that knocks at the backdoor?" Cry
55   you mercy, I thought you were an Italian captain.°

WARD: Zounds, leave your circumlocutions. I'll send your head to your
    heels else.

FRANCISCO: You parcel bawd, all usher! Answer directly who 'tis bears
    away the prize in your mistress's race, or I'll spoil your footing, cut you
60   off by the hams.

RABSHAKE: Alas, sir!

WARD: Speak—who are her suitors?

RABSHAKE: Voada's suitors? Oh sir, a barber, sir.

FRANCISCO: I'll make you have need of a surgeon ere I have done with you.
65   How do you know he is a barber?

RABSHAKE: He smells strong of rosewater, and he hath never money in his
    purse but on Saturday nights.

WARD: What other suitor, slave?

RABSHAKE: Another sweet youth, too. I take it a comfit-maker, and it
70   seems hath rotten teeth, for he dares not come in sight so long as
    the barber's in the way.

FRANCISCO: This dog deludes us. I'll tear thy throat out, villain, unless
    thou instantly name him she loves.

RABSHAKE: Her page, sir, the little Christian the good-faced captain gave
75   her, Fidelio.

WARD: My slave, the French shipboy?

FRANCISCO: I saw him leave her now. How dost thou know she loves him?

RABSHAKE: She makes him sing bawdy songs to her, looks fortunes in his
    fist and babies in his eyes, makes dialogues betwixt him, her little dog,
80   and herself, lies upon her back, puts his hand in her hand, and wrings
    it till the tears come again.

WARD: Insatiate monster! Could her swollen blood reach such a height?
    None but my page must suit her!

FRANCISCO: Contain yourself awhile. This slave can speak one of her
85   dialogues.

RABSHAKE: It is my practice, sir. You shall stand for the lady, you for her
    dog, and I the page. You and that dog looking one upon another, the
    page presents himself.

---

58 **parcel bawd**] part pimp.

58 **usher**] a male attendant on a lady, especially one who has charge of a door and admits people; thus,
a procurer or pimp.

FRANCISCO: Good.

90 RABSHAKE: The best is behind, sir. *Runs away.*

FRANCISCO: Jew, slave, dog!

WARD: The horned Devil follow him! A skipper's boy?
    The shame of woman! Rather than be baffled thus
    I will betray this town, blow up the castle.

95   Francisco, do but second me.

FRANCISCO: First repossess yourself of your stronghold.
    I fear some treachery: the governor
    With all the janissaries of the town°
    I met in their way thither.

100 WARD: Blast them, ye powers, first. The governor
    Make towards the castle? I am betrayed! Away,
    I see that heaven forgets not, though I delay.   *[Enter janissaries.]*
    Thrust out by janissaries?

JANISSARY: Pack hence, false runagate! Slave, beggar!

[Ward runs and hides by throwing himself on the ground.]
[Exit Francisco, pursued by janissaries.]

105 WARD: Disgracious vassals! What mountain covers me?
    Wink, wink, thou day-star! Hide my guilty shame!
    Make me as if I ne'er had been, whose name
    Succeeding times will curse. Should I confess my sin,
    There's not an ear that can with pity hear
110   A man so wicked miserable. Should I bear up,
    Outlook my crimes, I want means to support me.
    To die I dare not: the jaws of hell do yawn
    To swallow me. Live, I cannot: famine threats,
    And that the worst of poverty—contempt and scorn.
115   Never on man Fate cast so black a frown.
    Up I am denied to fly, unpitied down.
    Rest, restless soul, on this accursed soil
    And teach the world into how sad a toil

---

92 **skipper**] sailor.
105 **Disgracious**] discourteous.
111 **Outlook**] overlook, look beyond.
118 **toil**] net, trap.

Ambition and swift riot run when mean content
120   Sits low, yet happy; and when their day is spent
All that they get is labor and unrest,
A hateful grave, and worst, a troubled breast.

Enter Francisco.

FRANCISCO: Where shall I find this most unfortunate wretch?
There is a part in him called man, which we should pity
125   Howe'er his merit stands. Nor will I leave him,
Though he hath left himself. See where he lies,
Best suiting with his fortunes. Could we our fate foreknow,
Men were as gods, nor need we have lain so low.
How fare you, brother? Why with so sad an eye
130   Do you behold me, that in your miseries
Bear equal part?
WARD: Can there remain a soul that will vouchsafe
Compassion on me? Thou dost but flatter,
Or hast forgot. I have lost all, and poverty,
135   When no ill else will do't, makes all friends fly.
FRANCISCO: Were you entitled to no other guilt,
How willing for you should my blood be spilt!
Here sir, accept this poor relief.
Bootless, alas! Distress recounts those errors
140   To think what might have been cures, not the terrors,
Of present suffering.
WARD: True, true, Francisco, could I redeem the time,
The world should speak my penitence.
Could I call back but one seven years,
145   Though all my life were servile after,
Were my soul but free
From innocent blood and fearful blasphemy,
On the condition I might live an age
Tortured upon a wheel. I tell thee, friend,
150   Were I this city's viceroy, I would give
My crown, despoil myself of all, only to live
One month with that content this soul did know
When a poor fisherman possessed it.

FRANCISCO: You are too low dejected.
155   Men that with sufferance their wrongs do bear
        Are held but weak, and states, more oft for fear
        Than love unto the right, redress men's ills
        Who stoutly down his enemies. Malice kills,
        Who basely wounds himself.
160 WARD: No less than truth. I have been too low indeed.
        Each one the yielding grass doth dare to tread
        That flies resisting thorns. False Voada,   [*He rises.*]
        Thy lamb is turned a lion. I feel revenge
        Give a new life to me. I'll only stay
165   Till I have spoke thy brother. I think he'll blush
        To hear thy shame, tell thee thou hast not played
        A woman's part with me. Suppose the worse—
        That he turn villain, too. He had better curse
        His grandsire's ashes. If once more I fall in,
170   I'll be unparalleled at least for sin.

                [Enter Alizia disguised as Fidelio.]

FRANCISCO: Stay! See the strumpet's love, Fidelio.
ALIZIA: Captain, you are the man I seek. I have a suit to you.
WARD: Concerning Voada, is't not?
ALIZIA: Concerning her that hates you for my sake,
175   Neglects your merit. This night gives full revenge
        To all her injuries.
WARD: Repeat that happy word again, I am wholly thine.
ALIZIA: Know her vassaliate lust hath long pursued
        And with such violence attempted me,
180   That with my oaths tonight to sate her heat
        I hardly have delayed her.
WARD: What's this to my revenge?
ALIZIA: It follows: give me but way
        Through your castle. There's a Hollander

---

165 **thy brother**] Voada's brother, Crosman.
175–76 **gives full revenge to all her injuries**] offers an opportunity for you to avenge yourself completely on Voada.
178 **vassaliate**] subjugating.

185   This evening makes from hence
     That gives them passage. I have tied him to't.
     WARD: Thou art forever free—the hour name.
     ALIZIA: I'll speak your worth yet, in spite of fame.
     About three, watch the word "Fidelio."
190 WARD: Avoid suspicion and till then be gone.
     ALIZIA: Nay then, my joys do flow.   *Exit.*
     FRANCISCO: Whither tends this? What passage? Come you for him?
     WARD: To heaven. I once more must exact
     Thy trust and diligence.
195 FRANCISCO: Speak it.
     WARD: Make instantly to Voada; tell her
     This night a skipper doth attend to steal aboard
     Her love Fidelio. Give her the hour and place;
     Wish her to pistol him.
200 FRANCISCO: Wouldst have her kill her love, too?
     WARD: Aye, and run mad for't. Meanwhile I'll walk the streets. I shall meet
     some will know me, to whom I will relate my wrongs. Wilt do't
     Francisco?
     FRANCISCO: My soul to gage.
205 WARD: This comfort then (in spite of hell) I'll have:
     Ward went not unrevenged unto his grave.   *Exeunt.*

SCENE 14.
MARSEILLES.

Enter Chorus

CHORUS: How black a path unbounded riot treads,
     Your gentler eyes have viewed. Our scene now leads
     To give him rest, that from his ills had learnt
     To know his misery, and at least had earned
5   This lesson from the extremes that others passed:
     No course that violent is, secure can last.
     This clew doth wind him back, and Dansiker

---

186 **that gives them passage**] this must refer to Alizia's fiancé, Raymond, and the other slaves.
200 **have her kill her love**] have Voada kill Alizia/Fidelio.
1 **riot**] unrestrained sin, loose living.

(The wealth of Tunis) now is become their fear,
Strives to redeem his infamy and with success
10 Makes through their bowels to his happiness.
No sooner he arrives in France but his sad ears
(Instead of welcomes) entertain new fears.
The agèd oak that Atlas-like sustained
The weight of France, that with his blood regained
15 Her wasted body (like the pelican),
By one that from his life took breath is slain.
This fatal blow astonisheth the hopes
Of Dansiker and his, to make return
Impossible.° Those fires yet fresh do burn
20 Would threaten them with utmost tortures here.
To make abode they find themselves beset
With many they by their spoil made foes; yet
Twixt two extremes they chose the better part:
Take land and to the governor present
25 Themselves and fortunes, show their act, intent
And penitence, their promised pardon. What befell
This show presents, which words deny to tell.

Enter governor [of Provence] in state, takes his seat. Dansiker and his followers
with ropes about their necks, their weapons with the points towards them, deliver
their petition. The governor reads and salutes them, [and they] put up their
swords. Suddenly rush in diverse, like merchants with followers, [who] seem to
threaten the governor, who defends Dansiker, labors betwixt them. [The
merchants] seem pacified, and Dansiker swears by his sword, [then] offer[s] to go
out to meet his wife and child. They [are] persuaded, [and] he delivers them to the
governor's trust. All exit.

CHORUS: 'Twixt hope and dread, as suited former merit,
The governor receives them, gives new spirit
30 Unto their drooping hopes, when (with the name
Of Dansiker's arrival) swift-winged Fame

---

18 **Danisker and his**] Danisker, his family, and followers.
here] in France.
s.d.   the governor] this is the French governor of Provence in the provincial capital, Marseilles, and
not the governor of Tunis who appears elsewhere in the play.
s.d.   diverse, like] various people, dressed like.

Brings in the oppressed merchants whose spoil
Had fed his hungry sword and with their toil
Made rich his rapines. These crave law, his life.
35   The opposing governor almost ends the strife
With his own blood; informs them the king's death
Stood only bar to his safety, that his breath
Would recompense all former injuries.
To approve it, gives them notice of the prize
40   Brought from Tunis, and more to assuage their ire,
Dansiker dares what act they can desire
Man to accomplish to redeem his peace
And their great losses. All their furies cease,
And with one voice demand Benwash the Jew
45   As his just ransom. They need no more renew
This their request: by oath themselves they tie
To bring him prisoner, or in the action die.
No motives from his wife or child dissuade
This his resolve. Suppose he now hath made
50   His back-return and in some apt disguise
Attends success unto his enterprise.
His end and strange prevention briefly show
Designs are men's; their sway the gods do owe.   *Exeunt.*

SCENE 15.
A DARK PASSAGEWAY INSIDE THE CASTLE OF TUNIS.°

Enter [Raymond (the younger)].

[RAYMOND]:   This is the place. A cold blood thwarts my heart.
My fleeting soul in her disturbed passion
Proclaims some ill near. Let me suppose the worst—
Alizia's dead. False tongue, how durst thou name

---

37 **stood only bar**] was the only obstacle.
37 **his safety . . . his breath**] Dansiker's . . . the governor's.
39 **approve**] prove.
46 **themselves**] Dansiker and his followers.
51 **attends success unto his enterprise**] waits for a chance to carry out his plan successfully.
53 **Designs are men's; their sway the gods do owe**] man proposes; the gods dispose.
1 **thwarts**] passes across.

5   So great a mischief? Alas, this bracelet speaks it.
This which I tied unto her ivory wrist,
The witness of those vows confirmed us one.
The news of my captivity took all her hopes
And life away, and dying she bequeathed

10   This loyal gift again, with my sad ransom.
'Tmay be this youth may be Alizia,
Herself a prisoner. Yet she's too virtuous
To outlive her honor and her chastity,
Which her captivity must needs endanger.   *Enter Ward and Voada.*

15   I hear his footsteps.

VOADA: We are not far off from the place. Softly, softly!
The night is dark and friendly to mine ends.

[RAYMOND]: Fidelio, Fidelio!

VOADA: 'Tis he would rob me of Fidelio!

20 [RAYMOND]: Fidelio, I say! Young Raymond here!

[Voada shoots Raymond.]

[RAYMOND]: So—I am slain.

VOADA: Thus dost thou bear Fidelio back again.

WARD: Ha, ha, ha.

[RAYMOND]: Oh false, false Alizia—thy watchwords as thyself,

25   Deceiving! Didst think my slavery
Was not an ill sufficient, but my blood
Must pay thy falsehood tribute? Or couldst not wish
So great a plague to me, that I should hear
Thou wert turned prostitute? Ungentle, cruel woman!

30 WARD: 'Tis not the boy, sure: his voice, his passion
Speaks him another.   *[Enter Alizia.]*
More projects yet—I hear some foot stir.

ALIZIA: How fearful is the night! Heaven's angry sure,
And having drawn the day up, chid her thus

35   For giving light to men's impieties.
'Tis much about the hour of my appoint.
What sad groan wounds my ears? Fidelio!
Raymond, friend Fidelio!

---

11 'Tmay] It may.
32 projects] plots.

[RAYMOND]: Or rather Infidelio! Whate'er thou art,
40   Thou needst not doubt thy task. Thou hast made me sure,
           Or if thou doubt'st it, here discharge one bullet more.
ALIZIA: 'Tis not his voice. Thou liest, false thoughts.
         Raymond, Fidelio!
[RAYMOND]: My name is Raymond, that Fidelio unjustly murdered.
45 ALIZIA: No marvel though thou thund'rest heaven
           And darts thy flashes down! Oh! Why is not
           This world a universal fire? What one good
           Keeps back thy flames?
[RAYMOND]: Oh speak! What art thou? Whose sad speech
50   Makes death stay yet to hear thee?
ALIZIA: My friend, my Raymond, by my means murdered!
         I have lived too long, too long.
[RAYMOND]: Oh speak! What art thou whose sad accents force
           Pale death to stay and hear thee?
55 ALIZIA: Alas, I am nothing, nothing.
[RAYMOND]: As thou hast hope in heaven, tell me thy name!
ALIZIA: I will. My name's Alizia, thy constant loyal, loyal friend, that in
         her passage unto thee will not be long.   [*Stabs herself.*]
[RAYMOND]: O save thy life!
60 ALIZIA: Wish me not so much ill. I love thee better.
           Miracle of thy sex, O let me embrace thee yet!
[RAYMOND]: Here, here! Fly hence, vain breath.
ALIZIA: No other good is known to me but death.

                    [They die together.]

WARD: Francisco, thou'rt a villain! Forgiveness, Voada!
65   The words of these two innocents with purple eyes
       Dart terror through me. Fidelio turned a woman!

           [Shouts from] within: Follow, follow, follow!

VOADA: I will rather give an ear to the black shrieks
        Of mandrakes! Thou knewst I loved him,

---

65 **purple**] blood-stained.
68–69 **shrieks of mandrakes**] The mandrake is a plant with a root resembling the human form. According to folk belief, it emits a deadly shriek when uprooted.

70   And that hath forced his wound, at sight whereof
      Methinks reflecting heaven should spread itself
      In a deep crimson veil, blush to have created
      A wretch so monstrous. But my revenge sleeps. Know, boy,
      I will repay thy death. [*To Ward*] Slave, I will famish thee,
75   And when thy fainting eyelids 'gin to crack,
      My satisfied lust, by him most hates thee,
      Shall be thy object.
WARD: You wrong me to suppose I should be guilty
      Of such an impious deed.
80 VOADA: Doth not thy bloodstained poniard speak it,
      With which thy accursed arm did force his breast?
      His too, too gentle breast!
WARD: Thyself be witness.   [*Offers her his dagger.*]
VOADA: That I am revenged on thee! *[Voada] stabs at him [with the dagger].*
                                      Ward beats it back and wounds her.
85   Murder, murder! The slave will murder me!
WARD: What mean you, wife?

                    Enter watch.

VOADA: As you are men, make rescue of me!
WARD: I am betrayed, outgone by a she-devil.
VOADA: He hath not only slain his innocent page,
90   But thus assailed my life. Lay hands on him,
      Dear countrymen! Revenge my wrongs, my blood,
      On this false runagate! I faint, I faint.
      Convey me to a chirurgeon! Make him safe!   *Exit Voada.*
FIRST OFFICER: In the governor's name, I do command you give your
95   weapons up.
WARD: S'heart, gentlemen, you know Francisco killed him. I'll make it good.
SECOND OFFICER: We have nothing to charge you with about your page.
      It is the wounding of your wife with an unlawful weapon.
FIRST OFFICER: You have most unmanly thrust in a woman.
100 WARD: Honest friends, Turks, and officers—if ever I laid hands on her,
      may I never see light more.

---

88 **outgone**] outwitted, defeated.
93 **chirurgeon**] surgeon.
99 **thrust in**] stabbed.

FIRST OFFICER: We'll take a reasonable order for that. You never laid
            hands on her! Out, impudence! Away to the dungeon with him.
WARD: 'Sheart, carry me to the governor that I may have justice first.
105 SECOND OFFICER: The fellow raves. He thinks men in office have nothing
            to do but to give him justice. You must be punished and then talk of
            justice when you have cause.
FIRST OFFICER: Away with him! He shall know what 'tis to marry into a
            great tribe, an honorable tribe. You use a great woman as if she were
110   your wife! Y'are a base fellow indeed. You, a courtier?
WARD: Nay, then I see my end draws. I shall rave,
            Run mad. Have you e'er a Bedlam, that I may not famish
            But show tricks to get meat with, or rail against the state?
            And when I have eased my gall a month or two,
115   Come out again? Zounds, let me beat hemp,
            Do anything, rather than famish! That death
            She hath vowed me, and I'll prevent it: allow me
            But every week a Christian. I am content
            To feed upon raw flesh. If't be but once a month
120   A Briton, I'll be content with him.
SECOND OFFICER: Nay, then you are mad indeed! Away with him.
WARD: As you are true Turks, I will put you in sureties. I know the Devil
            will provide me bail, rather then lose my employment. As you are
            pitiful Turks!
125 FIRST OFFICER: Nay, then we shall be troubled with you.
WARD: Plagues, pestilences, all fall upon my head.
            Rather than by a whore be famishèd.
            I do conjure you!   *Exeunt.*

SCENE 16.
AT THE HOUSE OF BENWASH THE JEW.

Enter Benwash, Rabshake, at several doors.

BENWASH: Rabshake?
RABSHAKE: Here, sir.

---

112 Have you e'er a Bedlam?] do you have a madhouse like Bedlam (London's Bethlehem Hospital)?
114 eased my gall] purged my angry humors.
122 put you in sureties] give you a legal guarantee or contract.

BENWASH: Is this child of Adam coming yet? He that will eat of the
forbidden fruit though he lose Paradise for't? Is he coming?

5 RABSHAKE: As fast as his legs will bear him, considering the use he means
to put them to. I have provided a caudle to comfort him with.

BENWASH: That's my dear precious villain! How sweet art thou, Revenge!
The thought of thee turns all my blood to air.

RABSHAKE: And your horns, too, sir?

10 BENWASH: All light, Rabshake.

RABSHAKE: They were begot light, but methinks they should be heavy in
the wearing.

BENWASH: I will make them abortives, man, smother them in the womb.

RABSHAKE: Though you lop the branches, you will preserve the tree to bear
15 more fruit, I hope—your wife, sir.

BENWASH: She shall down, too. I will let her blood in a new vein. She shall
turn up the white of the eye and die the death of a sinner.

RABSHAKE: How will you dispense with your oaths, sir?

BENWASH: Tush, by equivocation man. I will not hurt her, but thou shalt
20 by equivocation. Behind the arras, my dear Rabshake.

[Benwash and Rabshake conceal themselves.]

RABSHAKE: That word (by equivocation) lies on my stomach, I would be
loath it should make me cast up my gall. I would not have my throat
cut by equivocation.

[Enter Gallop and Agar, while Benwash and Rabshake speak aside.]

BENWASH: The game is roused—take thy stand and strike, Rabshake.

25 RABSHAKE: Strike you, sir? You are the keeper, and have the fees in
possession. I have no money upon this equivocation.

BENWASH: So the hour of my redemption is at hand—for man's worst hell,
a whore.

GALLOP: You put me to a sweet purgation the other night. 'Twas well fear
30 took away some of my senses—I had smelt for't else.

AGAR: You saw the necessity of it, sir.

GALLOP: You may call it necessity; I thought of the Day of Judgment—and

---

6 caudle] a warm medicinal drink.

22 cast up my gall] literally, to vomit bile; here, be purged of my angry spirit.

30 I had smelt for't else] Gallop refers to his escape through the foul-smelling sewers.

that was more than ever I did in my life before! What with the fire
above, and the ram-headed devil your husband below, I imagined
35   damnation could not be far off.

BENWASH: [aside] Good, excellent good.

GALLOP: And whither is that golden calf of Horeb, that Jew of the tribe of
Israel gone, that it is jubilee with you now, all open?°

AGAR: He is rid to the Goletto about taking in a commodity.

40   GALLOP: And in the meantime thou wilt utter one at home. I am thy
merchant, wench, and will deal with thee by wholesale.

BENWASH: [aside] Rather by retail, sir, retail.

GALLOP: Where is your pimp, Rabshake? Taking a nap at the stairfoot?
Committing sin in conceit, whilst we are at it in action? Hath he the
45   two qualities of an usher, a good ear, and to endure cold of his feet?
Have you given him instructions?

BENWASH: [aside] I see how it did work. I feel it.

RABSHAKE: [aside] He'll make the old Jew believe I was his wife's bawd.

GALLOP: The slave was born pander, his mother was midwife, and then he
50   must needs be bawd to set his mother's trade awork.

RABSHAKE: [aside] You will groan for this anon, sir.

AGAR: I pray you, sir, sit down—a small banquet, sir.

[Agar brings out wine and food.]

GALLOP: Provocatives and whetters on? One liquorous thing draws out
another. Who will not swear venery is a sweet sin now? Bacchus and
55   Venus, two gods—the Devil is far enough off then.

[Benwash and Rabshake reveal themselves.]

BENWASH: You are deceived, sir. He is at your elbow.

RABSHAKE: Is Dun in the mire? For old acquaintance sake we'll drag you out,
sir. You are in travail: I am the son of a midwife; I'll help to deliver you.

GALLOP: It cannot be. I am in a dream.

---

38 **open**] (sexually) accessible.

39 **is rid**] has ridden.

39 **Goletto**] La Goletta, the harbor adjacent to the city of Tunis.

57 **Is Dun in the mire?**] refers to the proverb "Dun (the horse) is in the mire," meaning that things are
stuck or at a standstill. This phrase refers to a traditional Christmas game called "drawing Dun out of
the mire" in which a heavy log was lifted.

60 RABSHAKE: A good belief doth well. Were I in your case, I should be past dreaming—but I'll cast you in a slumber, sir.

BENWASH: You must be at your sweetmeats. Cannot mutton serve your turn, but you must have sauce to it?

GALLOP: This whore hath betrayed me: now she hath wrung what she
65 can out of me, she hangs me up for a dried neat's tongue. She is an insatiate whore, sir, hath enticed me by the pander, your man: I was chaste before I knew her, sir.

RABSHAKE: Believe him not, sir. He is a mere goat—look on his beard else.

AGAR: You may see by his hair he is a man of hot liver. He came over me
70 with such violence I had not the heart to resist him.

BENWASH: I believe you, wife, I believe you, and thou shalt justify it to his teeth before the greatest devil in hell. Rabshake, give her a mittimus— strangle her.

AGAR: Have you forgot your oaths, sir?

75 BENWASH: I sware as I was a Turk, and I will cut your throat as I am a Jew.

AGAR: Villain, keep off, I say.

RABSHAKE: You should have said so when time was, mistress.

AGAR: [to Rabshake] Thou betrayest thyself, slave, makest way to thine own destruction.

80 BENWASH: Stop her throat, I say! Give no ear to her.

AGAR: I do confess my sin—I have wrongfully betrayed thee.

GALLOP: I find myself in bonds for't, lady. It is some comfort yet, that I die not unrevenged.   [*Rabshake kills her.*]

BENWASH: Thou speakest charitably. Is she gone? Is her lust satisfied now?

85 RABSHAKE: Do a woman to death, and she will be satisfied—nothing else will.

BENWASH: Now for you, Mr. Gallop. You gave it me with tilting, and I will return your courtesy.

GALLOP: Save my life, sir, and I will be your slave, sell myself in open
90 market, brand me.

BENWASH: That were *Lex talion* indeed—one mark for another! But it will not serve the turn. Have at you!

---

69 his hair] red hair?

69 of hot liver] irascible.

72 mittimus] L., "we send," the first word of a legal warrant or order of dismissal; used jocularly to mean a death sentence.

87 tilting] jousting with lances, a metaphor for phallic prowess.

91 Lex talion] L., "law of retaliation," referring to the Judaic law of an eye for an eye (see Exodus xxi).

[Benwash] kills him.

RABSHAKE: Ha, ha, ha. How the ox gores him!

GALLOP: 'Sdeath! Villains, treacherous villains, the plague, pox—   [*Dies.*]

95 RABSHAKE: He died a true lecher, with the pox in his mouth. Why this was valiantly done, sir, in single opposition.

BENWASH: Why, now my brow begins to smooth. How lik'st this tragedy, Rabshake?

RABSHAKE: Rarely! If it do not prove a tragedy to us, sir; it's but a comedy
100   hitherto: the setting off is all.

BENWASH: Tush, the best is behind, man: dost think I do not bear a brain about me? Beware a politician, man. Here, bind me, bind me—hard, hard!

RABSHAKE: Aye, marry, sir. I like this well. A man may trust you when
105   your hands are tied behind you.

BENWASH: I cannot choose but laugh to think how happy I am in my project. It will amaze thee when thou hear'st it, Rabshake. We shall so gull the innocent world, laugh at the silly world.

RABSHAKE: If you gull me now, I'll give you leave to make mummy of me.
110   What's next, sir?

BENWASH: Here, take this dagger. Stab me an inch into the breast and arm.

RABSHAKE: Do you call this gulling of the world?

BENWASH: I cannot but laugh at the gentleman's lecherous voyage to Lucifer. There, there. Now, Rabshake, let me bind thee.

115 RABSHAKE: How? Bind me?

BENWASH: Thou art not capable of the mystery. Thou art shallow, Rabshake.

RABSHAKE: I do not desire to wade deeper in, I thank you, sir. I am no politician, bear no brain about me, sir. Yet I can dive into a knave's
120   pockets as well as any man, your worship knows.

BENWASH: What dost thou mean by this?

RABSHAKE: To rob you as I am a Turk, and cut your throat as I am a Jew. You have forgot your equivocation. I'll chop logic with you. Come,

---

99 **Rarely**] Exceptionally.

100 **setting off**] carrying it through to completion (?).

102 **politician**] "a shrewd schemer; a crafty plotter" (*O.E.D.*).

108 **silly**] simple, naive.

109 **mummy**] powder allegedly made from dried mummies' flesh.

116 **the mystery**] the craft (of concealing murder).

your rings, your chain: do you not laugh? Have you not gulled the
125   world fairly?

BENWASH: Thou hast mistaken me: know thou art all my care.

RABSHAKE: And you would be rid of me. I conceive you, sir; though
I am no politician: I have seen the play of Pedringano, sir—of
Pedringano, sir.°

130 BENWASH: Dear Rabshake, upon my knees I do entreat thee: hear me! For
whom have I ta'en thought, outwatched the night, out-toiled the day,
but for my Rabshake? What friend, what kinsman, what heir had I but
Rabshake?

RABSHAKE: Yes, you meant I should have been your heir.

135 BENWASH: Nay, thou shouldst have had all in possession. My purpose
was to have lived a private life, done penance for my sins, and given
thee all.

RABSHAKE: You would have parted with this chain, these rings and gold?

BENWASH: They are thine own—on whom should I bestow them else?

140 RABSHAKE: And you have a trick to come off clear with this business?

BENWASH: In spite of jealousy, without suspicion, man! You being bound,
your head thrust in this circle, as if tied up for starting; I had cried out,
"thieves, murder!" raised the street, transferred the act upon some
stranger.

145 RABSHAKE: And I should have been your heir.

BENWASH: Thou wrongst me to make question of't.

RABSHAKE: If I should try him, it is beyond my compass if he outsail me.
This chain and gold is mine?

BENWASH: 'Sfoot, myself too!

150 RABSHAKE: For once I'll try you. Here, bind me. If you do outreach me, I'll
n'er trust Jew more.

BENWASH: Here, here. Is thy head in?

RABSHAKE: It is, sir.

BENWASH: Have I caught you? Are you in the noose? You have seen the
155   play of Pedringano, sir. I'll play with you!

RABSHAKE: 'Sheart, I am your slave, sir. I did it to make your worship
merry.

BENWASH: Tush, you are my heir. I'll hang you up a airing!

RABSHAKE: As you are a man, hear me, sir!

---

142 **this circle**] this noose.
142 **for starting**] to prevent escape by running away.

[Benwash strangles Rabshake.]

160 BENWASH: You must have your chains; you shall be chained. I could even
         crack my sides with laughter. This will afford me mirth unto my dying
         day. The play of Pedringano? How the weasel hangs! Ha, ha, ha.
         Thieves, thieves! Murder, murder! I shall betray myself with laughter.
         Were you caught, Reynard? Are you in the noose? Murder, murder!
165   Thieves! Murder!

Enter Mufti, Mulli, and officers.

MULLI: Break ope the doors! The voice speaks from this room.
BENWASH: Murder, murder, murder!
MUFTI: Inhuman deed! What hand could be so bloody?
MULLI: Speak, who was the murderer?
170 BENWASH: Help me to a surgeon!
MUFTI: Run for a surgeon! Tell by what monster was this act (so full of
         horror) done?
BENWASH: Three strangers rushed in suddenly, we being at supper, all my
         servants forth, save honest Rabshake. And having rifled us, did act
175   this horrible act of murther.
FIRST OFFICER: Here is a surgeon.   *[Enter Surgeon.]*
MUFTI: The prophet Mahomet reveal the homicides!

Enter Governor, other officers, Sares, Ferdinand, Albert, Dansiker disguised.

GOVERNOR: What moves these outcries?
MULLI: Behold a bloody murder—Benwash, his wife, this captain, and his
180   servant.
BENWASH: My honest servant, honest Rabshake.
DANSIKER: *[aside]* Benwash murdered? He hath saved me a labor.
GOVERNOR: Is there any hope of life in him?
SURGEON: His wounds are slight, sir. Only his faint heart makes them
185   dangerous.
GOVERNOR: Take courage, man. Speak! Hast thou any knowledge of the
         murderers?
MUFTI: Only he says they are strangers, men of the sea.

---

164 **Reynard**] the proverbially clever, hard-to-catch fox.

SARES: Canst thou remember in what habit, what manner of person and
190   complexion they were?

DANSIKER: What means the slave to eye me so?

BENWASH: That fellow in the stammel hose is one of them.

GOVERNOR: Lay hands on him.

DANSIKER: On me? Villain, thou buy'st my blood   [*Stabs Benwash.*]
195   At a dear rate. O thou immortal God,
           Who know'st my innocence! That for his former sins
           Hast given up Dansiker into the hands
           Of these damned miscreants.

ALL: Dansiker?

200 DANSIKER: Aye, Dansiker! That would with all your deaths
           Have canceled his former infamy,
           Left to the world a precedent of valor
           Writ in your sad confusions. But heaven is just:
           Christians did fall by me, by slaves I must.

205 GOVERNOR: Call forth the common hangman. By this time he hath done
           his office on Francisco. Dansiker? Unlooked for!

BENWASH: Hear me before I die. I do confess
           Mine own hand did these murthers. Dansiker
           Hath justly done me vengeance.

210 GOVERNOR: How's this? Thou done these murthers thyself, being
           bound and hurt? Thou rav'st sure.

BENWASH: I did them, sir. The cause? My wife proved false, untrue.
           Bear witness, though I lived a Turk, I die a Jew.   [*Dies.*]

ALL: Out, dog! Devil!

215 GOVERNOR: Unheard of monster! Cast his loathed carcass
           Unto the common air. Never did day discover
           Two such inhuman caitiffs! Stretch out his arms.
           You have your trains and fireworks: apply your torches
           Unto his breast. We'll know what project now
220   Led you unto this second venture.

DANSIKER: I will confess it willingly: it was to have conveyed
           This Jew from hence, have made a massacre
           Of the whole town, dashed out the miscreant brains
           Of your young infidels.

225 MUFTI: And art not sorry, dog?

---

192 **stammel hose**] hose made of red woolen cloth.

DANSIKER: Yes, dog, I am sorry—and confess my crimes
    Prevented such a merit: I was not worthy
    To do heaven so good a service.
GOVERNOR: Pull off his hateful flesh! Dig out his heart
230   By piecemeal!
MUFTI: Wilt thou turn Turk and save thy soul yet?
DANSIKER: Yes, pagan; villain, I will. Forgiveness, heaven!

              [Stabs himself.]

    Let my example move all pirates, robbers,
    To think how heavy thy revenging hand
235   Will sit upon them. I feel thy justice now.
    Receive my soul; accept my intended vow. *Dies.*
GOVERNOR: So, convey his hateful body to the same place
    The Jew doth lie unburied.

       Enter at several doors Voada and Ward.

VOADA: Justice! Let me have justice, worthy governor!
240 WARD: Give her no ear. She is all woman—dissimulation.
    I am a Turk, and I do crave the law.
TURK: He hath wounded here a Turk, a lady, and
    We crave sentence according to his merit.
    He may receive the bastinado, pay a fine.
245 WARD: Pay a fine! What fine, from one that's famished?
    For want of a poor asper, set me to sea again.
    The tenth of what I'll bring you in shall countervail
    The revenue of the Indies.
GOVERNOR: The slave is mad. We'll send you far enough.
250   Lady, depose thee for't: you shall have justice.
VOADA: By our great prophet, Mahomet!
WARD: You do me wrong. Let me in private speak to her
    Ere she betray my life. It is no less
    Than your own law affords me.

---

244 **bastinado**] corporal punishment administered with a stick or cudgel.
246 **asper**] a small Turkish coin of silver, worth about two pence.
247 **countervail**] equal.
250 **depose thee**] make a formal complaint.

255   TURK: The weakness of her body brooks it not.

   GOVERNOR: How say you, Voada? Can you afford him speech?

   VOADA: I'll give his vain words hearing, though to much pain.
   Oh, my deep wound! Let all remove from hence.

   WARD: Had she a heart of brass, I'd pierce it. Leave us all.

[The others stand apart.]

260 VOADA: Now sir, your motion.

   WARD: Wherein hath my desert strewed so much ill
   To strain thy hate to this, a height beyond
   What we deem malice? I loved that face so well,
   To purchase it I exchanged my heaven with hell.
265   And to be barred what I so dearly paid for,
   Is't not a plague sufficient? But thy faith
   Must now be sold, to be a vengeance greater,
   To pay me ungrateful hire. Canst thou behold
   These eyes struck inward, as ashamed to view
270   The fires which first betrayed them? This mind, body,
   That doth contain a soul more black and dismal
   Than is the raven night? These arms, that have so oft
   Made to thee rules of love, now famished
   For want of what thou surfeit'st on—canst without tears
275   Behold my miseries?

   VOADA: Ha, ha, ha!

   WARD: Prodigy of woman, dost laugh?

   VOADA: This is true music! Could I enjoy these tunes,
   Myself would be thy jailor.

280 WARD: Why then, thy wound is not dangerous?

   VOADA: A mere scratch. Know that I am revenged
   Of my Fidelio's death, and as thy tortures
   Each hour increase, so shall my harmony
   Till vengeance period give unto thy destiny.

285 WARD: I will discover thy hypocrisy.

   VOADA: You are prevented. Help! I swound! I fall!

---

260 **motion**] proposal.

261 **strewed**] piled up.

284 **Till vengeance period give unto thy destiny**] until vengeance brings your life to its appointed end.

286 **swound**] faint.

WARD: As low as hell, there keep thy festival.
GOVERNOR: Hold, murderous villain! All tortures man e'er knew
 Shall be inflicted on thee.
290 OMNES: Inhuman dog!
WARD: Ha, ha, ha. I laugh at you.
 Here's a preservative against all your poisons,
 True balsamum for villainy. Who will soar high
 First lesson that he learns must be to die.
295 Here's precedent for him.   *[Stabs himself.]*
 You're slaves of Mahomet,
 Ungrateful curs, that have repaid me thus
 For all the service that I have done for you.
 He that hath brought more treasure to your shore
300 Than all Arabia yields! He that hath shown you
 The way to conquer Europe—did first impart
 What your forefathers knew not, the seaman's art;
 Which had they attained, this universe had been
 One monarchy. May all your seed be damned!
305 The name of Ottoman be the only scorn
 And by-word to all nations; may his own slaves
 Tear out the bowels of the last remains
 Unto his blood-propped throne; may ye cut each other's throats;
 Or may, O may, the force of Christendom
310 Be reunited and all at once requite
 The lives of all that you have murdered,
 Beating a path out to Jerusalem
 Over the bleeding breasts of you and yours.
ALL: Unheard of monster!
315 WARD: Lastly, O may I be the last of my country
 That trust unto your treacheries, seducing treacheries.
 All you that live by theft and piracies,
 That sell your lives and souls to purchase graves,
 That die to hell, and live far worse then slaves,

---

287 **there keep thy festival**] The 1612 text does not give any stage directions here, but it was probably
intended that Ward would kill Voada at this point.
293 **balsamum**] balm, cure.
306 **by-word**] word or name attached to an object of public contempt.
306 **his own**] the Ottoman sultan's.

320   Let dying Ward tell you that heaven is just,
        And that despair attends on blood and lust.   [*Dies.*]
    ALL: Down with the villain!
    GOVERNOR: Tear the wretch piecemeal! Throw his accursed limbs
        Into the raging bowels of the sea!
325   His monument in brass we'll thus engrave:
        "Ward sold his country, turned Turk, and died a slave."   [*Exeunt.*]

EPILOGUE

[Enter Chorus.]

[CHORUS]: Who writes and thinks to please the general taste,
        Where eyes and ears are fed, shall find he hath placed
        His work with the fond painter who did mend
        So long, that (striving to please others) gave no end
5   To his own labors. For us, and if not all,
        We know we have pleased some, whose judgments fall
        Beyond the common rank, to whom we humbly yield
        Ourselves and labors. They best deserve to shield
        The worthy works of Time and with their view
10   To grace choice pens; and such we hope are you,
        To whom we owe our toil and willing give
        All right in this. Your favor makes it live.
        Stand fair unto our ends then still, and crown
        With gentle hand this work which now's your own.

FINIS.

Notes

~

DEDICATORY EPISTLE

poesy   In early modern English the term "poesy" refers to any form of imaginative writing including poetry, drama, and prose fiction. Cf. Sir Philip Sidney, *Apology for Poesy* (1581): "It is not rhyming and versing that maketh poesy. One may be a poet without versing, and a versifier without poetry."

this oppressed and much martyred tragedy.   Daborne's defensive rhetoric throughout this epistle to the reader indicates that when the play was performed it was controversial, unpopular, or unsuccessful. It is quite likely that its portrayal of pirates like Ward and Dansiker as sympathetic, even heroic, may have been criticized or condemned, or that the staging of Ward's conversion to Islam was deemed offensive.

PROLOGUE

8. **ours is Ward turned Turk.**   Here Daborne refers to other contemporary texts—perhaps including other plays—that featured the career of Ward. The "Prologue" announces that this play will feature not the relatively "trivial" crime of turning pirate, which, after all, was only a degree or two removed from legitimate activity as a privateer, but rather the damnable, apostatical crime of conversion to Islam that Ward commits in the central scene of the play.

SCENE I

4–5. **She hath turned . . . hath soaked me!**   The opening lines of the play contain a series of puns referring to the game of chance called "hazard," a popular form of gambling in English society. Hazard was played with dice and sometimes (as here) with cards as well. As Massinger's play begins, Ward, Gismund, and the merchants, Ferdinand and Albert, have finished one hand and are preparing to deal another. Gismund complains of his bad luck: he has repeatedly thrown the ace and "crapped out." Gismund personifies Fortune (Lady Luck) as a whore, whose excessive sexual demands have drained and exhausted him—body and purse. Here "ace," in bawdy slang, refers to the vulva, as well as to the die cast. When Gismund says, "I have ne'er an eye to see with," he alludes to the belief that excessive sexual activity caused a weakening of the eyes. The verb "to soak" means to draw out by means of soaking, to suck out, to exhaust, to drain, or to impoverish, thereby suggesting both sexual and financial "soaking."

6–7. **deal merchant-like . . . throw at all.** Albert challenges Ward and Gismund to bet all they have on this last hand. His language connects the game of hazard to another form of financial risk—venturing life, limb, and investment in a merchant marine voyage on the high seas or "main." "Main" refers to 1) the open ocean, 2) the principal part (of one's assets) and 3) "in the game of hazard, a number . . . called by the 'caster' before the dice are thrown" (*O.E.D.*).

67. **These children have been at Saint Antholin's.** "St. Antholin" is an English derivation of "St. Antoine" or "St. Anthony." The reference here is to a school in London at St. Anthony's Hospital in Threadneedle Street. During its heyday in the sixteenth century, boys from St. Anthony's competed annually for prizes with their rivals from St. Thomas Acon, and the boys from St. Anthony's usually won. After 1540 the school declined, however, and by 1550 its chapel was being used as the French Protestant Church.

83–85. **The first that . . . us for succor.** If unable to outrun pirates in pursuit, a fleeing merchant vessel might try to sail toward another ship in the hope of protection. Identifying the nationality and status of other ships in the Mediterranean was a tricky business, though, and there are accounts of merchants who escape one group of pirates only to be captured by another. Daborne may be thinking of the incident described in *News from the Sea*, when two English ships, having already been ransacked by Ward, attempted to seek refuge with a group of friendly ships, but were then attacked by Dansiker's pirates.

Scene 2

55–56. **Lace the netting . . . the small shot** A series of commands to prepare a ship for close combat. "Lace the netting" is an order to lash on "small ropes which are seized together with rope yarns in the form of a net with meshes." "The fights" are screens used in naval engagements "wherein men may cover themselves and yet use their arms" (from Mainwaring's definitions of "netting" and "fights," in his *Seaman's Dictionary*, 1644).

Scene 4

97–101. **You are not . . . oyster voice** Francisco taunts Ward for his low origins as a fisherman from Faversham in Kent. Ward's "rags to riches" transformation from fisherman and naval conscript to the leadership of a pirate fleet is recounted with a mixture of admiration and condemnation in contemporary pamphlets and ballads. (See Appendix 1.)

Scene 5

2–6. These letters . . . King Henry of France! Eminent pirates like Ward and Dansiker were offered amnesty by various rulers and sometimes were permitted to keep part of their ill-gotten wealth if they agreed to cease piratical activities. Henry IV of France did in fact grant a pardon to Dansiker.

37. The renegado Jew The term "renegado," used in early modern English, is derived from a Spanish form of "renegade" and suggests a particularly Mediterranean phenomenon—the activities of European Christians who converted to Islam and lived under Muslim authorities in the Ottoman empire or the Barbary ports of North Africa. In this case, the word describes a Jew who has converted to Islam, but it was more commonly used to refer to Christians who had "turned Turk." Those who changed religion in order to gain freedom, wealth, and patronage in Muslim society were considered to be both apostates and traitors. The term "renegado" carried both a political and a religious signification, referring to the turncoat's betrayal of one's country as well as his renunciation of his faith. The *O.E.D.* cites Hakluyt, from the *Voyages:* "He was a renegado, which is one that was first a Christian and afterwards becometh a Turk." See also in the *O.E.D.* the term "runagado," where W. Davies' *Travels* (1614) is cited: "He is circumcised . . . denying his Christian name, so that ever after he is called a runagado."

Scene 6

99–100. I would use . . . opened the bags Voada plays upon the legal and sexual meanings of "overseer." She tells Agar to let Rabshake act as a legal "overseer," a person appointed by a testator to supervise the executor of a will, while the "executioner" (i.e., executor) "opens" the lawyer's "bag" containing the will. Voada suggests that Rabshake will look on and "stand by" as a sexually aroused voyeur while Agar makes herself sexually "open" to Gallop.

141–46. stay his pace . . . to the Devil A series of equestrian metaphors that carry erotic innuendo. To "trot in your ring" (literally referring to horseback riding on a circular track) alludes to coital movement in Agar's genital "ring." "Courser," a racehorse, puns upon the notion of a "course" as a sexual bout, and to "be jaded" (referring to a horse that has been tired out or worn out by over-riding) means to be made into a worn-out whore. Continuing the equine wordplay, "to go post" means to ride at top speed. Metaphorically, Rabshake expresses his fear that he will go straight to hell and implies that Benwash is "the Devil" who will damn him.

150. St. Anthony's purgatory Dansiker alludes to the hellish visions of St. Anthony's temptation, but also to the inflammatory skin diseases collectively and popularly known as "St. Anthony's fire" (erysipelas, ergotism, and other inflammatory conditions causing redness and swelling).

379–82. He's all for rem in re . . . present business. *"Rem in re"* ("the thing in the thing") is a Latin legal euphemism for copulation. This phrase was used in the churchwarden's court to describe the ocular proof necessary to convict in a case of adultery. Benwash implies that Rabshake will wait until his master is made "a cuckold by law." That is, Rabshake will not report anything to Benwash until he witnesses "the thing in the thing" (i.e., observes Gallop and Agar in the act). A "book case" is "a law case found in the books or on record, a precedent" (*O.E.D.*); "to moot" is "to argue (a legal case)"; and to "prize him but to the present business" suggests that Rabshake believes he will be valued or rewarded only if the "present business"—the sexual tryst arranged between Gallop and Agar—takes place. Benwash says he will argue on precedent that his jealousy and suspicion are justified, and therefore precautions must be taken. He fears that Rabshake will wait until the legal evidence is established before claiming his reward for his service as "supervisor."

425. **you oxgall** A play on Gallop's name. To "gall" is to touch on a sore point, to irritate a wound; an "ox" is a castrated male bovine. This term refers to the way in which Gallop is "galling" or vexing Benwash, the castrated and horned cuckold-ox.

451. **usher his own crest** The metaphor here refers to the neo-chivalric practice whereby an "usher" bearing a "crest" (heraldic figure or device) would precede the coming of a dignitary, making way for him and announcing his title. Gallop implies that Benwash is acting as his own usher, announcing and introducing himself by the heraldic title of "cuckold" whose device is a "crest" or pair of (cuckold's) horns.

SCENE 7

216. **this boy's words trouble me.** In this scene, Alizia/Fidelio's lines are misattributed to "Francisco" in the 1612 quarto. This statement, and others later in this scene, refer to Ward's interlocutor as a "boy." It is difficult to determine exactly the nature of the textual problem here, but it is unlikely that the pirate captain Francisco would be described as a mere "boy." It is either a case of misattribution (and these lines were intended for the boy actor playing the role of Alizia/Fidelio), or it is a set of allusions, lost on us, to the child actors of the Queen's Revels company, for whom Daborne originally wrote this play. Under the assumption of misattribution, the speech headings have been changed here from "Francisco" to "Alizia" (as indicated by the brackets). This makes sense because Alizia is employed as Ward's "page" and is disguised as a boy in other scenes.

224. **Think on Ulysses' constancy.** An allusion to the hero of Homer's *Odyssey*, Ulysses, who faced a series of trials and temptations (some feminine—Circe, Calypso, the Sirens) in faraway, foreign lands but maintained his loyalty to his homeland and succeeded in returning to his household and family in Ithaca.

SCENE 8

1–2. **Here could I . . . acts of men.** The Chorus, addressing the audience directly, wishes that the shocking events about to be represented in the dumb show were only a fiction, and not true. In fact, there is no description of Ward undergoing such a circumcision ceremony in either Andrew Barker's *True and Certain Report of the Beginning, Proceedings, Overthrows, and now present estate of Captains Ward and Danseker* (1609) or the anonymous *News from Sea, Of Two Notorious Pirates, Ward . . . and Danseker* (1609).

7–8. **he dares to . . . more to show.**   What he (Ward) has done is so shocking that it is unthinkable, and so horrible that it cannot be fully dramatized on stage. Here, Daborne puns on "dumb show," a scene enacted without words, introducing the dumb show that will "show" without speech the execrable actions of Ward. The Chorus may be hinting that the surgical procedure of circumcision (considered by early modern Englishmen to be a bizarre rite of mutilation) is too grisly to be imagined, much less staged.

s.d.   Daborne's stage directions for the ceremony of conversion are similar to the description of the rites performed for those who "turn Turk" in a contemporary captivity narrative, *A True Relation of the Travails and most miserable captivity . . . of William Davies* (1614):

> The manner of a Christian turning Turk is thus. He is put upon a horse
> with his face towards the tail, and a bow and an arrow in his hand.
> Then the picture of Christ is carried before him with his feet upwards,
> at the which he draws his bow with the arrow therein, and thus he rid-
> eth to the place of circumcision, cursing his father that begat him and
> his mother that bore him, his country, and all his kindred. Then com-
> ing to the place of circumcision, he is circumcised, receiving a name and
> denying his Christian name, so that ever after he is called a renegado;
> that is, a Christian denying Christ and turned Turk; of which sort there
> are more in Turkey and Barbary than of natural Turks (B3v).

s.d. a Mahomet's head   A standard stage property of the London companies, probably a grotesque, oversized, angry-eyed, turbaned head, like the "Turk's heads" used in England as tavern signs or archery targets. The 1598 playhouse inventory of the Lord Admiral's Men includes an entry for "owld Mahametes head" (see Carol Rutter, ed., *Documents of the Rose Playhouse* [Manchester: Manchester University Press, 1984], 136).

s.d. swears him on the Mahomet's head   The misperception of "Mahomet" as a pagan idol, worshipped by "Saracens" and "paynim knights," goes back to the *Chanson de Roland* and other medieval romance tales. The notion that Mahomet was just another pagan god continued to appear in English writings about Islam throughout the seventeenth century.

17. **their pagan tribes**   Although Muslims are monotheist iconoclasts, and not "pagan" idol worshippers, Christians in Western Europe continued to refer to them as "pagan," "heathen," and the like, well into the eighteenth century. Cf. Shakespeare,

Richard II: "Streaming the ensign of the Christian cross, against black pagans, Turks, and Saracens" (4.1.95).

22. **In wars 'gainst Christians.** Many renegades who had converted to Islam aided the crews of Turkish or Barbary ships by helping to reproduce the latest military technologies known in Western Europe.

Scene 9

2. **I saw him Turk to the circumcision.** He went so far in his Islamic zeal as to be circumcised. Here "Turk" means "Muslim." According to the theology of early modern Christianity, circumcision was considered to be an Abrahamic practice, abrogated by the coming of Christ and the new covenant:

> . . . as the Jews have showed themselves most obstinate in the blindness
> of their hearts by the retaining of this ceremony and their old traditions:
> so the Turks likewise, no less vain in the idleness of their own imagina-
> tions, have and do use circumcision, as a special token or mark of their
> fond and superstitious sect. (*The Policy of the Turkish Empire*, London,
> 1597, 22.)

4. **I heard he . . . an ape's tail.** He tricked them by substituting the end of an ape's tail for his foreskin. Jews, like Muslims, are required to undergo circumcision, and according to the anti-Semitic stereotype maintained by early modern Christians, Jews were proverbial deceivers and oathbreakers. Thus Sares is punning on the idea of "playing the Jew": Ward "played" (i.e., faked) the part of the circumcised Jew, cheating them of his foreskin.

Scene 10

51. **Press her in a dumb show!** A puzzling line, but it seems to be a sudden call for silence. Perhaps the first sailor means that it is time to cease the banter (to make like a "dumb show") and "press" themselves into service as thieves (picking up on the earlier references to what poor sailors are forced to do to avoid starving or begging).

64–67. **A woman's lower . . . man's part uppermost.** The two sailors come upon Agar and Gallop while they are having sex. The sailors are standing near the exit to the upper playing area, where they look in on the copulating couple and emerge holding pieces of clothing and underwear discarded by Agar and Gallop. "Part" is both an article of clothing and the "private part." That it is "in fashion" for women to "be light about the bum," refers to women wearing lightweight clothing but also suggests a feminine tendency toward sexual promiscuity. The first sailor holds up Gallop's "doublet," which is his upper garment, but the sailor's words also imply that he has just seen the other half of the copulating couple. The women's "request to have the man's part uppermost" may refer to a contemporary trend for cross-dressing, but also has bawdy signification: the sailor implies that women like men to assume the "upper-most" sexual position and they want "the man's part" to be standing up, erect.

Scene 13

9–10. **Your brother being . . . shall enjoy thee.**   In order to protect her fiancé, Raymond, and redeem him from captivity, Alizia pretends that Raymond is her brother so as not to arouse Voada's jealousy. Voada agrees to pay the ransom of Alizia's "brother" if Alizia/Fidelio will sleep with her.

52–54. **Poor fellow . . . an Italian captain.**   Rabshake taunts Ward, making light of his conversion and the painful circumcision he has just undergone. Rabshake jok-ingly implies that the removal of Ward's foreskin has rendered the amorous captain incapable of consummating his marriage with Voada, and that, instead, Ward has been a passive participant in what early modern Englishmen often called the "Italian" prac-tice of anal sex. This is implied in the reference to the line, presumably from a contem-porary ballad, "Who's that knocks at the back door?"

97–98. **the governor / With all the janissaries of the town**   In Tunis there was a governor or viceroy appointed by the Ottoman sultan to supervise commerce and taxa-tion, maintain Turkish sovereignty over the local peoples, and perform other duties. The power and authority of this Turkish governor was supported by a garrison of "janissaries," soldiers from an elite corps of the Turkish military who were captured or purchased as slaves when young and then trained from childhood in military discipline.

Scene 14

13–19. **The agèd oak . . . make return / Impossible.**   "The agèd oak" is King Henri IV of France, who was assassinated on May 14, 1610, by Ravaillac. In fact, Dan-siker arrived in Paris with the duke of Guise before the king's murder and was officially pardoned by the king.

Scene 15

The intricacy of the plot intensifies at this point in the play. A brief synopsis may help to clarify the events of this scene for the reader: Voada has agreed to ransom Raymond if Alizia/Fidelio will spend the night with her (see 13.9–10). Alizia, to es-cape Voada's lust and still save her fiancé, has deceived Voada and made a deal with Ward: Ward agrees to help Alizia meet with Raymond so that the lovers can escape with the "Hollander" (Dansiker?). Ward promises to let the young couple flee through the castle (of which he still retains the keys, given to him by Crosman). But Ward, in turn, double-crosses Alizia: he sends Francisco to tell Voada that a "skipper" (the "Hollander") is planning to meet Alizia/Fidelio and flee from Tunis with her. Instead of helping Alizia, Ward (who does this to avenge himself on Voada for her incon-stancy) guides Voada to the rendezvous point inside the castle, where Voada subsequently shoots Raymond. Ward was hoping that Voada would unintentionally shoot and kill Alizia/Fidelio, his rival for Voada's attention. Instead, she mistakenly murders Raymond, who arrives first and gives the password "Fidelio" in the dark. When Alizia appears on the scene, she discovers Raymond mortally wounded and commits suicide, dying with him. Ward then betrays his friend Francisco when he lies and tells the Turks that Francisco has murdered Alizia and Raymond.

SCENE 16

37–38. **And whither is . . . all open?** Gallop asks Agar where Benwash, "that golden calf of Horeb," has gone, referring to the golden idol worshipped by the backsliding Israelites while Moses received the commandments. "Golden calf" also implies a wealthy, feeble-hearted fool and cuckold. (See *O.E.D.*, "calf," "Applied to human beings: a stupid fellow, a dolt; sometimes a meek, inoffensive person.") The allusion to the Judaic "jubilee" refers to the year when property outside the walls reverted to previous owners (see Leviticus 25).

128. **I have seen the play of Pedringano, sir** Rabshake refers to Kyd's *Spanish Tragedy*, in which Lorenzo orders his faithful servant Pedringano to murder Serberine. When Pedringano is sentenced to be hanged for this crime, he expects to receive a pardon but is betrayed and executed on stage (see *Spanish Tragedy* 3.6). Rabshake declares that he has seen this play, learned not to trust a master who asks his servant to commit a murder, and so refuses to be "gulled" like Pedringano.

THE RENEGADO,

A TRAGÆCOMEDIE.

As it hath beene often acted by the
Queenes Maiesties seruants, at
the priuate Play-house in
Drurye-Lane.

By PHILIP MASSINGER.

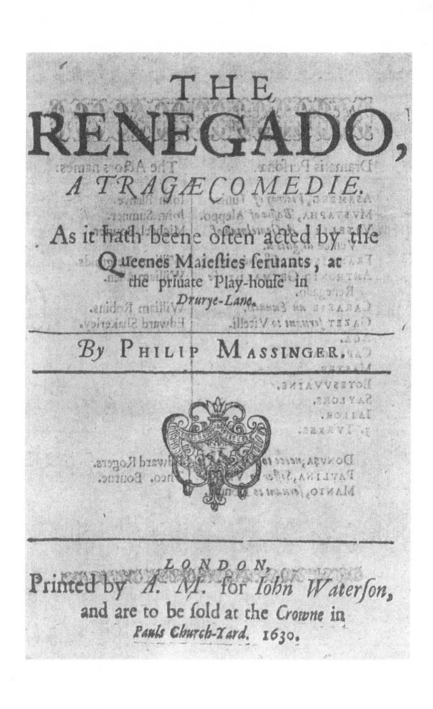

LONDON,
Printed by *A. M.* for *Iohn Waterson,*
and are to be sold at the *Crowne* in
Pauls Church-Yard. 1630.

The Renegado

A Tragicomedy.

As it hath often been acted by the
Queen's Majesty's servants, at
the private playhouse in
Drury Lane

By Philip Massinger

LONDON,
PRINTED BY A. M. FOR JOHN WATERSON,
AND ARE TO BE SOLD AT THE CROWN IN
PAUL'S CHURCHYARD. 1630.

TO THE RIGHT HONORABLE GEORGE HARDING,

Baron Berkeley, of Berkeley Castle,
and Knight of the Honorable Order of the Bath.°

My good lord,

To be honored for old nobility or hereditary titles is not alone proper to
yourself but to some few of your rank who may challenge the like privilege
with you: but in our age to vouchsafe (as you have often done) a ready hand
to raise the dejected spirits of the contemned sons of the Muses, such as
would not suffer the glorious fire of poesy to be extinguished, is so remark-
able and peculiar to your lordship, that with a full vote and suffrage it is
acknowledged that the patronage and protection of the dramatic poem is
yours—and almost without a rival. I despair not, therefore, but that my ambition to present my service in this kind may in your clemency meet with a
gentle interpretation. Confirm it, my good lord, in your gracious acceptance
of this trifle, in which if I were not confident there are some pieces worthy
the perusal, it should have been taught in an humbler flight, and the writer
(your countryman) never yet made happy in your notice and favor, had not
made this an advocate to plead for his admission among such as are wholly
and sincerely devoted to your service. I may live to tender my humble thank-
fulness in some higher strain, and till then comfort myself with hope that
you descend from your height to receive,

Your Honor's Commanded Servant,
Philip Massinger

To My Honored Friend, Master Philip Massinger,
  upon His *Renegado*

Dabblers in poetry that only can
Court this weak lady, or that gentleman,
    With some loose wit in rhyme;
    Others that fright the time
Into belief with mighty words that tear
    A passage through the ear;
        Or nicer men,
That through a perspective will see a play
    And use it the wrong way
        (Not worth thy pen);
Though all their pride exalt 'em, cannot be
Competent judges of thy lines or thee.

I must confess I have no public name
To rescue judgment; no poetic flame
    To dress thy Muse with praise,
    And Phoebus his own bays;
Yet I commend this poem and dare tell
    The world I liked it well,
        And if there be
A tribe who in their wisdoms dare accuse
    This offspring of thy Muse,
        Let them agree,
Conspire one comedy, and they will say
'Tis easier to commend than make a play.
                              James Shirley°

---

nicer] fussier.
perspective] an optical instrument for viewing or magnifying objects, sometimes designed to produce
special effects (for example, by distortion of images).

To his worthy friend Master Philip Massinger,
   on his play, called *The Renegado*

The bosom of a friend cannot breathe forth
A flattering phrase to speak the noble worth
Of him that hath lodged in his honest breast
So large a title: I, among the rest
That honor thee, do only seem to praise,
Wanting the flowers of art to deck that bays
Merit has crowned thy temple with. Know, friend,
Though there are some who merely do commend
To live i'th' world's opinion such as can
Censure with judgment, no such piece of man
Makes up my spirit; where desert does live,
There will I plant my wonder, and there give
My best endeavors to build up his story
That truly merits. I did ever glory
To behold virtue rich, though cruel Fate
In scornful malice does beat low their state
That best deserve, when others that but know
Only to scribble, and no more, of't grow
Great in their favors that would seem to be
Patrons of wit and modest poesy.
Yet with your abler friends, let me say this:
Many may strive to equal you but miss
Of your fair scope. This work of yours men may
Throw in the face of envy and then say
To those that are in the great men's thoughts more blest,
"Imitate this and call that work your best."
Yet wise men, in this, and too often, err
When they their love before the work prefer.
If I should say more, some may blame me for't,
Seeing your merits speak you, not report.
                                        Daniel Lakyn°

Dramatis Personae

~

Asambeg	*viceroy of Tunis.*°
Mustapha	*basha of Aleppo.*°
Vitelli	*a Venetian gentleman disguised as a merchant.*
Francisco	*a Jesuit.*
Antonio Grimaldi	*the renegado.*
Carazie	*an eunuch.*
Gazet	*servant to Vitelli.*
Aga	*captain of the Janissaries.*
Capiaga	*Turkish officer and chief porter of the viceregal palace.*
Donusa	*niece to the Ottoman emperor, Amurath.*
Paulina	*sister to Vitelli.*
Manto	*servant to Donusa.*

Master, Boatswain, Jailor, Guards, Sailors, Turks, Janissaries.

Gazet] a humorous name derived from the word for a Venetian coin of small value that circulated throughout the Levant; also a cheap newspaper containing gossip.
Aga] see plate 11.

THE SCENE, TUNIS

ACT ONE

SCENE 1.
A STREET NEAR THE BAZAAR.

VITELLI: You have hired a shop, then?

GAZET: Yes, sir; and our wares,
    Though brittle as a maidenhead at sixteen,
    Are safe unladen; not a crystal cracked
    Or china dish needs soldering; our choice pictures,
5   As they came from the workman, without blemish;
    And I have studied speeches for each piece
    And, in a thrifty tone, to sell them off,
    Will swear by Mahomet and Termagant°
    That this is mistress to the great Duke of Florence,
10 That, niece to old King Pippin, and a third,
    An Austrian princess by her Roman lip,
    However my conscience tells me they are figures
    Of bawds and common courtesans in Venice.

VITELLI: You make no scruple of an oath, then?

---

10 **King Pippin**] probably refers to Pepin III, the Carolingian monarch and father of Charlemagne.

GAZET: Fie, sir!
15   'Tis out of my indentures. I am bound there
        To swear for my master's profit, as securely
        As your intelligencer must for his prince
        That sends him forth an honorable spy,
        To serve his purposes. And if it be lawful
20   In a Christian shopkeeper to cheat his father,
        I cannot find but to abuse a Turk
        In the sale of our commodities must be thought
        A meritorious work.
VITELLI: I wonder, sirrah,
        What's your religion?
GAZET: Troth, to answer truly,
25   I would not be of one that should command me
        To feed upon poor John when I see pheasants
        And partridges on the table. Nor do I like
        The other, that allows us to eat flesh
        In Lent, though it be rotten, rather than be
30   Thought superstitious; as your zealous cobbler
        And learned botcher preach at Amsterdam,
        Over a hotchpotch.° I would not be confined
        In my belief: when all your sects and sectaries
        Are grown of one opinion, if I like it
35   I will profess myself—in the mean time,
        Live I in England, Spain, France, Rome, Geneva:
        I'm of that country's faith.
VITELLI: And what in Tunis?
        Will you turn Turk here?
GAZET: No, so I should lose
        A collop of that part my Doll enjoined me
40   To bring home as she left it: 'tis her venture,
        Nor dare I barter that commodity
        Without her special warrant.

_____

17 intelligencer] spy.
26 poor John] dried herring; thus, Lenten fare.
31 botcher] professional mender of clothing.
32 hotchpotch] a mixture of heterogeneous or incongruous components.
39 collop] small piece of flesh.

VITELLI: You are a knave, sir!
　　　Leaving your roguery, think upon my business:
　　　It is no time to fool now.
45　　Remember where you are, too: though this mart-time
　　　We are allowed free trading, and with safety,
　　　Temper your tongue and meddle not with the Turks,
　　　Their manners, nor religion.
GAZET: Take you heed, sir,
　　　What colors you wear. Not two hours since, there landed
50　　An English pirate's whore with a green apron,
　　　And as she walked the streets, one of their muftis
　　　(We call them priests at Venice) with a razor
　　　Cut it off—petticoat, smock, and all—and leaves her
　　　As naked as my nail; the young fry wondering
55　　What strange beast it should be. I 'scaped a scouring—
　　　My mistress' busk-point, of that forbidden color,
　　　Then tied my codpiece. Had it been discovered
　　　I had been caponed.
VITELLI: And had been well served.
　　　Haste to the shop and set my wares in order:
　　　I will not long be absent.
60 GAZET: Though I strive, sir,
　　　To put off melancholy, to which you are ever
　　　Too much inclined, it shall not hinder me,
　　　With my best care, to serve you.   *Exit.*
VITELLI: I believe thee.

Enter Francisco.

　　　O welcome, sir! Stay of my steps in this life,
65　　And guide to all my blessed hopes hereafter.
　　　What comforts, sir? Have your endeavors prospered?

---

56 **busk-point**] lace designed to secure a woman's corset or busk.

56 **that forbidden color**] green is the color sacred to Islam, traditionally worn by those who claim descent from the Prophet, and green clothing was sometimes prohibited for non-Muslims living under Islamic rule.

57 **codpiece**] a pouch fastened over the front opening of the tight breeches worn by men.

58 **caponed**] castrated (a capon being a castrated rooster), implying circumcision.

Have we tried Fortune's malice with our sufferings?
Is she at length, after so many frowns,
Pleased to vouchsafe one cheerful look upon us?
70 FRANCISCO: You give too much to Fortune and your passions,
O'er which a wise man, if religious, triumphs.
That name fools worship; and those tyrants, which
We arm against our better part, our reason,
May add, but never take, from our afflictions.
75 VITELLI: Sir, as I am a sinful man, I cannot
But like one suffer.

FRANCISCO: I exact not from you
A fortitude insensible of calamity,
To which the saints themselves have bowed and shown
They are made of flesh and blood; all that I challenge
80 Is manly patience. Will you, that were trained up
In a religious school, where divine maxims,
scorning comparison with moral precepts,
Were daily taught you, bear your constancy's trial,
Not like Vitelli, but a village nurse,
85 With curses in your mouth, tears in your eyes?
How poorly it shows in you!

VITELLI: I am schooled, sir,
And will hereafter, to my utmost strength,
Study to be myself.

FRANCISCO: So shall you find me
Most ready to assist you. Neither have I
90 Slept in your great occasions: since I left you,
I have been at the viceroy's court and pressed
As far as they allow a Christian entrance.
And something I have learned that may concern
The purpose of this journey.

VITELLI: Dear sir, what is it?
95 FRANCISCO: By the command of Asambeg, the viceroy,
The city swells with barbarous pomp and pride
For the entertainment of stout Mustapha,
The basha of Aleppo, who in person

---

72 **those tyrants**] refers to "Fortune and your passions," in line 70.

Comes to receive the niece of Amurath,
The fair Donusa, for his bride.

100 VITELLI: I find not
How this may profit us.

FRANCISCO: Pray you, give me leave.
Among the rest that wait upon the viceroy,
Such as have, under him, command in Tunis,
Who, as you've often heard, are all false pirates;
105 I saw the shame of Venice, and the scorn
Of all good men, the perjured renegado,
Antonio Grimaldi.

VITELLI: Ha! His name
Is poison to me.

FRANCISCO: Yet again?

VITELLI: I have done, sir.

FRANCISCO: This debauched villain, whom we ever thought
110 (After his impious scorn done in St. Mark's,
To me, as I stood at the holy altar)
The thief that ravished your fair sister from you,
The virtuous Paulina, not long since,
As I am truly given to understand,
115 Sold to the viceroy a fair Christian virgin;
On whom, maugre his fierce and cruel nature,
Asambeg dotes extremely.

VITELLI: 'Tis my sister!
It must be she; my better angel tells me
'Tis poor Paulina. Farewell, all disguises!
120 I'll show, in my revenge, that I am noble.

FRANCISCO: You are not mad?

VITELLI: No, sir; my virtuous anger
Makes every vein an artery. I feel in me
The strength of twenty men; and being armed
With my good cause, to wreak wronged innocence,

---

110 St. Mark's] cathedral in Venice.
116 maugre] despite.
118 better angel] guardian angel.
122 Makes every vein an artery] arteries, not veins, were thought to distribute the energizing "vital spirits" that the passionate heart pumped into the blood.

125   I dare alone run to the viceroy's court
        And with this poniard, before his face,
        Dig out Grimaldi's heart.

FRANCISCO: Is this religious?

VITELLI: Would you have me tame now? Can I know my sister
        Mewed up in his seraglio and in danger
130   Not alone to lose her honor, but her soul;
        The hell-bred villain by, too, that has sold both
        To black destruction, and not haste to send him
        To the Devil, his tutor? To be patient now
        Were, in another name, to play the pander
135   To the viceroy's loose embraces and cry "ay me!"
        While he, by force or flattery, compels her
        To yield her fair name up to his foul lust,
        And after, turn apostata to the faith
        That she was bred in.

140 FRANCISCO: Do but give me hearing,
        And you shall soon grant how ridiculous
        This childish fury is. A wise man never
        Attempts impossibilities: 'tis as easy
        For any single arm to quell an army
        As to effect your wishes. We come hither
145   To learn Paulina's fate and to redeem her.
        Leave your revenge to heaven. I oft have told you
        Of a relic that I gave her which has power,
        if we may credit holy men's traditions,
        To keep the owner free from violence.
150   This on her breast she wears and does preserve
        The virtue of it by her daily prayers.
        So, if she fall not by her own consent
        (Which it were sin to think), I fear no force.
        Be, therefore, patient. Keep this borrowed shape
155   Till time and opportunity present us
        With some fit means to see her; which performed,
        I'll join with you in my desperate course
        For her delivery.

VITELLI: You have charmed me, sir,
        And I obey in all things. Pray you, pardon
        The weakness of my passion.

160 FRANCISCO: And excuse it.
    Be cheerful, man; for know that good intents
    Are, in the end, crowned with as fair events.   *Exeunt.*

SCENE 2.
A ROOM IN DONUSA'S SECTION OF THE PALACE.

Enter Donusa, Manto, and Carazie.

DONUSA: Have you seen the Christian captive
    The great basha is so enamored of?
MANTO: Yes, an' t please your excellency,
    I took a full view of her when she was
    Presented to him.
DONUSA: And is she such a wonder
    As 'tis reported?
5 MANTO: She was drowned in tears then,
    Which took much from her beauty; yet in spite
    Of sorrow, she appeared the mistress of
    Most rare perfections and, though low of stature,
    Her well-proportioned limbs invite affection.
10   And when she spoke, each syllable is music
    That does enchant the hearers. But your Highness,
    That are not to be paralleled, I yet never
    Beheld her equal.
DONUSA: Come, you flatter me;
    But I forgive it. We that are born great
15   Seldom distaste our servants, though they give us
    More than we can pretend to. I have heard
    That Christian ladies live with much more freedom
    Than such as are born here. Our jealous Turks
    Never permit their fair wives to be seen
20   But at the public bagnios or the mosques,
    And even then, veiled and guarded. Thou, Carazie,
    Wert born in England. What's the custom there,

---

3 **an 't**] and it.
20 **bagnios**] bathhouses.

Among your women? Come, be free and merry:
I am no severe mistress, nor hast thou met with
A heavy bondage.

25 CARAZIE: Heavy! I was made lighter
By two stone weight, at least, to be fit to serve you!
But to your question, madam. Women in England,
For the most part, live like queens. Your country ladies
Have liberty to hawk, to hunt, to feast,
30   To give free entertainment to all comers,
To talk, to kiss; there's no such thing known there
As an Italian girdle. Your city dame,
Without leave, wears the breeches, has her husband
At as much command as her 'prentice, and if need be
35   Can make him cuckold by her father's copy.

DANUSA: But your court lady?

CARAZIE: She, I assure you, madam,
Knows nothing but her will; must be allowed
Her footmen, her caroche, her ushers, pages,
Her doctor, chaplains; and, as I have heard,
40   They're grown of late so learned that they maintain
A strange position, which their lords with all
Their wit cannot confute.

DONUSA: What's that, I prithee?

CARAZIE: Marry, that it is not only fit, but lawful,
Your madam there (her much rest and high feeding
45   Duly considered) should, to ease her husband,
Be allowed a private friend. They have drawn a bill
To this good purpose and, the next assembly,
Doubt not to pass it.

DONUSA: We enjoy no more
That are of the Ottoman race, though our religion
50   Allows all pleasure. I am dull: some music.
Take my chapines off. So, a lusty strain.

_____

25–26 made lighter by two stone weight] Carazie refers to his castration by punning on the double meaning of "stone" as a weight and as "testicle."
28 queens] a pun, meaning either female monarchs or "queans" (whores).
32 Italian girdle] chastity belt.
32 city dame] wife of a London merchant.
51 chapines] woman's shoe with a thick cork sole.

A galliard. [Knocking within.]

Who knocks there?   [*Manto goes to the door and returns.*]
MANTO: 'Tis the basha of Aleppo,
Who humbly makes request he may present
His service to you.
DONUSA: Reach a chair. We must
55   Receive him like ourself and not depart with
One piece of ceremony, state, and greatness
That may beget respect and reverence
In one that's born our vassal. Now admit him.

Enter Mustapha. [He] puts off his yellow pantofles.

MUSTAPHA: The place is sacred; and I am to enter
60   The room where she abides, with such devotion
As pilgrims pay at Mecca when they visit
The tomb of our great prophet.   [*He kneels.*]
DONUSA: Rise; the sign
That we vouchsafe your presence.

[Carazie] takes up the pantofles.°

MUSTAPHA: May those powers
That raised the Ottoman empire, and still guard it,
65   Reward your highness for this gracious favor
You throw upon your servant! It hath pleased
The most invincible, mightiest Amurath°
(To speak his other titles would take from him
That in himself does comprehend all greatness)
70   To make me the unworthy instrument
Of his command. Receive, divinest lady,   *Delivers a letter.*
This letter, signed by his victorious hand
And made authentic by the imperial seal.
There, when you find me mentioned, far be it from you

---

s.d.   **galliard**] lively French dance.
s.d.   **pantofles**] slippers.

75   To think it my ambition to presume
At such a happiness, which his powerful will,
From his great mind's magnificence, not my merit,
Hath showered upon me. But if your consent
Join with his good opinion and allowance,
80   To perfect what his favors have begun,
I shall, in my obsequiousness and duty,
Endeavor to prevent all just complaints
Which want of will to serve you may call on me.
DONUSA: His sacred majesty writes here that your valor
85   Against the Persian hath so won upon him,
That there's no grace or honor in his gift
Of which he can imagine you unworthy;
And, what's the greatest you can hope or aim at,
It is his pleasure you should be received
90   Into his royal family—provided,
For so far I am unconfined, that I
Affect and like your person. I expect not
The ceremony which he uses in
Bestowing of his daughters and his nieces;
95   As that he should present you for my slave,
To love you if you pleased me; or deliver
A poniard, on my least dislike, to kill you.
Such tyranny and pride agree not with
My softer disposition. Let it suffice,
100   For my first answer, that thus far I grace you.

Gives him her hand to kiss.

Hereafter, some time spent to make inquiry
Of the good parts and faculties of your mind,
You shall hear further from me.
MUSTAPHA: Though all torments
Really suffered, or in hell imagined
105   By curious fiction, in one hour's delay
Are wholly comprehended; I confess

---

81 **obsequiousness**] obedience.

That I stand bound in duty not to check at
Whatever you command or please to impose
For trial of my patience.

DONUSA: Let us find
110 Some other subject; too much of one theme cloys me.
Is't a full mart?

MUSTAPHA: A confluence of all nations
Are met together. There's variety, too,
Of all that merchants traffic for.

DONUSA: I know not—
I feel a virgin's longing to descend
115 So far from my own greatness as to be,
Though not a buyer, yet a looker on
Their strange commodities.

MUSTAPHA: If without a train
You dare be seen abroad, I'll dismiss mine
And wait upon you as a common man
And satisfy your wishes.

120 DONUSA: I embrace it.
Provide my veil and at the postern gate
Convey us out unseen. I trouble you.

MUSTAPHA: It is my happiness you deign to command me.   *Exeunt.*

SCENE 3.
THE MARKETPLACE.

A shop discovered, Gazet in it; Francisco and Vitelli walking by.

GAZET: What do you lack? Your choice China dishes, your pure Venetian
crystal of all sorts, of all neat and new fashions, from the mirror of the
madam to the private utensil of her chambermaid, and curious pictures
of the rarest beauties of Europa. What do you lack, gentlemen?

5 FRANCISCO: Take heed, I say! Howe'er it may appear
Impertinent, I must express my love

---

117 train] retinue.

In my advice and counsel. You are young
And may be tempted, and these Turkish dames
(Like English mastiffs that increase their fierceness
10   By being chained up), from the restraint of freedom,
If lust once fire their blood from a fair object,
Will run a course the fiends themselves would shake at
To enjoy their wanton ends.

VITELLI: Sir, you mistake me:
I am too full of woe to entertain
15   One thought of pleasure, though all Europe's queens
Kneeled at my feet and courted me, much less
To mix with such whose difference of faith
Must of necessity (or I must grant
Myself neglectful of all you have taught me)
Strangle such base desires.

20 FRANCISCO: Be constant in
That resolution. I'll abroad again
And learn, as far as is possible,
What may concern Paulina. Some two hours
Shall bring me back.   *Exit.*

VITELLI: All blessings wait upon you!

25 GAZET: Cold doings, sir: a mart, do you call this? 'Slight!
A puddingwife, or a witch with a thrum cap
That sells ale underground to such as come
To know their fortunes in a dead vacation,
Have ten to one more stirring.

VITELLI: We must be patient.

30 GAZET: Your seller by retail ought to be angry
But when he's fingering money.

Enter Grimaldi, Master, Boatswain, Sailors, and Turks.

---

26 **puddingwife**] female sausage seller.
26 **thrum cap**] cheap cap made from the thrums or waste ends of the yarn used in weaving.
28 **dead vacation**] here "dead" meaning commercially inactive. The economic slowdown of the "vacation" periods was contrasted with the busy period of the "term," when London law courts were in session and people flocked to the city.

VITELLI: Here are company—
    [*aside*] Defend me, my good angel; I behold
    A basilisk!

GAZET: What do you lack? What do you lack? Pure China
    dishes, clear crystal glasses, a dumb mistress to make love to? What do
35   you lack, gentlemen?

GRIMALDI: Thy mother for a bawd or, if thou hast
    A handsome one, thy sister for a whore!
    Without these, do not tell me of your trash,
    Or I shall spoil your market.

VITELLI: [*aside*] Old Grimaldi!

40 GRIMALDI: 'Zounds, wherefore do we put to sea, or stand
    The raging winds aloft, or piss upon
    The foamy waves when they rage most? Deride
    The thunder of the enemy's shot, board boldly
    A merchant's ship for prize, though we behold
45   The desperate gunner ready to give fire
    And blow the deck up? Wherefore shake we off
    Those scrupulous rags of charity and conscience
    Invented only to keep churchmen warm
    Or feed the hungry mouths of famished beggars;
50   But, when we touch the shore, to wallow in
    All sensual pleasures?

MASTER: Aye, but noble captain,
    To spare a little for an after-clap
    Were not improvidence.°

GRIMALDI: Hang consideration!
    When this is spent, is not our ship the same,
55   Our courage, too, the same, to fetch in more?
    The earth where it is fertilest returns not
    More than three harvests while the glorious sun
    Posts through the zodiac and makes up the year,
    But the sea, which is our mother (that embraces
60   Both the rich Indies in her outstretched arms),

---

33 **basilisk**] legendary serpent or dragon whose glance was said to kill.
33 **What do you lack?**] traditional cry of London street vendors.

Yields every day a crop, if we dare reap it.
No, no, my mates! Let tradesmen think of thrift
And usurers hoard up. Let our expense
Be as our comings in are—without bounds.
65   We are the Neptunes of the ocean,
And such as traffic shall pay sacrifice
Of their best lading. I'll have this canvas
Your boy wears lined with tissue, and the cates
You taste served up in gold. Though we carouse
70   The tears of orphans in our Greekish wines,
The sighs of undone widows paying for
The music bought to cheer us, ravished virgins
To slavery sold for coin to feed our riots,
We will have no compunction.

GAZET: Do you hear, sir?
We have paid for our ground.

GRIMALDI: Hum!

75 GAZET: And hum, too!
For all your big words, get you further off
And hinder not the prospect of our shop,
Or—

GRIMALDI: What will you do?

GAZET: Nothing, sir—but pray
Your worship to give me handsel.

GRIMALDI: By the ears,
Thus, sir, by the ears.   [*Grimaldi seizes Gazet by the ears.*]

MASTER: Hold, hold!

80 VITELLI: [*To Gazet*] You'll still be prating.

GRIMALDI: Come, let's be drunk! Then each man to his whore.
'Slight, how do you look! You had best go find a corner
To pray in and repent—do, do, and cry:
It will show fine in pirates.   *Exit.*

MASTER: We must follow,
Or he will spend our shares.

---

69 carouse] drink up entirely.
73 riots] unrestrained revelry; immoral excesses.
79 handsel] first money taken by a merchant in the morning.

85 BOATSWAIN: I fought for mine.
MASTER: Nor am I so precise but I can drab, too:
    We will not sit out for our parts.
BOATSWAIN: Agreed.

Exeunt Master, Boatswain, Sailors.

GAZET: The devil gnaw off his fingers! If he were
    In London among the clubs, up went his heels
90   For striking of a 'prentice. What do you lack?
    What do you lack, gentlemen?
FIRST TURK: I wonder how the viceroy can endure
    The insolence of this fellow.
SECOND TURK: He receives profit
    From the prizes he brings in, and that excuses
95   Whatever he commits. Ha! what are these?

Enter Mustapha, and Donusa veiled.

FIRST TURK: They seem of rank and quality. Observe 'em.
GAZET: What do you lack? See what you please to buy!
    Wares of all sorts, most honorable madonna.
VITELLI: Peace, sirrah, make no noise: these are not people
    To be jested with.
100 DONUSA: Is this the Christians' custom
    In the venting their commodities?
MUSTAPHA: Yes, best madam.
    But you may please to keep your way; here's nothing
    But toys and trifles not worth your observing.
DONUSA: Yes, for variety's sake pray you show us, friends,
    The chiefest of your wares.
105 VITELLI: Your ladyship's servant;
    And if in worth or title you are more,
    My ignorance plead my pardon.

---

86 precise] morally fastidious.
86 drab] go with prostitutes.
89 the clubs] groups of young men in London, mainly apprentices, who would gather at the cry of
"clubs" to take violent action against others.

DONUSA: He speaks well.

VITELLI: [*To Gazet*] Take down the looking-glass. [*To Donusa*] Here is
          a mirror
          Steeled so exactly, neither taking from
110   Nor flattering the object it returns
          To the beholder, that Narcissus might
          (And never grow enamored of himself)
          View his fair feature in it.

DONUSA: Poetical, too!

VITELLI: Here China dishes to serve in a banquet,
115   Though the voluptuous Persian sat a guest.
          Here crystal glasses, such as Ganymede
          Did fill with nectar to the Thunderer
          When he drank to Alcides and received him
          In the fellowship of the gods—true to the owners.
120   Corinthian plate studded with diamonds
          Concealed oft deadly poison; this pure metal
          So innocent is and faithful to the mistress
          Or master that possesses it, that, rather
          Than hold one drop that's venomous, of itself
125   It flies in pieces and deludes the traitor.

DONUSA: How movingly could this fellow treat upon
          A worthy subject, that finds such discourse
          To grace a trifle!

VITELLI: Here's a picture, madam;
          The masterpiece of Michaelangelo,
130   Our great Italian workman. Here's another
          So perfect at all parts that had Pygmalion
          Seen this, his prayers had been made to Venus
          To have given it life and his carved ivory image
          By poets ne'er remembered. They are indeed

---

109 **steeled**] made of polished steel.
111 **Narcissus**] figure from classical legend who fell in love with his own image reflected in the water of
a pond.
116 **Ganymede**] cupbearer to the classical gods on Mount Olympus.
117 **the Thunderer**] Zeus or Jove.
118 **Alcides**] another name for Hercules, who was made immortal after completing his twelve labors.
131 **Pygmalion**] legendary sculptor and king of Cyprus who fell in love with one of his statues. Venus
granted his prayer for the statue to come to life.

135 The rarest beauties of the Christian world
And nowhere to be equaled.

DONUSA: You are partial
In the cause of those you favor. I believe
I instantly could show you one, to theirs
Not much inferior.

VITELLI: With your pardon, madam,
I am incredulous.

140 DONUSA: Can you match me this? *Unveils herself.*

VITELLI: What wonder look I on! I'll search above
And suddenly attend you. *Exit.*

DONUSA: Are you amazed?
I'll bring you to yourself. *Breaks the glasses.*

MUSTAPHA: Ha! what's the matter?

GAZET: My master's ware! We are undone! O strange!

145 A lady to turn roarer and break glasses!
'Tis time to shut up shop then.

MUSTAPHA: [*To Donusa*] You seem moved.
If any language of these Christian dogs
Have called your anger on, in a frown show it,
And they are dead already.

DONUSA: The offense

150 Looks not so far. The foolish paltry fellow
Showed me some trifles and demanded of me,
For what I valued at so many aspers,
A thousand ducats. I confess he moved me;
Yet I should wrong myself, should such a beggar
Receive the least loss from me.

155 MUSTAPHA: Is it no more?

DONUSA: No, I assure you. [*To Gazet*] Bid him bring his bill
Tomorrow to the palace and enquire
For one "Donusa." That word gives him passage
Through all the guard. Say there he shall receive
Full satisfaction. [*To Mustapha*] Now, when you please.

---

145 **roarer**] a noisy, riotous bully.
153 **aspers**] small Turkish coins of silver, worth about two pence each.
154 **ducats**] valuable gold coins.

160 MUSTAPHA: I wait you.

FIRST TURK: We must not know them—let's shift off and vanish.

Exeunt Mustapha, Donusa, Turks.

GAZET: The swine's pox overtake you! There's a curse
   For a Turk that eats no hog's flesh.   *Re-enter Vitelli.*

VITELLI: Is she gone?

GAZET: Yes—you may see her handiwork.

VITELLI: No matter.
   Said she ought else?

165 GAZET: That you should wait upon her
   And there receive court payment, and to pass
   The guards she bids you only say you come
   To one Donusa.

VITELLI: How! Remove the wares;
   Do it without reply. The sultan's niece!

170 I have heard among the Turks for any lady
   To show her face bare argues love or speaks
   Her deadly hatred. What should I fear? My fortune
   Is sunk so low, there cannot fall upon me
   Aught worth my shunning. I will run the hazard:

175 She may be a means to free distressed Paulina;
   Or if offended, at the worst, to die
   Is a full period to calamity.   [*Exeunt.*]

ACT TWO

SCENE 1.
A ROOM IN DONUSA'S SECTION OF THE PALACE.

Enter Carazie and Manto.

CARAZIE: In the name of wonder, Manto, what hath my lady
   Done with herself since yesterday?

---

161 **shift off**] remove ourselves, withdraw.

MANTO: I know not.
    Malicious men report we are all guided
    In our affections by a wandering planet,
5   But such a sudden change in such a person
    May stand for an example to confirm
    Their false assertion.

CARAZIE: She's now pettish, froward;
    Music, discourse, observance—tedious to her.

MANTO: She slept not the last night and yet prevented
10   The rising sun in being up before him;
    Called for a costly bath, then willed the rooms
    Should be perfumed; ransacked her cabinets
    For her choice and riches jewels; and appears now
    Like Cynthia in full glory, waited on
    By the fairest of the stars.

15 CARAZIE: Can you guess the reason
    Why the aga of the janissaries and he
    That guards the entrance of the inmost port
    Were called before her?

MANTO: They are both her creatures
    And by her grace preferred, but I am ignorant
    To what purpose they were sent for.   *Enter Donusa.*

20 CARAZIE: Here she comes,
    Full of sad thoughts: we must stand further off.
    What a frown was that!

MANTO: Forbear.

CARAZIE: I pity her.

DONUSA: What magic hath transformed me from myself?
    Where is my virgin pride? How have I lost
25   My boasted freedom? What new fire burns up
    My scorched entrails? What unknown desires
    Invade and take possession of my soul,
    All virtuous objects vanished? Have I stood
    The shock of fierce temptations, stopped mine ears
30   Against all siren notes' lust ever sung,
    To draw my bark of chastity (that with wonder
    Hath kept a constant and an honored course)

---

31 **bark**] small ship.

Into the gulf of a deserved ill fame,
Now to fall unpitied? And in a moment
35   With mine own hands dig up a grave to bury
The monumental heap of all my years
Employed in noble actions? O my fate!
But there is no resisting. I obey thee,
Imperious god of love, and willingly
40   Put mine own fetters on to grace thy triumph.
'Twere, therefore, more than cruelty in thee
To use me like a tyranne. What poor means
Must I make use of now? And flatter such
To whom, till I betrayed my liberty,
45   One gracious look of mine would have erected
An altar to my service! How now, Manto?
My ever careful woman! And Carazie—
Thou hast been faithful, too.

CARAZIE: I dare not call
My life mine own, since it is yours, but gladly
50   Will part with it whene'er you shall command me
And think I fall a martyr, so my death
May give life to your pleasures.

MANTO: But vouchsafe
To let me understand what you desire
Should be effected: I will undertake it
55   And curse myself for cowardice if I pause
To ask a reason why.

DONUSA: I am comforted
In the tender of your service but shall be
Confirmed in my full joys in the performance.
Yet trust me: I will not impose upon you
60   But what you stand engaged for to a mistress
(Such as I have been to you). All I ask
Is faith—and secrecy.

CARAZIE: Say but you doubt me,
And, to secure you, I'll cut out my tongue;
I am libbed in the breech already.

---

42 **use me like a tyranne**] treat me tyrannically.
63 **libbed in the breech**] castrated.

MANTO: Do not hinder
  Yourself by these delays.
65 DONUSA: Thus then I whisper
  Mine own shame to you—O that I should blush
  To speak what I so much desire to do!
  And, further— *Whispers and uses vehement actions.*
MANTO: Is this all?
DONUSA: Think it not base
  Although I know the office undergoes
  A coarse construction.
70 CARAZIE: Coarse? 'Tis but procuring;
  A smock employment, which has made more knights
  (In a country I could name) than twenty years
  Of service in the field.°
DONUSA: You have my ends.
MANTO: Which say you have arrived at: be not wanting
  To yourself and fear not us.
75 CARAZIE: I know my burthen;
  I'll bear it with delight.
MANTO: Talk not, but do.

Exit Carazie and Manto.

DONUSA: O Love, what poor shifts thou dost force us to! *Exit.*

SCENE 2.
IN THE VICEREGAL PALACE.

Enter Aga, Capiaga and Janissaries.

AGA: She was ever our good mistress and our maker,
  And should we check at a little hazard for her,
  We were unthankful.

---

71 **smock employment**] sexual service, a "smock" being a woman's chemise or linen undergarment.
2 **check at a little hazard**] hesitate because of a small risk or danger.

CAPIAGA: I dare pawn my head,
    'Tis some disguisèd minion of the court,
5   Sent from great Amurath to learn from her
    The viceroy's actions.
AGA: That concerns not us:
    His fall may be our rise. Whate'er he be,
    He passes through my guards.
CAPIAGA: And mine—provided
    He give the word.   *Enter Vitelli.*
VITELLI: To faint now, being thus far,
    Would argue me of cowardice.
10 AGA: Stand—the word.
    Or, being a Christian, to press thus far
    Forfeits thy life.
VITELLI: Donusa.
AGA: Pass in peace.

Exit Aga and Janissaries.

VITELLI: What a privilege her name bears! 'Tis wondrous strange!
    The captain of the janissaries! If the great officer,
15 The guardian of the inner port, deny not—
CAPIAGA: Thy warrant—speak, or thou art dead.
VITELLI: Donusa.
CAPIAGA: That protects thee. Without fear, enter.
    So: discharge the watch.   *Exeunt.*

SCENE 3.
AN OUTER ROOM IN THE PALACE.

Enter Carazie and Manto.

CARAZIE: Though he hath passed the aga and chief porter,
    This cannot be the man.

---

15 **port**] door.
1 **chief porter**] the capiaga, an officer and doorkeeper who controlled comings and goings in the palace. This was a position of privilege and power.

MANTO: By her description,
  I am sure it is.
CARAZIE: O women, women,
  What are you? A great lady dote upon
  A haberdasher of small wares!
5 MANTO: Pish! Thou hast none.
CARAZIE: No; if I had, I might have served the turn:
  This 'tis to want munition, when a man
  Should make a breach and enter.   *Enter Vitelli.*
MANTO: Sir, you are welcome.
  Think what 'tis to be happy and possess it.
10 CARAZIE: Perfume the rooms there and make way. Let music
  With choice notes entertain the man the princess
  Now purposes to honor.
VITELLI: I am ravished.   *Exeunt.*

SCENE 4.
A ROOM OF STATE IN DONUSA'S SECTION
OF THE PALACE.

A table set forth, with jewels and bags upon it. Loud music.
Enter Donusa, [who] takes a chair. [Enter] Carazie, Vitelli and Manto,
[who approach her].

DONUSA: Sing o'er the ditty that I last composed
  Upon my lovesick passions. Suit your voice
  To the music that's placed yonder: we shall hear you
  With more delight and pleasure.
CARAZIE: I obey you.   *[Carazie sings.]*
5 VITELLI: Is not this Tempe? Or the blessed shades
  Where innocent spirits reside? Or do I dream,
  And this a heavenly vision? Howsoever,
  It is a sight too glorious to behold
  For such a wretch as I am.   *Stands amazed.*

---

5 Tempe] valley in Arcadian Greece, a pastoral paradise.
5 blessed shades] the Elysian fields in the classical underworld.

CARAZIE: He is daunted.

10 MANTO: Speak to him, madam; cheer him up, or you
       Destroy what you have builded.

CARAZIE: [*aside*] Would I were furnished
       With his artillery, and if I stood
       Gaping as he does, hang me.

[Exit Carazie and Manto.]

VITELLI: That I might ever dream thus!   *He kneels.*

DONUSA: Banish amazement,
15   You wake! Your debtor tells you so, your debtor,
       And to assure you that I am a substance
       And no aerial figure, thus I raise you.   [*She raises him to his feet.*]
       Why do you shake? My soft touch brings no ague.
       No biting frost is in this palm, nor are
20   My looks like to the Gorgon's head that turn
       Men into statues; rather they have power
       (Or I have been abused) where they bestow
       Their influence (let me prove it truth in you)
       To give to dead men motion.

VITELLI: Can this be?
25   May I believe my senses? Dare I think
       I have a memory or that you are
       That excellent creature that of late disdained not
       To look on my poor trifles?

DONUSA: I am she.

VITELLI: The owner of that blessed name, Donusa,
30   Which, like a potent charm, although pronounced
       By my profane but much unworthier tongue,
       Hath brought me safe to this forbidden place
       Where Christian yet ne'er trode.

DONUSA: I am the same.

VITELLI: And to what end—great lady, pardon me
35   That I presume to ask—did your command

---

17 aerial figure] spirit made of air.
20 Gorgon's head] the head of Medusa, who had snakes for hair and eyes that turned anyone looking
into them to stone.

Command me hither? Or what am I, to whom
You should vouchsafe your favors—nay, your angers?
If any wild or uncollected speech,
Offensively delivered, or my doubt
40 Of your unknown perfections, have displeased you,
You wrong your indignation to pronounce,
Yourself, my sentence. To have seen you only
And to have touched that fortune-making hand
Will with delight weigh down all tortures that
45 A flinty hangman's rage could execute
Or rigid tyranny command with pleasure.
DONUSA: How the abundance of good flowing to thee
Is wronged in this simplicity! And these bounties,
Which all our Eastern kings have kneeled in vain for,
50 Do, by thy ignorance, or willful fear,
Meet with a false construction! Christian, know
(For till thou art mine by a nearer name,
That title, though abhorred here, takes not from
Thy entertainment) that 'tis not the fashion
55 Among the greatest and the fairest dames
This Turkish empire gladly owes and bows to,
To punish where there's no offense, or nourish
Displeasures against those without whose mercy
They part with all felicity. Prithee, be wise
60 And gently understand me. Do not force her,
That ne'er knew aught but to command, nor e'er read
The elements of affection but from such
As gladly sued to her, in the infancy
Of her newborn desires to be at once
Importunate and immodest.
65 VITELLI: Did I know,
Great lady, your commands or to what purpose
This personated passion tends (since 'twere
A crime in me deserving death to think
It is your own) I should, to make you sport,

---

38 uncollected] unpremeditated.
45 flinty] hard and unrelenting; merciless.
48 simplicity] humbleness.
56 owes] acknowledges.

70   Take any shape you please t'impose upon me
        And with joy strive to serve you.

DONUSA: Sport? Thou art cruel,
        If that thou canst interpret my descent
        From my high birth and greatness but to be
        A part, in which I truly act myself!
75   And I must hold thee for a dull spectator,
        If it stir not affection and invite
        Compassion for my sufferings. Be thou taught
        By my example to make satisfaction
        For wrongs unjustly offered. Willingly
80   I do confess my fault: I injured thee
        In some poor petty trifles; thus I pay for
        The trespass I did to thee. Here—receive
        These bags stuffed full of our imperial coin,
        Or if this payment be too light, take here
85   These gems for which the slavish Indian dives
        To the bottom of the main; or if thou scorn
        These as base dross (which take but common minds),
        But fancy any honor in my gift
        (Which is unbounded as the sultan's power)
        And be possessed of 't.

90 VITELLI: I am overwhelmed
        With the weight of happiness you throw upon me.
        Nor can it fall in my imagination
        What wrong you e'er have done me, and much less
        How, like a royal merchant, to return
        Your great magnificence.

95 DONUSA: They are degrees,
        Not ends, of my intended favors to thee.
        These seeds of bounty I yet scatter on
        A glebe I have not tried—but be thou thankful,
        The harvest is to come.

VITELLI: What can be added
100   To that which I already have received,
        I cannot comprehend.

---

86 main] sea.
98 a glebe I have not tried] a piece of land I have not yet cultivated.

DANUSA: The tender of
    Myself. Why dost thou start? And in that gift,
    Full restitution of that virgin freedom
    Which thou hast robbed me of. Yet I profess,
105   I so far prize the lovely thief that stole it,
    That, were it possible thou couldst restore
    What thou unwittingly hast ravished from me,
    I should refuse the present.

VITELLI: How I shake
    In my constant resolution! And my flesh,
110   Rebellious to my better part, now tells me
    (As if it were a strong defense of frailty)
    A hermit in a desert trenched with prayers
    Could not resist this battery.

DONUSA: Thou an Italian?
    Nay more—I know't—a natural Venetian,
115   Such as are courtiers born to please fair ladies,
    Yet come thus slowly on?

VITELLI: Excuse me, madam.
    What imputation soe'er the world
    Is pleased to lay upon us, in myself
    I am so innocent that I know not what 'tis
    That I should offer.

120 DONUSA: By instinct I'll teach thee
    And with such ease as love makes me to ask it.
    When a young lady wrings you by the hand, thus,
    Or with an amorous touch presses your foot,
    Looks babies in your eyes, plays with your locks,
125   Do not you find without a tutor's help
    What 'tis she looks for?

VITELLI: I am grown already
    Skillful in the mystery.

DONUSA: Or if thus she kiss you,
    Then tastes your lips again—   *[She kisses him.]*

---

110 **better part**] rational soul or mind.
118 **us**] Venetian courtiers.
124 **Looks babies in your eyes**] stares intently into your eyes and sees her own "baby-sized" image reflected there.
127 **mystery**] skilled trade or craft.

VITELLI: That latter blow
Has beat all chaste thoughts from me.
DONUSA: Say she points to
130   Some private room the sunbeams never enter,
Provoking dishes passing by to heighten
Declined appetite, active music ushering
Your fainting steps, the waiters, too, as born dumb,
Not daring to look on you.   *Exit, inviting him to follow.*
VITELLI: Though the Devil
135   Stood by and roared, I follow! Now I find
That virtue's but a word, and no sure guard
If set upon by beauty and reward.   *Exit.*

SCENE 5.
A HALL IN ASAMBEG'S PALACE.

Enter Aga, Capiaga, Grimaldi, Master, Boatswain and others.

AGA: The Devil's in him, I think.
GRIMALDI: Let him be damned, too.
I'll look on him, though he stared as wild as hell.
Nay, I'll go near to tell him to his teeth
If he mends not suddenly and proves more thankful,
5   We do him too much service. Were't not for shame now
I could turn honest and forswear my trade,
Which, next to being trussed up at the mainyard
By some Low Country butterbox, I hate
As deadly as I do fasting, or long grace
When meat cools on the table.
10 CAPIAGA: But take heed:
You know his violent nature.
GRIMALDI: Let his whores
And catamites know't. I understand myself
And how unmanly 'tis to sit at home

---

7 trussed up] hung.
8 butterbox] derisive term for a Dutchman.

And rail at us, that run abroad all hazards,
15   If every week we bring not home new pillage
For the fatting his seraglio.

Enter Asambeg and Mustapha.

AGA: Here he comes.
CAPIAGA: How terrible he looks!
GRIMALDI: To such as fear him.
The viceroy, Asambeg! Were he the sultan's self,
He will let us know a reason for his fury,
20   Or we must take leave without his allowance
To be merry with our ignorance.
ASAMBEG: Mahomet's hell
Light on you all! You crouch and cringe now! Where
Was the terror of my just frowns when you suffered
Those thieves of Malta,° almost in our harbor,
25   To board a ship and bear her safely off
While you stood idle lookers on?
AGA: The odds
In the men and shipping, and the suddenness
Of their departure, yielding us no leisure
To send forth others to relieve our own,
Deterred us, mighty sir.
30 ASAMBEG: Deterred you? Cowards!
How durst you only entertain the knowledge
Of what fear was, but in the not performance
Of our command? In me great Amurath spake!
My voice did echo to your ears his thunder
35   And willed you, like so many sea-born tritons,
Armed only with the trumpets of your courage,
To swim up to her and (like remoras
Hanging upon her keel) to stay her flight

15–16 **new pillage / For the fatting his seraglio**] captives sold to Asembeg to serve as slaves and con-
cubines in his harem.
26 **lookers on**] spectators.
31–33 **How durst you . . . Of our command**] How did you dare to let your fear of the Maltese attack-
ers outweigh your fear of disobeying me?

Till rescue, sent from us, had fetched you off.

40   You think you are safe now. Who durst but dispute it

Or make it questionable, if this moment

I charged you from yon hanging cliff that glasses

His rugged forehead in the neighboring lake

To throw yourselves down headlong? Or, like faggots,

45   To fill the ditches of defended forts

While on your backs we marched up to the breach?

GRIMALDI: That would not I.

ASAMBEG: Ha?

GRIMALDI: Yet I dare as much

As any of the sultan's boldest sons

(Whose heaven and hell hang on his frown or smile),

His warlike janissaries.

50 ASAMBEG: Add one syllable more,

Thou dost pronounce upon thyself a sentence

That earthquake-like will swallow thee.

GRIMALDI: Let it open—

I'll stand the hazard. Those contemned thieves,

Your fellow-pirates, sir, the bold Maltese,

55   Whom with your looks you think to quell, at Rhodes

Laughed at great Solyman's anger, and if treason

Had not delivered them into his power,

He had grown old in glory as in years

At that so fatal siege, or risen with shame,

His hopes and threats deluded.°

60 ASAMBEG: Our great prophet!

How have I lost my anger and my power?

GRIMALDI: Find it and use it on thy flatterers,

And not upon thy friends that dare speak truth.

These knights of Malta, but a handful to

65   Your armies that drink rivers up, have stood

Your fury at the height, and with their crosses

Struck pale your horned moons. These men of Malta,

---

42 **glasses**] mirrors, reflects.

59 **risen**] withdrawn, retreated.

67 **horned moons**] crescent moons displayed on Turkish military banners.

Since I took pay from you, I have met and fought with,
Upon advantage, too; yet to speak truth,
70　By the soul of honor I have ever found them
As provident to direct and bold to do
As any trained up in your discipline,
Ravished from other nations.°

MUSTAPHA:　　　　　　　　I perceive
The lightning in his fiery looks; the cloud
Is broke already.

75　GRIMALDI:　　　　Think not, therefore, sir,
That you alone are giants, and such pigmies
You war upon.

ASAMBEG:　　　　Villain, I'll make thee know
Thou hast blasphemed the Ottoman power, and safer
At noonday might have given fire to St. Mark's,
80　Your proud Venetian temple. Seize upon him!
I am not so near reconciled to him
To bid him die: that were a benefit
The dog's unworthy of. To our use confiscate
All that he stands possessed of. Let him taste
85　The misery of want, and his vain riots,
Like to so many walking ghosts, affright him
Where'er he sets his desperate foot. Who is't
That does command you?

GRIMALDI:　　　　　　　　Is this the reward
For all my service and the rape I made
On fair Paulina?

90　ASAMBEG:　　　　Drag him hence—he dies
That dallies but a minute.

Grimaldi [is] dragged off, his head covered.

BOATSWAIN:　　　　　　　　What's become
Of our shares now, Master?

MASTER:　　　　　　　　Would he had been born dumb!
The beggar's cure, patience, is all that's left us.

89　**rape I made**] the abduction I carried out.

Exit Master and Boatswain.

MUSTAPHA: 'Twas but intemperance of speech. Excuse him;
95   Let me prevail so far. Fame gives him out
        For a deserving fellow.
ASAMBEG: At Aleppo,
        I durst not press you so far: give me leave
        To use my own will and command in Tunis,
        And if you please, my privacy.
MUSTAPHA: I will see you
        When this high wind's blown o'er.
100 ASAMBEG: So shall you find me
        Ready to do you service. Rage, now leave me.   *Exit Mustapha.*
        Stern looks, and all the ceremonious forms
        Attending on dread majesty, fly from
        Transformed Asambeg. Why should I hug   *Plucks out a gilt key.*
105   So near my heart what leads me to my prison,
        Where she that is enthralled commands her keeper
        And robs me of the fierceness I was born with?
        Stout men quake at my frowns, and in return
        I tremble at her softness. Base Grimaldi
110   But only named Paulina, and the charm
        Had almost choked my fury ere I could
        Pronounce his sentence. Would, when first I saw her,
        Mine eyes had met with lightning, and in place
        Of hearing her enchanting tongue the shrieks
115   Of mandrakes had made music to my slumbers!
        For now I only walk a loving dream
        And, but to my dishonor, never wake;
        And yet am blind but when I see the object
        And madly dote on it. Appear, bright spark

        Opens a door; Paulina [is] discovered [and] comes forth.

120   Of all perfection! Any simile
        Borrowed from diamonds or the fairest stars,

114–15 shrieks of mandrakes] the mandrake is a plant with a root resembling the human form. According to folk belief, it emits a deadly shriek when uprooted.

To help me to express how dear I prize
Thy unmatched graces, will rise up and chide me
For poor detraction.

PAULINA: I despise thy flatteries:

125   Thus spit at 'em and scorn 'em, and being armed
In the assurance of my innocent virtue,
I stamp upon all doubts, all fears, all tortures
Thy barbarous cruelty (or what's worse, thy dotage,
The worthy parent of thy jealousy)
Can shower upon me.

130 ASAMBEG: If these bitter taunts
Ravish me from myself and make me think
My greedy ears receive angelical sounds,
How would this tongue, turned to a loving note,
Invade and take possession of my soul,
Which then I durst not call my own!

135 PAULINA: Thou art false,
Falser than thy religion. Do but think me
Something above a beast—nay more, a monster
Would fright the sun to look on—and then tell me
If this base usage can invite affection?

140   If to be mewed up and excluded from
Human society, the use of pleasures,
The necessary—not superfluous—duties
Of servants to discharge those offices
I blush to name—

ASAMBEG: Of servants? Can you think

145   That I, that dare not trust the eye of heaven
To look upon your beauties, that deny
Myself the happiness to touch your pureness,
Will e'er consent an eunuch or bought handmaid
Shall once approach you? There is something in you

150   That can work miracles, or I am cozened,
Dispose and alter sexes. To my wrong,
In spite of nature, I will be your nurse,
Your woman, your physician, and your fool
Till with your free consent (which I have vowed

155   Never to force) you grace me with a name
That shall supply all these.

PAULINA: What is't?

ASAMBEG: Your husband.

PAULINA: My hangman when thou pleasest.

ASAMBEG: Thus I guard me
    Against your further angers.   [*Leads her to the door.*]

PAULINA: Which shall reach thee,
    Though I were in the center.

[Asambeg closes the door upon her] and locks it [with the key.]

ASAMBEG: Such a spirit
160   In such a small proportion I ne'er read of,
    Which time must alter. Ravish her, I dare not:
    The magic that she wears about her neck,
    I think, defends her. This devotion paid
    to this sweet saint, mistress of my sour pain,
165   'Tis fit I take mine own rough shape again.   *Exit.*

SCENE 6.
A STREET NEAR THE PALACE.

Enter Francisco and Gazet.

FRANCISCO: I think he's lost.

GAZET: 'Tis ten to one of that.
    I ne'er knew citizen turn courtier yet
    But he lost his credit, though he saved himself.
    Why, look you, sir; there are so many lobbies,
5   Out-offices, and disputations here
    Behind these Turkish hangings that a Christian
    Hardly gets off but circumcised.

FRANCISCO: I am troubled,

Enter Vitelli, [dressed in fine clothes, with] Carazie and Manto.

----

159 **the center**] center of the earth.

Troubled exceedingly. Ha! what are these?

GAZET: One, by his rich suit, should be some French ambassador;°
    For his train, I think they are Turks.

10 FRANCISCO: Peace! Be not seen.

CARAZIE: You are now past all the guards, and undiscovered
    You may return.

VITELLI: There's for your pains: forget not
    My humblest service to the best of ladies.

MANTO: Deserve her favor, sir, in making haste
    For a second entertainment.

15 VITELLI: Do not doubt me;
    I shall not live till then.   *Exit Carazie and Manto.*

GAZET: The train is vanished.
    They have done him some good office, he's so free
    And liberal of his gold. Ha, do I dream,
    Or is this mine own natural master?

FRANCISCO: 'Tis he,

20   But strangely metamorphosed. You have made, sir,
    A prosperous voyage. Heaven grant it be honest:
    I shall rejoice then, too.

GAZET: You make him blush
    To talk of honesty. You were but now
    In the giving vein and may think of Gazet,
    Your worship's 'prentice.

25 VITELLI: There's gold: be thou free, too,
    And master of my shop and all the wares
    We brought from Venice.

GAZET: Rivo, then!

VITELLI: Dear sir,
    This place affords not privacy for discourse,
    But I can tell you wonders. My rich habit

30   Deserves least admiration. There's nothing
    That can fall in the compass of your wishes
    (Though it were to redeem a thousand slaves
    From the Turkish galleys, or at home to erect

---

27 Rivo] according to the *O.E.D.,* "an exclamation used at revels or drinking-bouts."

Some pious work to shame all hospitals),
But I am master of the means.
35 FRANCISCO: 'Tis strange.
VITELLI: As I walk, I'll tell you more.
GAZET: Pray you, a word, sir;
And then I will put on. I have one boon more.
VITELLI: What is't? Speak freely.
GAZET: Thus, then: as I am master
Of your shop and wares, pray you, help me to some trucking
40   With your last she-customer. Though she crack my best piece,
I will endure it with patience.
VITELLI: Leave your prating.
GAZET: I may. You have been doing; we will do, too.
FRANCISCO: I am amazed, yet will not blame nor chide you
Till you inform me further. Yet must say,
45   They steer not the right course, nor traffic well,
That seek a passage to reach heaven through hell.   *Exeunt.*

ACT THREE

SCENE 1.
A ROOM IN DONUSA'S SECTION OF THE PALACE.

Enter Donusa and Manto.

DONUSA: When said he, he would come again?
MANTO: He swore
Short minutes should be tedious ages to him
Until the tender of his second service,
So much he seemed transported with the first.
5 DONUSA: I am sure I was. I charge thee, Manto, tell me—
By all my favors and my bounties, truly—
Whether thou art a virgin or, like me,
Hast forfeited that name?

---

39 **trucking**] commercial exchange, dealings.

MANTO: A virgin, madam?
At my years? Being a waiting-woman, and in court, too?
10   That were miraculous! I so long since lost
That barren burthen, I almost forget
That ever I was one.

DONUSA: And could thy friends
Read in thy face, thy maidenhead gone, that thou
Hadst parted with it?

MANTO: No, indeed. I passed
15   For current many years after, till, by fortune,
Long and continued practice in the sport
Blew up my deck. A husband then was found out
By my indulgent father, and to the world
All was made whole again. What need you fear, then,
20   That at your pleasure may repair your honor,
Durst any envious or malicious tongue
Presume to taint it?   *Enter Carazie.*

DONUSA: How now?

CARAZIE: Madam, the basha
Humbly desires access.

DONUSA: If it had been
My neat Italian, thou hadst met my wishes.
Tell him we would be private.

25 CARAZIE: So I did,
But he is much importunate.

MANTO: Best dispatch him:
His lingering here else will deter the other
From making his approach.

DONUSA: His entertainment
Shall not invite a second visit. Go;
Say we are pleased.

> *[Exit Carazie. Re-enter Carazie with] Mustapha.*

MUSTAPHA: All happiness—
30 DONUSA: Be sudden.
'Twas saucy rudeness in you, sir, to press

14–15 **passed for current**] was taken as a genuine coin (as a true virgin).

17 **Blew up my deck**] caused me to become pregnant. Here "deck" means "covering."

On my retirements, but ridiculous folly
To waste the time (that might be better spent)
In complimental wishes.

CARAZIE: [*aside*] There's a cooling
For his hot encounter.

35 DONUSA: Come you here to stare?
If you have lost your tongue and use of speech,
Resign your government: there's a mute's place void
In my uncle's court, I hear; and you may work me
To write for your preferment.

MUSTAPHA: This is strange!
40   I know not, madam, what neglect of mine
Has called this scorn upon me.

DONUSA: To the purpose—
My will's a reason, and we stand not bound
To yield account to you.

MUSTAPHA: Not of your angers,
But with erected ears I should hear from you
45   The story of your good opinion of me,
Confirmed by love and favors.

DONUSA: How deserved?
I have considered you from head to foot,
And can find nothing in that wainscot face
That can teach me to dote; nor am I taken
50   With your grim aspect or toadpool-like complexion.
Those scars you glory in, I fear to look on;
And had much rather hear a merry tale
Than all your battles won with blood and sweat,
Though you belch forth the stink, too, in the service
55   And swear by your mustachios all is true.
You are yet too rough for me: purge and take physic,
Purchase perfumers, get me some French tailor
To new-create you; the first shape you were made with

---

48 **wainscot face**] a face hardened or colored like old wainscot (oak paneling). The actor playing the role of Mustapha was probably made up in black face to look the part of a stage Saracen or Islamic warrior.
50 **toadpool-like complexion**] Donusa may be comparing the dark-skinned Mustapha's "complexion" to the black color of a tadpole's skin, or she may be suggesting that his face is as foul as a toad-breeding pond.

Is quite worn out. Let your barber wash your face, too:
60   You look yet like a bugbear to fright children.
Till when, I take my leave. Wait me, Carazie.

Exit Donusa and Carazie.

MUSTAPHA: Stay you, my lady's cabinet-key.
MANTO: How's this, sir!
MUSTAPHA: Stay and stand quietly, or you shall fall else;
Not to firk your belly up, flounder-like, but never
65   To rise again. Offer but to unlock
These doors that stop your fugitive tongue (observe me),
                                    [*Draws his sword.*]
And by my fury, I'll fix there this bolt
To bar thy speech forever.° So! Be safe now
And but resolve me, not of what I doubt,
70   But bring assurance to a thing believed;
Thou mak'st thyself a fortune, not depending
On the uncertain favors of a mistress,
But art thyself one. I'll not so far question
My judgment and observance as to ask
75   Why I am slighted and contemned, but in
Whose favor it is done. I that have read
The copious volumes of all women's falsehood,
Commented on by the heart-breaking groans
Of abused lovers, all the doubts washed off
80   With fruitless tears, the spider's cobweb veil
Of arguments alleged in their defense,
Blown off with sighs of desperate men, and they
Appearing in their full deformity,
Know that some other hath displanted me
85   With her dishonor. Has she given it up?
Confirm it in two syllables.

---

64 firk] stir up; set in motion.
64 flounder-like] flat as a flounder, suggesting a prone sexual position.
67 this bolt] this sword.
85 Has she given it up?] Has Donusa given up her virginity?

MANTO: She has.

MUSTAPHA: I cherish thy confession thus, and thus.   *Gives her jewels.*

    Be mine. Again I court thee thus, and thus.

    Now prove but constant to my ends.

MANTO: By all—

90 MUSTAPHA: Enough! I dare not doubt thee. O land crocodiles

    Made of Egyptian slime, accursed women!

    But 'tis no time to rail—come, my best Manto.   *Exeunt.*

SCENE 2.
STREET IN TUNIS.

Enter Vitelli and Francisco.

VITELLI: Sir, as you are my confessor, you stand bound

    Not to reveal whatever I discover

    In that religious way: nor dare I doubt you.

    Let it suffice you have made me see my follies

5   And wrought, perhaps, compunction; for I would not

    Appear an hypocrite. But when you impose

    A penance on me beyond flesh and blood

    To undergo, you must instruct me how

    To put off the conditions of a man;

10   Or if not pardon, at the least, excuse

    My disobedience. Yet despair not, sir;

    For though I take mine own way, I shall do

    Something that may hereafter, to my glory,

    Speak me your scholar.

FRANCISCO: I enjoin you not

    To go, but send.

15 VITELLI: That were a petty trial,

    Not worth one so long taught and exercised

    Under so grave a master. Reverend Francisco,

    My friend, my father, in that word, my all;

---

90 **crocodiles**] crocodiles were associated with hypocrisy because of the feigned "crocodile tears" they were said to shed while luring or devouring their victims.

2 **discover**] reveal.

14 **scholar**] student.

Rest confident you shall hear something of me
20 That will redeem me in your good opinion
Or judge me lost for ever. Send Gazet
(She shall give order that he may have entrance)
To acquaint you with my fortunes.   *Exit.*
FRANCISCO: Go, and prosper.
Holy saints guide and strengthen thee! Howsoever
25 As my endeavors are, so may they find
Gracious acceptance.

Enter Gazet, and Grimaldi in rags.

GAZET: Now you do not roar, sir;
You speak not tempests nor take ear-rent from
A poor shopkeeper. Do you remember that, sir?
I wear your marks here still.
FRANCISCO: Can this be possible?
All wonders are not ceased then.
30 GRIMALDI: Do: abuse me,
Spit on me, spurn me, pull me by the nose,
Thrust out these fiery eyes that yesterday
Would have looked thee dead.
GAZET: O save me, sir!
GRIMALDI: Fear nothing:
I am tame and quiet. There's no wrong can force me
35 To remember what I was. I have forgot
I e'er had ireful fierceness, a steeled heart
Insensible of compassion to others;
Nor is it fit that I should think myself
Worth mine own pity. Oh!
FRANCISCO: Grows this dejection
From his disgrace, do you say?
40 GAZET: Why, he's cashiered, sir.
His ships, his goods, his livery punks, confiscate;
And there is such a punishment laid upon him!

---

27 **take ear-rent**] suggests 1. charge rent for keeping a stall in the market, 2. collect a "tax" imposed on
a listener's patience by a noisy speaker, and 3. tear or pull the ears.
40 **cashiered**] suddenly and disgracefully dismissed from a position of command.
41 **livery punks**] servant-prostitutes.

The miserable rogue must steal no more,
Nor drink, nor drab.

FRANCISCO: Does that torment him?

GAZET: O sir!

45   Should the state take order to bar men of acres
From these two laudable recreations,
Drinking and whoring, how should panders purchase,
Or thrifty whores build hospitals? 'Slid, if I,
That since I am made free may write myself
50   A city gallant, should forfeit two such charters,
I should be stoned to death and ne'er be pitied
By the liveries of those companies.°

FRANCISCO: You'll be whipped, sir,
If you bridle not your tongue. Haste to the palace:
Your master looks for you.

GAZET: My quondam master.

55   Rich sons forget they ever had poor fathers;
In servants 'tis more pardonable. As a companion,
Or so, I may consent. But is there hope, sir,
He has got me a good chapwoman? Pray you write
A word or two in my behalf.

FRANCISCO: Out, rascal!

GAZET: I feel some insurrections.

FRANCISCO: Hence!

60 GAZET: I vanish.   *Exit.*

GRIMALDI: Why should I study a defense or comfort,
In whom black guilt and misery, if balanced,
I know not which would turn the scale? Look upward
I dare not; for should it but be believed
65   That I (dyed deep in hell's most horrid colors)
Should dare to hope for mercy, it would leave
No check or feeling in men innocent

---

45 **men of acres**] wealthy landowners.
49 **made free**] made a property-owning citizen, no longer a servant.
50 **city gallant**] a high-spirited man about town, prone to amorous exploits.
54 **quondam**] former.
58 **chapwoman**] female hawker or dealer in petty merchandise.
60 **insurrections**] "rebellious impulses and sexual desires ('risings')" (Edwards and Gibson).

To catch at sins the devil ne'er taught mankind yet.
No, I must downward, downward! Though repentance
70　Could borrow all the glorious wings of grace,
My mountainous weight of sins would crack their pinions
And sink them to hell with me.
FRANCISCO:　　　　　　　　　Dreadful! Hear me,
Thou miserable man.
GRIMALDI:　　　　　Good sir, deny not
But that there is no punishment beyond
Damnation.

Enter Master and Boatswain.

75　MASTER:　　　Yonder he is. I pity him.
BOATSWAIN: Take comfort, captain; we live still to serve you.
GRIMALDI: Serve me? I am a devil already: leave me,
Stand further off—you are blasted else! I have heard
Schoolmen affirm man's body is composed
80　Of the four elements and, as in league together
They nourish life, so each of them affords
Liberty to the soul when it grows weary
Of this fleshy prison. Which shall I make choice of?
The fire? No—I shall feel that hereafter.
85　The earth will not receive me. Should some whirlwind
Snatch me into the air, and I hang there,
Perpetual plagues would dwell upon the earth;
And those superior bodies that pour down
Their cheerful influence deny to pass it
90　Through those vast regions I have infected.
The sea? Aye, that is justice. There I ploughed up
Mischief as deep as hell; there, there, I'll hide
This cursèd lump of clay. May it turn rocks
Where plummet's weight could never reach the sands,
95　And grind the ribs of all such barks as press

---

71 **pinions**] wing bones.
79 **Schoolmen**] theologians.
88 **superior bodies**] planets and stars.

The ocean's breast in my unlawful course!
I haste then to thee: let thy ravenous womb,
Whom all things else deny, be now my tomb!   *Exit.*
MASTER: Follow him and restrain him.   *Exit Boatswain.*
FRANCISCO: Let this stand
100   For an example to you. I'll provide
           A lodging for him and apply such cures
           To his wounded conscience as heaven hath lent me.
           He's now my second care, and my profession
           Binds me to teach the desperate to repent
105   As far as to confirm the innocent.   *Exeunt.*

                              SCENE 3.
                    A ROOM IN ASAMBEG'S PALACE.

                Enter Asambeg, Mustapha, Aga, and Capiaga.

ASAMBEG: Your pleasure?
MUSTAPHA: 'Twill exact your private ear,
          And when you have received it, you will think
          Too many know it.
ASAMBEG: Leave the room; but be
          Within our call.   *Exit Aga and Capiaga.*
                        Now, sir, what burning secret
5   Brings you (With which, it seems, you are turned cinders)
          To quench in my advice or power?
MUSTAPHA: The fire
          Will rather reach you.
ASAMBEG: Me?
MUSTAPHA: And consume both.
          For 'tis impossible to be put out
          But with the blood of those that kindle it;
10   And yet one vial of it is so precious,
          It being borrowed from the Ottoman spring,

---

1 'Twill exact your private ear] It is something that must be heard privately.
11 Ottoman spring] the bloodline of the Ottoman royal family.

That better 'tis, I think, both we should perish
Than prove the desperate means that must restrain it
From spreading further.
ASAMBEG: To the point—and quickly.
15 These winding circumstances in relations
Seldom environ truth.
MUSTAPHA: Truth, Asambeg?
ASAMBEG: Truth, Mustapha! I said it, and add more:
You touch upon a string that to my ear
Does sound "Donusa."
MUSTAPHA: You then understand
Who 'tis I aim at.
20 ASAMBEG: Take heed, Mustapha!
Remember what she is, and whose we are.
'Tis her neglect, perhaps, that you complain of,
And should you practice to revenge her scorn
With any plot to taint her in her honor—
MUSTAPHA: Hear me.
25 ASAMBEG: I will be heard first: there's no tongue
A subject owes that shall out-thunder mine.
MUSTAPHA: Well, take your way.
ASAMBEG: I then again repeat it:
Mustapha dares with malicious breath
(On jealous suppositions) presume
30 To blast the blossom of Donusa's fame
Because he is denied a happiness
Which men of equal, nay, of more desert,
Have sued in vain for—
MUSTAPHA: More?
ASAMBEG: More. 'Twas I spake it.
The basha of Natolia and myself
35 Were rivals for her. Either of us brought
More victories, more trophies, to plead for us
To our great master than you dare lay claim to;
Yet still by his allowance she was left
To her election. Each of us owed nature
40 As much for outward form and inward worth
To make way for us to her grace and favor

As you brought with you. We were heard, repulsed,
Yet thought it no dishonor to sit down
With the disgrace, if not to force affection
May merit such a name.

45 MUSTAPHA: Have you done yet?

ASAMBEG: Be, therefore, more than sure the ground on which
You raise your accusation may admit
No undermining of defense in her:
For if, with pregnant and apparent proofs
50 Such as may force a judge more than inclined
Or partial in her cause to swear her guilty,
You win not me to set off your belief,
Neither our ancient friendship nor the rites
Of sacred hospitality (to which
55 I would not offer violence) shall protect you.
Now, when you please.

MUSTAPHA: I will not dwell upon
Much circumstance, yet cannot but profess,
With the assurance of a loyalty
Equal to yours, the reverence I owe
60 The sultan and all such his blood makes sacred;
That there is not a vein of mine, which yet is
Unemptied in his service, but this moment
Should freely open, so it might wash off
The stains of her dishonor. Could you think,
65 Or (though you saw it) credit your own eyes,
That she, the wonder and amazement of
Her sex, the pride and glory of the empire,
That has disdained you, slighted me, and boasted
A frozen coldness which no appetite
70 Or height of blood could thaw, should now so far
Be hurried with the violence of her lust,
As in it burying her high birth and fame,
Basely descend to fill a Christian's arms
And to him yield her virgin honor up—
Nay, sue to him to take it?

ASAMBEG: A Christian?

75 MUSTAPHA: Temper
Your admiration. And what Christian, think you?

No prince disguised; no man of mark, nor honor;
No daring undertaker in our service;
But one whose lips her foot should scorn to touch—
A poor mechanic peddler.

ASAMBEG: He?

80 MUSTAPHA: Nay, more!
Whom do you think she made her scout, nay bawd,
To find him out, but me? What place makes choice of
To wallow in her foul and loathsome pleasures,
But in the palace? Who the instruments
85 Of close conveyance, but the captain of
Your guard, the aga, and that man of trust,
The warden of the inmost port? I'll prove this,
And though I fail to show her in the act,
Glued like a neighing mare to her proud stallion,
90 Your incredulity shall be convinced
With proofs I blush to think on.

ASAMBEG: Never yet
This flesh felt such a fever. By the life
And fortune of great Amurath, should our Prophet
(Whose name I bow to) in a vision speak this,
95 'Twould make me doubtful of my faith! Lead on,
And when my eyes and ears are, like yours, guilty,
My rage shall then appear; for I will do
Something—but what, I am not yet determined.   *Exeunt.*

SCENE 4.
AN OUTER ROOM IN DONUSA'S SECTION
OF THE PALACE.

Enter Carazie, Manto, and Gazet.

CARAZIE: They are private, to their wishes?

MANTO: Doubt it not.

GAZET: A pretty structure this! A court, do you call it?

---

78 **undertaker**] one who is hired to carry out a task or business for another.
80 **mechanic peddler**] vulgar tradesman who works with his hands.

Vaulted and arched! O here has been old jumbling
Behind this arras.

CARAZIE: [*to Manto*] Prithee let's have some sport
With this fresh codshead.

5 MANTO: I am out of tune,
But do as you please. [*aside*] My conscience! Tush, the hope
Of liberty throws that burthen off. I must
Go watch and make discovery.   *Exit.*

CARAZIE: [*aside*] He's musing
And will talk to himself. He cannot hold:
The poor fool's ravished.

10 GAZET: I am in my master's clothes.
They fit me to a hair, too. Let but any
Indifferent gamester measure us inch by inch
Or weigh us by the standard, I may pass.
I have been proved and proved again true metal.

CARAZIE: [*aside*] How he surveys himself!

15 GAZET: I have heard that some
Have fooled themselves at court into good fortunes
That never hoped to thrive by wit in the city
Or honesty in the country. If I do not
Make the best laugh at me, I'll weep for myself—

20 If they give me hearing. 'Tis resolved: I'll try
What may be done. By your favor, sir, I pray you,
Were you born a courtier?

CARAZIE: No, sir. Why do you ask?

GAZET: Because I thought that none could be preferred
But such as were begot there.

CARAZIE: O, sir! Many,

25 And howsoe'er you are a citizen born,
Yet if your mother were a handsome woman
And ever longed to see a masque at court,
It is an even lay but that you had

---

3 **jumbling**] mixing together by shaking; thus a euphemism for sexual intercourse.
4 **arras**] tapestry used as a wall hanging.
5 **codshead**] stupid person.
23 **preferred**] given a lucrative position.
28 **even lay**] even wager; fifty per cent chance.

A courtier to your father; and I think so,
You bear yourself so sprightly.

30 GAZET: It may be.
But pray you, sir, had I such an itch upon me
To change my copy, is there hope a place
May be had here for money?

CARAZIE: Not without it—
That I dare warrant you.

GAZET: I have a pretty stock
35   And would not have my good parts undiscovered.
What places of credit are there?

CARAZIE: There's your beglerbeg.

GAZET: By no means that: it comes too near the beggar,
And most prove so that come there.

CARAZIE: Or your sanzacke.°

GAZET: Sans jack! Fie, none of that.

CARAZIE: Your chiaus.°

GAZET: Nor that.

CARAZIE: Chief gardener.

40 GAZET: Out upon't!
'Twill put me in mind my mother was an herb-woman.
What is your place, I pray you?

CARAZIE: Sir, an eunuch.

GAZET: An eunuch! Very fine, i'faith—an eunuch!
And what are your employments? Neat and easy?

45 CARAZIE: In the day, I wait on my lady when she eats,
Carry her pantofles, bear up her train;
Sing her asleep at night, and when she pleases
I am her bedfellow.

GAZET: How! Her bedfellow?
And lie with her?

CARAZIE: Yes, and lie with her.

GAZET: O rare!

---

32 **change my copy**] spend my wealth, plenty.
36 **beglerbeg**] governor of an Ottoman province.
39 **Sans jack**] without a penis.
44 **Neat**] clean and orderly.

50 I'll be an eunuch, though I sell my shop for't
    And all my wares.
CARAZIE: It is but parting with
    A precious stone or two: I know the price on't.
GAZET: I'll part with all my stones; and when I am
    An eunuch, I'll so toss and touse the ladies!
    Pray you, help me to a chapman.
55 CARAZIE: The court surgeon
    Shall do you that favor.
GAZET: I am made! an eunuch!   *Enter Manto.*
MANTO: Carazie, quit the room.
CARAZIE: Come, sir; we'll treat of
    Your business further.
GAZET: Excellent! An eunuch!   *Exeunt.*

SCENE 5.
AN INNER ROOM IN DONUSA'S SECTION
OF THE PALACE.

Enter Donusa and Vitelli.

VITELLI: Leave me, or I am lost again: no prayers,
    No penitence, can redeem me.
DONUSA: Am I grown
    Old or deformed since yesterday?
VITELLI: You are still,
    Although the sating of your lust hath sullied
5   The immaculate whiteness of your virgin beauties,
    Too fair for me to look on. And though pureness,
    The sword with which you ever fought and conquered,
    Is ravished from you by unchaste desires,
    You are too strong for flesh and blood to treat with,
10 Though iron grates were interposed between us
    To warrant me from treason.

---

52 **stone**] gemstone; testicle.
54 **touse**] tousle.
55 **chapman**] negotiator, broker.

DONUSA: Whom do you fear?

VITELLI: That human frailty I took from my mother
That as my youth increased grew stronger on me,
That still pursues me and though once recovered,
15   In scorn of reason, and what's more, religion,
Again seeks to betray me.

DONUSA: If you mean, sir,
To my embraces, you turn rebel to
The laws of Nature, the great queen and mother
Of all productions, and deny allegiance
Where you stand bound to pay it.

20 VITELLI: I will stop
Mine ears against these charms, which if Ulysses
Could live again and hear this second siren,
Though bound with cables to his mast (his ship, too,
Fastened with all her anchors), this enchantment
25   Would force him, in despite of all resistance,
To leap into the sea and follow her,
Although destruction with outstretched arms
Stood ready to receive him.

DONUSA: Gentle sir,
Though you deny to hear me, yet vouchsafe
30   To look upon me. Though I use no language,
The grief for this unkind repulse will print
Such a dumb eloquence upon my face
As will not only plead but prevail for me.

VITELLI: I am a coward. I will see and hear you:
35   The trial, else, is nothing; nor the conquest
My temperance shall crown me with hereafter
Worthy to be remembered. Up, my virtue!
And holy thoughts and resolutions arm me
Against this fierce temptation! Give me voice,
40   Tuned to a zealous anger, to express
At what an overvalue I have purchased
The wanton treasure of your virgin bounties

---

22 **this second siren**] Vitelli compares Donusa to a siren and his temptation to that of Ulysses, whose
crew tied him to the mast while their ears were plugged with wax, so that he could listen to the son of
the sirens. Ulysses struggled and begged to be released, but his crew sailed on.

That in their false fruition heap upon me
Despair and horror. That I could with that ease
45   Redeem my forfeit innocence or cast up
The poison I received into my entrails
From the alluring cup of your enticements
As now I do deliver back the price   *Returns the casket [of jewels].*
And salary of your lust! Or thus unclothe me
50   Of sin's gay trappings, the proud livery *Throws off his cloak and doublet.*
Of wicked pleasure, which but worn and heated
With the fire of entertainment and consent,
Like to Alcides' fatal shirt, tears off
Our flesh and reputation both together,
55   Leaving our ulcerous follies bare and open
To all malicious censure!

DONUSA: You must grant,
If you hold that a loss to you, mine equals
If not transcends it. If you then first tasted
That poison (as you call it), I brought with me
60   A palate unacquainted with the relish
Of those delights, which most (as I have heard)
Greedily swallow; and then the offense
(If my opinion may be believed)
Is not so great; howe'er, the wrong's no more
65   Than if Hippolytus and the virgin huntress
Should meet and kiss together.°

VITELLI: What defenses
Can lust raise to maintain a precipice

Enter Asambeg and Mustapha above.

To the abyss of looseness! But affords not
The least stair, or the fastening of one foot,
70   To reascend that glorious height we fell from.

MUSTAPHA: By Mahomet, she courts him!   *[Donusa] kneels.*
ASAMBEG: Nay, kneels to him!
Observe: the scornful villain turns away, too,

---

53 **Alcides' fatal shirt**] poisoned shirt that was given to Hercules.

As glorying in his conquest.
DONUSA: Are you marble?
If Christians have mothers, sure they share in
75   The tigress' fierceness, for if you were owner
Of human pity, you could not endure
A princess to kneel to you, or look on
These falling tears which hardest rocks would soften,
And yet remain unmoved. Did you but give me
80   A taste of happiness in your embraces,
That the remembrance of the sweetness of it
Might have perpetual bitterness behind it?
Or showed me what it was to be a wife,
To live a widow ever?
ASAMBEG: She has confessed it!
Seize on him, villains. O the Furies!

Enter Capiaga and Aga, with [Janissaries].
[Exit] Asambeg and Mustapha [who] descend [from above].

85 DONUSA: How!
Are we betrayed?
VITELLI: The better—I expected
A Turkish faith.
DONUSA: Who am I, that you dare this?
'Tis I that do command you to forbear
A touch of violence.
AGA: We already, madam,
90   Have satisfied your pleasure further than
We know to answer it.
CAPIAGA: Would we were well off!
We stand too far engaged, I fear.
DONUSA: For us?
We'll bring you safe off: who dares contradict
What is our pleasure?

Enter Asambeg and Mustapha [below].

---

87 **A Turkish faith**] false, pretended faith; double-dealing.

ASAMBEG: Spurn the dog to prison.

[*To Donusa*] I'll answer you anon.

95 VITELLI: What punishment

Soe'er I undergo, I am still a Christian.   *Exit Guard with Vitelli.*

DONUSA: What bold presumption's this? Under what law

Am I to fall, that set my foot upon

Your statutes and decrees?

MUSTAPHA: The crime committed

Our Alcoran calls death.

100 DONUSA: Tush! who is here

That is not Amurath's slave, and so, unfit

To sit a judge upon his blood?

ASAMBEG: You have lost

And shamed the privilege of it; robbed me, too,

Of my soul, my understanding, to behold

105   Your base unworthy fall from your high virtue.

DONUSA: I do appeal to Amurath.

ASAMBEG: We will offer

No violence to your person till we know

His sacred pleasure; till when, under guard

You shall continue here.

DONUSA: Shall?

ASAMBEG: I have said it.

DONUSA: We shall remember this.

The Guard leads off Donusa.

110 ASAMBEG: It ill becomes

Such as are guilty to deliver threats

Against the innocent. I could tear this flesh now,

But 'tis in vain; nor must I talk, but do.

Provide a well-manned galley for Constantinople.

115   Such sad news never came to our great master.

As he directs, we must proceed and know

No will but his, to whom what's ours we owe.   *Exeunt.*

ACT FOUR

SCENE 1.
A ROOM IN GRIMALDI'S HOUSE.

Enter Master and Boatswain.

MASTER: He does begin to eat?

BOATSWAIN: A little, Master,
But our best hope for his recovery is that
His raving leaves him and those dreadful words,
"Damnation" and "despair," with which he ever
5   Ended all his discourses, are forgotten.

MASTER: This stranger is a most religious man sure,
And I am doubtful whether his charity
In the relieving of our wants, or care
To cure the wounded conscience of Grimaldi,
Deserves more admiration.

10 BOATSWAIN: Can you guess
What the reason should be that we never mention
The church or the high altar but his melancholy
Grows and increases on him?

MASTER: I have heard him,
When he gloried to profess himself an atheist,
15   Talk often, and with much delight and boasting,
Of a rude prank he did ere he turned pirate;
The memory of which, as it appears,
Lies heavy on him.

BOATSWAIN: Pray you, let me understand it.

MASTER: Upon a solemn day when the whole city
20   Joined in devotion and with barefoot steps
Passed to St. Mark's, the duke and the whole signiory,
Helping to perfit the religious pomp

---

21 **the duke and the whole signiory**] the doge of the republic of Venice and all of the high government officials of the city.

22 **perfit**] to perfect or complete.

With which they were received; when all men else
Were full of tears and groaned beneath the weight
25   Of past offenses (of whose heavy burden
They came to be absolved and freed); our captain,
Whether in scorn of those so pious rites
He had no feeling of, or else drawn to it
Out of a wanton, irreligious madness
30   (I know not which), ran to the holy man
As he was doing of the work of grace,
And, snatching from his hands the sanctified means,
Dashed it upon the pavement.
BOATSWAIN: How escaped he,
It being a deed deserving death with torture?
35 MASTER: The general amazement of the people
Gave him leave to quit the temple, and a gundelo,
(Prepared, it seems, before) brought him aboard;
Since which he ne'er saw Venice. The remembrance
Of this, it seems, torments him; aggravated
40   With a strong belief he cannot receive pardon
For this foul fact but from his hands against whom
It was committed.
BOATSWAIN: And what course intends
His heavenly physician, reverend Francisco,
To beat down this opinion?
MASTER: He promised
45   To use some holy and religious fineness
To this good end, and in the meantime charged me
To keep him dark and to admit no visitants,
But on no terms to cross him. Here he comes.

Enter Grimaldi with a book.

---

31 **doing of the work of grace**] performing the high mass.
32 **the sanctified means**] the bread and wine of communion.
36 **gundelo**] gondola.
45 **fineness**] subtle strategy.
47 **dark**] "in the dark," i.e., uninformed.
48 **cross**] contradict; oppose.

GRIMALDI: For theft! He that restores treble the value
50   Makes satisfaction; and for want of means
        To do so, as a slave must serve it out
        Till he hath made full payment. There's hope left here.
        O with what willingness would I give up
        My liberty to those that I have pillaged
55   And wish the numbers of my years, though wasted
        In the most sordid slavery, might equal
        The rapines I have made; till with one voice
        My patient sufferings might exact from my
        Most cruel creditors a full remission,
60   An eye's loss with an eye, limb's with a limb.
        A sad account!° Yet to find peace within here,
        Though all such as I have maimed and dismembered
        In drunken quarrels, or o'ercome with rage
        When they were given up to my power, stood here now
65   And cried for restitution; to appease 'em
        I would do a bloody justice on myself:
        Pull out these eyes that guided me to ravish
        Their sight from others; lop these legs that bore me
        To barbarous violence; with this hand cut off
70   This instrument of wrong; till nought were left me
        But this poor bleeding limbless trunk, which gladly
        I would divide among them.

Enter Francisco in a cope, like a bishop.°

                  Ha! what think I
        Of petty forfeitures! In this reverend habit
        (All that I am turned into eyes) I look on
75   A deed of mine so fiend-like that repentance,
        Though with my tears I taught the sea new tides,
        Can never wash off. All my thefts, my rapes,
        Are venial trespasses compared to what
        I offered to that shape, and in a place, too,
        Where I stood bound to kneel to't.   *Kneels.*

---

74 **All that I am turned into eyes**] my whole state of being, made manifest in this sight.

80 FRANCISCO: 'Tis forgiven!
      I with his tongue (whom in these sacred vestments
      With impure hands thou didst offend) pronounce it.
      I bring peace to thee: see that thou deserve it
      In thy fair life hereafter.
      GRIMALDI: Can it be?
85   Dare I believe this vision? Or hope
      A pardon e'er may find me?
      FRANCISCO: Purchase it
      By zealous undertakings, and no more
      'Twill be remembered.
      GRIMALDI: What celestial balm   [*Rises.*]
      I feel now poured into my wounded conscience!
90   What penance is there I'll not undergo,
      Though ne'er so sharp and rugged, with more pleasure
      Than flesh and blood e'er tasted! Show me true Sorrow,
      Armed with an iron whip, and I will meet
      The stripes she brings along with her, as if
95   They were the gentle touches of a hand
      That comes to cure me. Can good deeds redeem me?
      I will rise up a wonder to the world
      When I have given strong proofs how I am altered.
      I, that have sold such as professed the faith
100   That I was born in to captivity,
      Will make their number equal that I shall
      Deliver from the oar and win as many,
      By the clearness of my actions, to look on
      Their misbelief and loathe it.° I will be
105   A convoy for all merchants, and thought worthy
      To be reported to the world hereafter,
      The child of your devotion, nursed up
      And made strong by your charity to break through
      All dangers hell can bring forth to oppose me.
110   Nor am I, though my fortunes were thought desperate,
      Now you have reconciled me to myself,
      So void of worldly means, but in despite

---

94 **stripes**] marks of the whip.

Of the proud viceroy's wrongs I can do something
To witness my good change. When you please, try me,
115 And I will perfit what you shall enjoin me
Or fall a joyful martyr.

FRANCISCO: You will reap
The comfort of it. Live yet undiscovered
And with your holy meditations strengthen
Your Christian resolution. Ere long,
You shall hear further from me. *Exit.*

120 GRIMALDI: I'll attend
All your commands with patience. Come, my mates,
I hitherto have lived an ill example
And as your captain led you on to mischief,
But now will truly labor, that good men
125 May say hereafter of me to my glory
(Let but my power and means stand with my will),
"His good endeavors did weigh down his ill."

Exit Grimaldi, Master, and Boatswain.
Re-enter Francisco, [in his usual attire].

FRANCISCO: This penitence is not counterfeit: howsoever,
Good actions are in themselves rewarded.
130 My travail's to meet with a double crown:
If that Vitelli come off safe and prove
Himself the master of his wild affections— *Enter Gazet.*
O, I shall have intelligence! How now, Gazet,
Why these sad looks and tears?

GAZET: Tears, sir? I have lost
135 My worthy master. Your rich heir seems to mourn for
A miserable father; your young widow,
Following a bedrid husband to his grave,
Would have her neighbors think she cries and roars
That she must part with such a goodman do-nothing,

---

115 **perfit**] accomplish; bring to completion.
139 **goodman**] a title given to the head of a household who is below the rank of gentleman. It was
sometimes prefixed to designations of occupation ("goodman tailor," for example).

140   When 'tis because he stays so long above ground
    And hinders a rich suitor. All is come out, sir.
    We are smoked for being cunny-catchers: my master
    Is put in prison; his she-customer
    Is under guard, too. These are things to weep for;
145   But mine own loss considered, and what a fortune
    I have had, as they say, snatched out of my chops,
    Would make a man run mad.

FRANCISCO: I scarce have leisure,
    I am so wholly taken up with sorrow
    For my loved pupil, to enquire thy fate;
    Yet I will hear it.

150 GAZET: Why, sir, I had bought a place,
    A place of credit, too, and had gone through with it;
    I should have been made an eunuch (there was honor
    For a late poor 'prentice!) when upon the sudden
    There was such a hurly-burly in the court
155   That I was glad to run away and carry
    The price of my office with me.

FRANCISCO: Is that all?
    You have made a saving voyage. We must think now,
    Though not to free, to comfort sad Vitelli.
    My grieved soul suffers for him.

GAZET: I am sad, too,
    But had I been an eunuch—
160 FRANCISCO: Think not on it.   *Exeunt.*

SCENE 2.
A HALL IN ASAMBEG'S PALACE.

Enter Asambeg. [He] unlocks the door and leads forth Paulina.

ASAMBEG: Be your own guard: obsequiousness and services
    Shall win you to be mine. Of all restraint

---

142 **smoked**] suspected.
142 **cunny-catchers**] swindlers, but also seducers of women. "Cunny" or "coney" (literally, a rabbit)
was a slang term for either a simple-minded, easily tricked person, or a woman as sexual object.
154 **hurly-burly**] uproar; noisy commotion.

Forever take your leave: no threats shall awe you,
No jealous doubts of mine disturb your freedom.
5   No feed spies wait upon your steps. Your virtue,
And due consideration in yourself
Of what is noble, are the faithful helps
I leave you as supporters to defend you
From falling basely.
PAULINA: This is wondrous strange.
Whence flows this alteration?
10 ASAMBEG: From true judgment
And strong assurance neither grates of iron
Hemmed in with walls of brass, strict guards, high birth,
The forfeiture of honor, nor the fear
Of infamy or punishment, can stay
15   A woman slaved to appetite from being
False and unworthy.
PAULINA: You are grown satirical
Against our sex. Why sir, I durst produce
Myself in our defense and from you challenge
A testimony that's not to be denied:
20   All fall not under this unequal censure.
I, that have stood your flatteries, your threats,
Bore up against your fierce temptations, scorned
The cruel means you practiced to supplant me,
Having no arms to help me to hold out
25   But love of piety and constant goodness.
If you are unconfirmed, dare again boldly;
Enter into the lists and combat with
All opposites man's malice can bring forth
To shake me in my chastity built upon
The rock of my religion.
30 ASAMBEG: I do wish
I could believe you; but when I shall show you
A most incredible example of
Your frailty in a princess sued and sought to
By men of worth, of rank, of eminence; courted

---

5 **feed**] paid, hired.
26 **unconfirmed**] uncertain.

35   By happiness itself, and her cold temper
Approved by many years; yet she to fall,
Fall from herself, her glories—nay, her safety—
Into a gulf of shame and black despair;
I think you'll doubt yourself, or in beholding
40   Her punishment, forever be deterred
From yielding basely.

PAULINA: I would see this wonder.
'Tis, sir, my first petition.

ASAMBEG: And thus granted:
Above, you shall observe all.   *Paulina steps aside.*°

Enter Mustapha.

MUSTAPHA: Sir, I sought you
And must relate a wonder. Since I studied,
45   And knew what man was, I was never witness
Of such invincible fortitude as this Christian
Shows in his sufferings: all the torments that
We could present him with to fright his constancy
Confirmed, not shook it; and those heavy chains
50   That eat into his flesh appeared to him
Like bracelets made of some loved mistress' hairs
We kiss in the remembrance of her favors.
I am strangely taken with it and have lost
Much of my fury.

ASAMBEG: Had he suffered poorly,
55   It had called on my contempt; but manly patience
And all-commanding virtue wins upon
An enemy. I shall think upon him. Ha!   *Enter Aga with a black box.*°
So soon returned! This speed pleads in excuse
Of your late fault, which I no more remember.
What's the Grand Signior's pleasure?

60 AGA: 'Tis enclosed here.
The box to, that contains it, may inform you
How he stands affected. I am trusted with

---

60 **Grand Signior**] the Ottoman emperor.

Nothing but this: on forfeit of your head,
She must have a speedy trial.

ASAMBEG: Bring her in

65   In black, as to her funeral. 'Tis the color   [*Exit Aga.*]
Her fault wills her to wear, and which in justice
I dare not pity. Sit, and take your place.
However in her life she has degenerated,
May she die nobly and in that confirm
Her greatness and high blood.

*Solemn music. [Re-enter] Aga, with Capiaga and a Guard. They lead in
Donusa in black, her train borne up by Carazie, and Manto.*

70 MUSTAPHA: I now could melt!
But soft compassion leave me.

MANTO: I am affrighted
With this dismal preparation. Should the enjoying
Of loose desires find ever such conclusions,
All women would be vestals.

DONUSA: That you clothe me

75   In this sad livery of death, assures me
Your sentence is gone out before, and I
Too late am called for, in my guilty cause
To use qualification or excuse—
Yet must I not part so with mine own strengths

80   But borrow from my modesty boldness to
Enquire by whose authority you sit
My judges and whose warrant digs my grave
In the frowns you dart against my life?

ASAMBEG: See here
This fatal sign and warrant! This, brought to

85   A general fighting in the head of his
Victorious troops, ravishes from his hand
His even then conquering sword; this, shown unto

---

74 **vestals**] virgins for life.
83 **See here**] Asembeg indicates the black box that the aga has brought from the imperial court in Istanbul.

The sultan's brothers or his sons, delivers
His deadly anger and (all hopes laid by)
90   Commands them to prepare themselves for heaven;
Which would stand with the quiet of your soul
To think upon and imitate.

DONUSA: Give me leave
A little to complain: first, of the hard
Condition of my fortune, which may move you,
95   Though not to rise up intercessors for me,
Yet in remembrance of my former life
(This being the first spot tainting mine honor),
To be the means to bring me to his presence;
And then I doubt not but I could allege
100   Such reasons in mine own defense or plead
So humbly (my tears helping) that it should
Awake his sleeping pity.

ASAMBEG: 'Tis in vain.
If you have aught to say, you shall have hearing;
And, in me, think him present.

DONUSA: I would thus then
105   First kneel and kiss his feet, and after, tell him
How long I had been his darling; what delight
My infant years afforded him; how dear
He prized his sister in both bloods, my mother;
That she, like him, had frailty that to me
110   Descends as an inheritance; then conjure him,
By her blest ashes and his father's soul,
The sword that rides upon his thigh, his right hand
Holding the scepter and the Ottoman fortune,
To have compassion on me.

ASAMBEG: But suppose
115   (As I am sure) he would be deaf. What then
Could you infer?

---

98 **his presence**] the presence of the Ottoman sultan, Amurath.
108 **in both bloods**] in the common blood of the Ottoman royal family, and in a hereditary tendency toward sensual "frailty."
116 **infer**] bring about; bring forward as an argument.

DONUSA: I then would thus rise up
And to his teeth tell him he was a tyrant,
A most voluptuous and insatiable epicure
In his own pleasures; which he hugs so dearly,
120   As proper and peculiar to himself,
That he denies a moderate lawful use
Of all delight to others. And to thee,
Unequal judge, I speak as much and charge thee
But with impartial eyes to look into
125   Thyself and then consider with what justice
Thou canst pronounce my sentence. Unkind Nature,
To make weak women servants, proud men masters!
Indulgent Mahomet, do thy bloody laws
Call my embraces with a Christian death?
130   Having my heat and May of youth to plead
In my excuse? And yet want power to punish
These that with scorn break through thy cobweb edicts
And laugh at thy decrees? To tame their lusts
There's no religious bit: let her be fair
135   And pleasing to the eye, though Persian, Moor,
Idolatress, Turk, or Christian, you are privileged
And freely may enjoy her. At this instant,
I know, unjust man, thou hast in thy power
A lovely Christian virgin. Thy offense
140   Equal if not transcending mine, why then
(We being both guilty) dost thou not descend
From that usurped tribunal and with me
Walk hand in hand to death?

ASAMBEG: She raves, and we
Lose time to hear her. Read the law.

DONUSA: Do, do—
145   I stand resolved to suffer.

AGA: [*Reads*] "If any virgin of what degree or quality soever, born a natural
Turk, shall be convicted of corporal looseness and incontinence with
any Christian, she is, by the decree of our great prophet, Mahomet, to
lose her head . . ."

---

128 **bloody laws**] laws that permit both violence and sexual freedom.

150 ASAMBEG: Mark that—then tax our justice!

AGA: "... Ever provided that if she, the said offender, by any reasons,
     arguments, or persuasion can win and prevail with the said Christian
     offending with her to alter his religion and marry her, that then the
     winning of a soul to the Mahometan sect shall acquit her from all
155   shame, disgrace and punishment whatsoever."

DONUSA: I lay hold on that clause and challenge from you
     The privilege of the law.

MUSTAPHA: What will you do?

DONUSA: Grant me access and means, I'll undertake
     To turn this Christian Turk and marry him.
     This trial you cannot deny.

160 MUSTAPHA: O base!
     Can fear to die make you descend so low
     From your high birth and brand the Ottoman line
     With such a mark of infamy?

ASAMBEG: This is worse
     Than the parting with your honor. Better suffer
165   Ten thousand deaths, and without hope to have
     A place in our great prophet's paradise,
     Than have an act to aftertimes remembered
     So foul as this is.

MUSTAPHA: Cheer your spirits, madam:
     To die is nothing. 'Tis but parting with
     A mountain of vexations.

170 ASAMBEG: Think of your honor:
     In dying nobly, you make satisfaction
     For your offense, and you shall live a story
     Of bold, heroic courage.

DONUSA: You shall not fool me
     Out of my life: I claim the law and sue for
175   A speedy trial. If I fail, you may
     Determine of me as you please.

ASAMBEG: Base woman!
     But use thy ways and see thou prosper in them;
     For if thou fall again into my power,
     Thou shalt in vain, after a thousand tortures,
180   Cry out for death—that death which now thou fliest from!

Unloose the prisoner's chains. Go, lead her on
To try the magic of her tongue. I follow.

[Exit all but Asambeg, and Paulina above.]

I'm on the rack. Descend, my best Paulina.   *[Exeunt.]*

SCENE 3.
A ROOM IN THE PALACE PRISON.

Enter Francisco and Jailor.

FRANCISCO: I come not empty-handed. I will purchase
  Your favor at what rate you please. There's gold.
JAILOR: 'Tis the best oratory. I will hazard
  A check for your content. Below there!
VITELLI: *[from] under the stage:* Welcome.
5   Art thou the happy messenger that brings me
  News of my death?
JAILOR: Your hand.   *Vitelli [is] plucked up.*
FRANCISCO: Now if you please,
  A little privacy.
JAILOR: You have bought it, sir:
  Enjoy it freely.   *Exit Jailor.*
FRANCISCO: O my dearest pupil!
  Witness these tears of joy! I never saw you,
10   Till now, look lovely; nor durst I ever glory
  In the mind of any man I had built up
  With the hands of virtuous and religious precepts
  Till this glad minute. Now you have made good
  My expectation of you. By my order,
15   All Roman caesars, that led kings in chains
  Fast bound to their triumphant chariots, if
  Compared with that true glory and full luster
  You now appear in, all their boasted honors

---

4 check] punishment or fine.

Purchased with blood and wrong would lose their names
And be no more remembered!

20 VITELLI: This applause
Confirmed in your allowance joys me more
Than if a thousand full-crammed theaters
Should clap their eager hands to witness that
The scene I act did please, and they admire it.

25 But these are, father, but beginnings, not
The ends of my high aims. I grant to have mastered
The rebel appetite of flesh and blood
Was far above my strength and still owe for it
To that great power that lent it. But when I

30 Shall make't apparent the grim looks of death
Affright me not, and that I can put off
The fond desire of life (that like a garment
Covers and clothes our frailty), hastening to
My martyrdom as to a heavenly banquet,

35 To which I was a choice invited guest;
Then you may boldly say you did not plough
Or trust the barren and ungrateful sands
With the fruitful grain of your religious counsel.

FRANCISCO: You do instruct your teacher. Let the sun

40 Of your clear life (that lends to good men light)
But set as gloriously as it did rise
(Though sometimes clouded), you may write nil ultra
To human wishes.

VITELLI: I have almost gained
The end of the race and will not faint or tire now.

Enter Aga and Jailor.

AGA: Sir, by your leave—nay, stay not—   [*Exit Jailor.*]
45   I bring comfort.
The viceroy, taken with the constant bearing
Of your afflictions and presuming, too,
You will not change your temper, does command

---

32 fond] foolish.
42 nil ultra] L., "nothing beyond."

Your irons should be ta'en off. Now arm yourself   *The chain taken off.*
50   With your old resolution: suddenly
You shall be visited. You must leave the room, too,
And do it without reply.
FRANCISCO: There's no contending.
Be still thyself, my son.   *Exit.*
VITELLI: 'Tis not in man

Enter Donusa, Asambeg, Mustapha, and Paulina.

To change or alter me.
PAULINA: [*aside*] Whom do I look on?
55   My brother? 'Tis he! But no more, my tongue;
Thou wilt betray all.
ASAMBEG: Let us hear this temptress.
The fellow looks as he would stop his ears
Against her powerful spells.
PAULINA: [*aside*] He is undone else.
VITELLI: I'll stand th'encounter—charge me home.
DONUSA: I come, sir,   *Bows herself.*
60   A beggar to you and doubt not to find
A good man's charity, which if you deny,
You are cruel to yourself; a crime a wise man
(And such I hold you) would not willingly
Be guilty of; nor let it find less welcome,
65   Though I (a creature you contemn) now show you
The way to certain happiness; nor think it
Imaginary or fantastical
And so not worth the acquiring, in respect
The passage to it is nor rough nor thorny;
70   No steep hills in the way which you must climb up,
No monsters to be conquered, no enchantments
To be dissolved by counter-charms, before
You take possession of it.
VITELLI: What strong poison
Is wrapped up in these sugared pills?

---

59 **charge me home**] a military metaphor. He challenges her to test his moral defenses with a frontal assault.

DONUSA: My suit is
75   That you would quit your shoulders of a burthen
       Under whose ponderous weight you willfully
       Have too long groaned; to cast those fetters off,
       With which, with your own hands, you chain your freedom.
       Forsake a severe, nay, imperious mistress
80   Whose service does exact perpetual cares,
       Watchings, and troubles; and give entertainment
       To one that courts you, whose least favors are
       Variety and choice of all delights
       Mankind is capable of.
VITELLI: You speak in riddles.
85   What burthen, or what mistress? Or what fetters
       Are those you point at?
DONUSA: Those which your religion,
       The mistress you too long have served, compels you
       To bear with slave-like patience.
VITELLI: Ha!
PAULINA: [*aside*] How bravely
       That virtuous anger shows!
DONUSA: Be wise and weigh
90   The prosperous success of things. If blessings
       Are donatives from heaven (which, you must grant,
       Were blasphemy to question) and that
       They are called down and poured on such as are
       Most gracious with the great disposer of 'em,
95   Look on our flourishing empire (if the splendor,
       The majesty and glory of it dim not
       Your feeble sight) and then turn back and see
       The narrow bounds of yours, yet that poor remnant
       Rent in as many factions and opinions
100   As you have petty kingdoms. And then, if
       You are not obstinate against truth and reason,
       You must confess the deity you worship
       Wants care or power to help you.
PAULINA: [*aside*] Hold out now,
       And then thou art victorious.
ASAMBEG: How he eyes her!
MUSTAPHA: As if he would look through her.

105 ASAMBEG: His eyes flame, too,
　　　　As threatening violence.
　　VITELLI: But that I know
　　　　The Devil, thy tutor, fills each part about thee
　　　　And that I cannot play the exorcist
　　　　To dispossess thee unless I should tear
110　　Thy body limb by limb and throw it to
　　　　The Furies that expect it, I would now
　　　　Pluck out that wicked tongue that hath blasphemed
　　　　That great omnipotency at whose nod
　　　　The fabric of the world shakes. Dare you bring
115　　Your juggling prophet in comparison with
　　　　That most inscrutable and infinite essence
　　　　That made this all and comprehends his work?
　　　　The place is too profane to mention him
　　　　Whose only name is sacred. O Donusa!
120　　How much, in my compassion, I suffer,
　　　　That thou, on whom this most excelling form,
　　　　And facilities of discourse, beyond a woman,
　　　　Were by his liberal gift conferred, shouldst still
　　　　Remain in ignorance of him that gave it!
125　　I will not foul my mouth to speak the sorceries
　　　　Of your seducer, his base birth, his whoredoms,
　　　　His strange impostures; nor deliver how
　　　　He taught a pigeon to feed in his ear,
　　　　Then made his credulous followers believe
130　　It was an angel that instructed him
　　　　In the framing of his Alcoran.° Pray you, mark me.
　　ASAMBEG: These words are death, were he in nought else guilty.
　　VITELLI: Your intent to win me
　　　　To be of your belief proceeded from
135　　Your fear to die. Can there be strength in that
　　　　Religion that suffers us to tremble
　　　　At that which every day—nay, hour—we haste to?
　　DONUSA: This is unanswerable, and there's something tells me
　　　　I err in my opinion.

---

115 **juggling**] deceiving by pretence of occult or magical powers.
119 **only name**] very name.

VITELLI: Cherish it—
140   It is a heavenly prompter! Entertain
        This holy motion and wear on your forehead
        The sacred badge he arms his servants with.
        You shall, like me, with scorn look down upon
        All engines tyranny can advance to batter
145   Your constant resolution. Then you shall
        Look truly fair, when your mind's pureness answers
        Your outward beauties.

DONUSA: I came here to take you,
        But I perceive a yielding in myself
        To be your prisoner.

VITELLI: 'Tis an overthrow
150   That will outshine all victories. O Donusa,
        Die in my faith, like me; and 'tis a marriage
        At which celestial angels shall be waiters,
        And such as have been sainted welcome us.
        Are you confirmed?

DONUSA: I would be—but the means
        That may assure me?

155 VITELLI: Heaven is merciful
        And will not suffer you to want a man
        To do that sacred office, build upon it.

DONUSA: Then thus I spit at Mahomet.

ASAMBEG: Stop her mouth!
        In death to turn apostata! I'll not hear
160   One syllable from any—wretched creature!
        With the next rising sun prepare to die.
        Yet Christian, in reward of thy brave courage,
        Be thy faith right or wrong, receive this favor:
        In person I'll attend thee to thy death
165   And boldly challenge all that I can give,
        But what's not in my grant, which is—to live.   *Exeunt.*

---

141 **motion**] impulse.
142 **sacred badge**] baptismal sign of the cross.
149 **overthrow**] defeat.
152 **waiters**] attendants.
154 **confirmed**] convinced.
156 **want**] lack.
159 **apostata**] a woman guilty of apostasy (desertion of the faith).

ACT FIVE

SCENE 1.
A ROOM IN THE PALACE PRISON.

Enter Vitelli and Francisco.

FRANCISCO: You are wondrous brave and jocund.
VITELLI: Welcome, father.
  Should I spare cost or not wear cheerful looks
  Upon my wedding day, it were ominous
  And showed I did repent it; which I dare not,
5 It being a marriage (howsoever sad
  In the first ceremonies that confirm it)
  That will forever arm me against fears,
  Repentance, doubts, or jealousies, and bring
  Perpetual comforts, peace of mind, and quiet
  To the glad couple.
10 FRANCISCO: I well understand you,
  And my full joy to see you so resolved
  Weak words cannot express. What is the hour
  Designed for this solemnity?
VITELLI: The sixth.
  Something before the setting of the sun
15 We take our last leave of his fading light
  And with our souls' eyes seek for beams eternal.
  Yet there's one scruple with which I am much
  Perplexed and troubled, which I know you can
  Resolve me of.
FRANCISCO: What is't?
VITELLI: This, sir: my bride,
20 Whom I first courted and then won (not with
  Loose lays, poor flatteries, apish compliments,
  But sacred and religious zeal) yet wants
  The holy badge that should proclaim her fit

---

21 **loose lays**] seductive songs.
21 **apish**] affected, insincere.

For these celestial nuptials. Willing she is,
25   I know, to wear it as the choicest jewel
On her fair forehead; but to you, that well
Could do that work of grace, I know the viceroy
Will never grant access. Now, in a case
Of this necessity, I would gladly learn
30   Whether, in me, a layman, without orders,
It may not be religious and lawful,
As we go to our deaths, to do that office?
FRANCISCO: A question in itself with much ease answered:
Midwives, upon necessity, perform it;
35   And knights that in the Holy Land fought for
The freedom of Jerusalem, when full
Of sweat and enemies' blood, have made their helmets
The fount out of which with their holy hands
They drew that heavenly liquor. 'Twas approved then
40   By the holy church, nor must I think it now,
In you, a work less pious.
VITELLI: You confirm me;
I will find a way to do it. In the meantime,
Your holy vows assist me!
FRANCISCO: They shall ever
Be present with you.
VITELLI: You shall see me act
This last scene to the life.
45 FRANCISCO: And though now fall,
Rise a blest martyr.
VITELLI: That's my end, my all.   *Exeunt.*

SCENE 2.
A STREET IN TUNIS NEAR THE HARBOR.

Enter Grimaldi, Master, Boatswain, and Sailors.

BOATSWAIN: Sir, if you slip this opportunity,
Never expect the like.

---

32 **do that office**] perform the rite of baptism (to convert Donusa to Christianity).
41 **confirm**] "make valid by formal authoritative assent" (*O.E.D.*).

MASTER: With as much ease now
We may steal the ship out of the harbor, captain,
As ever gallants in a wanton bravery
5 Have set upon a drunken constable
And bore him from a sleepy rug-gowned watch:
Be therefore wise.

GRIMALDI: I must be honest, too;
And you shall wear that shape, you shall observe me,
If that you purpose to continue mine.
10 Think you ingratitude can be the parent
To our unfeigned repentance? Do I owe
A peace within here kingdoms could not purchase
To my religious creditor, to leave him
Open to danger, the great benefit
15 Never remembered? No, though in her bottom
We could stow up the tribute of the Turk;
Nay, grant the passage safe, too; I will never
Consent to weigh anchor up, till he,
That only must, commands it.

BOATSWAIN: This religion
Will keep us slaves and beggars.

20 MASTER: The fiend prompts me
To change my copy. Plague upon't! We are seamen:
What have we to do with't, but for a snatch or so
At the end of a long Lent! *Enter Francisco.*

BOATSWAIN: Mum! See who is here?

GRIMALDI: My father!

FRANCISCO: My good convert. I am full
25 Of serious business which denies me leave
To hold long conferences with you. Only thus much
Briefly receive: a day or two, at the most,

---

6 rug-gowned] wearing a thick woolen cloak.
13 my religious creditor] Francisco.
16 the Turk] the Ottoman sultan.
21 change my copy] change my behavior; alter my intended course of action.
22 with't] with religion.
22–23 a snatch or so / At the end of a long Lent] a dismissive reference to Easter, the main festival of the Christian year, "snatch" meaning a brief period or a quick meal.

Shall make me fit to take my leave of Tunis
Or give me lost for ever.
GRIMALDI: Days nor years,
30   Provided that my stay may do you service,
But to me shall be minutes.
FRANCISCO: I much thank you.
In this small scroll you may in private read
What my intents are, and as they grow ripe
I will instruct you further. In the meantime
35   Borrow your late distracted looks and gesture:
The more dejected you appear, the less
The viceroy must suspect you.
GRIMALDI: I am nothing
But what you please to have me be.
FRANCISCO: Farewell, sir.
Be cheerful, Master. Something we will do
40   That shall reward itself in the performance,
And that's true prize indeed.
MASTER: I am obedient.
BOATSWAIN: And I—there's no contending.
FRANCISCO: Peace to you all.

Exit Grimaldi, Master, Boatswain, and Sailors.

Prosper, thou great Existence, my endeavors,
As they religiously are undertaken
45   And distant equally from servile gain

Enter Paulina, Carazie, and Manto.

Or glorious ostentation! I am heard
In this blest opportunity, which in vain
I long have waited for. I must show myself.
O, she has found me! Now if she prove right,
All hope will not forsake us.
50 PAULINA: [*To Carazie and Manto*] Farther off,
And in that distance know your duties, too.
You were bestowed on me as slaves to serve me

And not as spies to pry into my actions
And after to betray me. You shall find
55   If any look of mine be unobserved,
I am not ignorant of a mistress' power
And from whom I receive it.
CARAZIE: Note this, Manto!
The pride and scorn with which she entertains us,
Now we are made hers by the viceroy's gift!
60   Our sweet-conditioned princess, fair Donusa
(Rest in her death wait on her!), never used us
With such contempt. I would he had sent me
To the galleys or the gallows when he gave me
To this proud little devil.
MANTO: I expect
65   All tyrannous usage, but I must be patient;
And though ten times a day she tears these locks
Or makes this face her footstool, 'tis but justice.
PAULINA: 'Tis a true story of my fortunes, father.
My chastity preserved by miracle,
70   Or your devotions for me; and believe it,
What outward pride soe'er I counterfeit
Or state to these appointed to attend me,
I am not in my disposition altered,
But still your humble daughter and share with you
75   In my poor brother's sufferings—all hell's torments.
Revenge it on accursed Grimaldi's soul,
That in his rape of me gave a beginning
To all the miseries that since have followed!
FRANCISCO: Be charitable and forgive him, gentle daughter.
80   He's a changed man and may redeem his fault
In his fair life hereafter. You must bear, too,
Your forced captivity (for 'tis no better,
Though you wear golden fetters) and of him,
Whom death affrights not, learn to hold out nobly.

---

60 **sweet-conditioned**] gentle and sweet in temperament.
77 **rape**] abduction.
84 **of him**] from Vitelli.

PAULINA: You are still the same good counselor.

85 FRANCISCO: And who knows
(Since what above is proposed, is inscrutable)
But that the viceroy's extreme dotage on you
May be the parent of a happier birth
Than yet our hopes dare fashion. Longer conference
90 May prove unsafe for you and me, however.
Perhaps for trial he allows you freedom.
From this learn therefore what you must attempt,   *Delivers a paper.*
Though with the hazard of yourself. Heaven guard you
And give Vitelli patience! Then I doubt not
95 But he will have a glorious day, since some
Hold truly, such as suffer, overcome.   *Exeunt.*

SCENE 3.
A HALL IN ASAMBEG'S PALACE.

Enter Asambeg, Mustapha, Aga, and Capiaga.

ASAMBEG: What we commanded, see performed; and fail not
In all things to be punctual.
AGA: We shall, sir.   *Exit Aga and Capiaga.*
MUSTAPHA: 'Tis strange that you should use such circumstance
To a delinquent of so mean condition.
5 ASAMBEG: Had he appeared in a more sordid shape
Than disguised greatness ever deigned to mask in,
The gallant bearing of his present fortune
Aloud proclaims him noble.
MUSTAPHA: If you doubt him
To be a man built up for great employment
10 And as a cunning spy sent to explore
The city's strength or weakness, you by torture
May force him to discover it.

95–96 some / Hold truly, such as suffer, overcome] it is truly said that they who endure will overcome.
3 circumstance] elaborate ceremony.
8–9 doubt him / To be] suspect that he is.

ASAMBEG: That were base.
Nor dare I do such injury to virtue
And bold assured courage; neither can I
15   Be won to think, but if I should attempt it,
I shoot against the moon. He that hath stood
The roughest battery that captivity
Could ever bring to shake a constant temper;
Despised the fawnings of a future greatness
20   By beauty in her full perfection tendered;
That hears of death as of a quiet slumber;
And from the surplusage of his own firmness
Can spare enough of fortitude to assure
A feeble woman; will not, Mustapha,
25   Be altered in his soul for any torments
We can afflict his body with!

MUSTAPHA: Do your pleasure.
I only offered you a friend's advice,
But without gall or envy to the man
That is to suffer. But what do you determine
30   Of poor Grimaldi? The disgrace called on him,
I hear, has ran him mad.

ASAMBEG: There weigh the difference
In the true temper of their minds. The one,
A pirate sold to mischiefs, rapes, and all
That make a slave relentless and obdurate,
35   Yet of himself wanting the inward strengths
That should defend him, sinks beneath compassion
Or pity of a man; whereas this merchant,
Acquainted only with a civil life,
Armed in himself, entrenched and fortified
40   With his own virtue, valuing life and death
At the same price—poorly—does not invite
A favor, but commands us do him right;
Which unto him, and her we both once honored,

---

20 **tendered**] offered.
22 **surplusage**] surplus.

As a just debt I gladly pay. They enter.
Now sit we equal hearers.

A dreadful music. [Enter] at one door, the Aga, Janissaries, Vitelli, Francisco, and
Gazet; at the other, Donusa, Paulina, Carazie, and Manto.

45 MUSTAPHA: I shall hear
        And see, sir, without passion. My wrongs arm me.
    VITELLI: A joyful preparation! To whose bounty
        Owe we our thanks for gracing thus our hymen?
        The notes, though dreadful to the ear, sound here
50   As our epithalamium were sung
        By a celestial choir, and a full chorus
        Assured us future happiness. These that lead me
        Gaze not with wanton eyes upon my bride,
        Nor for their service are repaid by me
55   With jealousies or fears; nor do they envy
        My passage to those pleasures from which death
        Cannot deter me. Great sir, pardon me.
        Imagination of the joys I haste to
        Made me forget my duty; but the form
60   And ceremony past, I will attend you
        And with our constant resolution feast you,
        Not with coarse cates, forgot as soon as tasted,
        But such as shall, while you have memory,
        Be pleasing to the palate.
    FRANCISCO: Be not lost
        In what you purpose.   *Exit.*
65 GAZET: Call you this a marriage!
        It differs little from hanging—I cry at it.
    VITELLI: See where my bride appears! In what full luster!
        As if the virgins that bear up her train
        Had long contended to receive an honor

---

s.d.   dreadful] inspiring fear or reverence.
46 My wrongs arm me] The wrongs I have suffered give me strength to feel no pity.
48 hymen] marriage ceremony. From Hymen, the Roman god of marriage.
62 cates] food.

70   Above their births in doing her this service.
        Nor comes she fearful to meet those delights
        Which once passed o'er, immortal pleasures follow.
        I need not, therefore, comfort or encourage
        Her forward steps; and I should offer wrong
75   To her mind's fortitude, should I but ask
        How she can brook the rough high-going sea
        Over whose foamy back our ship, well rigged
        With hope and strong assurance, must transport us.
        Nor will I tell her, when we reach the haven
80   (Which tempests shall not hinder) what loud welcomes
        Shall entertain us; nor commend the place,
        To tell whose least perfection would strike dumb
        The eloquence of all boasted in story,
        Though joined together.
DONUSA: 'Tis enough, my dearest:
85   I dare not doubt you. As your humble shadow,
        Lead where you please, I follow.
VITELLI: One suit, sir,
        And willingly I cease to be a beggar.
        And that you may with more security hear it,
        Know 'tis not life I'll ask, nor to defer
        Our deaths but a few minutes.
90 ASAMBEG: Speak, 'tis granted.
VITELLI: We being now to take our latest leave
        And grown of one belief, I do desire
        I may have your allowance to perform it
        But in the fashion which we Christians use
        Upon the like occasions.
95 ASAMBEG: 'Tis allowed of.
VITELLI: My service: haste, Gazet, to the next spring
        And bring me of it.
GAZET: Would I could as well
        Fetch you a pardon! I would not run but fly
        And be here in a moment.   *Exit.*
MUSTAPHA: What's the mystery
        Of this? Discover it.

100 VITELLI: Great sir, I'll tell you.
           Each country hath its own peculiar rites:
           Some, when they are to die, drink store of wine,
           Which, poured in liberally, does oft beget
           A bastard valor, with which armed they hear
105   The not to be declined charge of death
           With less fear and astonishment. Others take
           Drugs to procure a heavy sleep, that so
           They may insensibly receive the means
           That casts them in an everlasting slumber;
           Others—   *Re-enter Gazet, with water.*
                O welcome!
110 ASAMBEG: Now, the use of yours?
      VITELLI: The clearness of this is a perfit sign
           Of innocence, and as this washes off
           Stains and pollutions from the things we wear,
           Thrown thus upon the forehead, it hath power
115   To purge those spots that cleave upon the mind,
           If thankfully received.   *Throws [water] on her face.*
      ASAMBEG: 'Tis a strange custom.
      VITELLI: How do you entertain it, my Donusa?
           Feel you no alteration, no new motives,
           No unexpected aids, that may confirm you
120   In that to which you were inclined before?
      DONUSA: I am another woman—till this minute
           I never lived, nor durst think how to die.
           How long have I been blind! Yet on the sudden
           By this blest means I feel the films of error
125   Ta'en from my soul's eyes. O divine physician
           That hast bestowed a sight on me which death,
           Though ready to embrace me in his arms,
           Cannot take from me! Let me kiss the hand
           That did this miracle and seal my thanks
130   Upon those lips from whence these sweet words vanished,
           That freed me from the cruelest of prisons,

---

100 **Discover**] reveal.
124 **films**] membranes.

Blind ignorance and misbelief. False prophet!
Impostor Mahomet!

ASAMBEG: I'll hear no more.
You do abuse my favors. Sever 'em.

135   Wretch, if thou hadst another life to lose,
This blasphemy deserved it—instantly
Carry them to their deaths!

VITELLI: We part now, blest one,
To meet hereafter in a kingdom where
Hell's malice shall not reach us.

PAULINA: Ha! ha! ha!

ASAMBEG: What means my mistress?

140 PAULINA: Who can hold her spleen
When such ridiculous follies are presented,
The scene, too, made religion? O my lord,
How from one cause two contrary effects
Spring up upon the sudden!

ASAMBEG: This is strange.

145 PAULINA: That which hath fooled her in her death, wins me,
That hitherto have barred myself from pleasure,
To live in all delight.

ASAMBEG: There's music in this.

PAULINA: I now will run as fiercely to your arms
As ever longing woman did, borne high
On the swift wings of appetite.

150 VITELLI: O devil!

PAULINA: Nay, more; for there shall be no odds betwixt us:
I will turn Turk.

GAZET: [*aside*] Most of your tribe do so
When they begin in whore.°

ASAMBEG: You are serious, lady?

PAULINA: Serious? But satisfy me in a suit

155   That to the world may witness that I have

---

140 **spleen**] laughter (because the spleen was believed to be the seat of mirth).

152 **turn Turk**] convert to Islam, but in this context also suggesting conversion to habitual indulgence in sexual sin.

Some power upon you, and tomorrow challenge
Whatever's in my gift; for I will be
At your dispose.

GAZET: [*aside*] That's ever the subscription
To a damned whore's false epistle.

ASAMBEG: Ask this hand,
160   Or if thou wilt, the heads of these. I am rapt
Beyond myself with joy. Speak, speak—what is it?

PAULINA: But twelve short hours reprieve for this base couple.

ASAMBEG: The reason, since you have them?

PAULINA: That I may
Have time to triumph o'er this wretched woman.
165   I'll be myself her guardian. I will feast,
Adorned in her choice and richest jewels.
Commit him to what guards you please. Grant this,
I am no more mine own, but yours.

ASAMBEG: Enjoy it.
Repine at it who dares. Bear him safe off
170   To the black tower,° but give him all things useful.
The contrary was not in your request?

PAULINA: I do contemn him.

DONUSA: Peace in death denied me!

PAULINA: Thou shalt not go in liberty to thy grave:
For one night a sultana is my slave.

MUSTAPHA: A terrible little tyranness.

175 ASAMBEG: No more—
Her will shall be a law. Till now ne'er happy!   *Exeunt.*

SCENE 4.
A STREET IN TUNIS.

Enter Francisco, Grimaldi, Master, Boatswain, and Sailors.

GRIMALDI: Sir, all things are in readiness: the Turks
That seized upon my ship, stowed under hatches;

---

158 **subscription**] signature at the end of a letter or text to which one has "subscribed."

My men resolved and cheerful. Use but means
To get out of the ports, we will be ready
5   To bring you aboard, and then (heaven be but pleased)
This for the viceroy's fleet!

FRANCISCO: Discharge your parts;
In mine I'll not be wanting. Fear not, Master,
Something will come along to fraught your bark,
That you will have just cause to say you never
Made such a voyage.

10 MASTER: We will stand the hazard.

FRANCISCO: What's the best hour?

BOATSWAIN: After the second watch.

FRANCISCO: Enough—each to his charge.

GRIMALDI: We will be careful.   *Exeunt.*

SCENE 5.
A ROOM IN ASAMBEG'S PALACE.

Enter Paulina, Donusa, Carazie, and Manto.

PAULINA: Sit, madam. It is fit that I attend you;
And pardon, I beseech you, my rude language,
To which the sooner you will be invited,
When you shall understand no way was left me
5   To free you from a present execution
But by my personating that which never
My nature was acquainted with.

DONUSA: I believe you.

PAULINA: You will, when you shall understand I may
Receive the honor to be known unto you
10   By a nearer name. And not to rack you further,

---

4 **the ports**] palace gates.

8 **fraught your bark**] load your ship.

1 **attend**] watch over; wait upon.

3 **to which the sooner you will be invited**] modifies "pardon" in the preceding line; thus, Paulina tells Donusa that as soon as she understands the secret reason for Paulina's "rude language," Donusa will be "invited" (or induced) to pardon Paulina.

The man you please to favor is my brother—
No merchant, madam, but a gentleman
Of the best rank in Venice.

DONUSA: I rejoice in't,
But what's this to his freedom? For myself,
Were he well off, I were secure.

15 PAULINA: I have
A present means, not plotted by myself,
But a religious man, my confessor,
That may preserve all, if we had a servant
Whose faith we might rely on.

DONUSA: She that's now
20 Your slave was once mine. Had I twenty lives,
I durst commit them to her trust.

MANTO: O madam,
I have been false! Forgive me! I'll redeem it
By anything, however desperate,
You please to impose upon me.

PAULINA: Troth, these tears,
25 I think, cannot be counterfeit. I believe her
And if you please will try her.

DONUSA: At your peril.
There is no further danger can look towards me.

PAULINA: This only then—canst thou use means to carry
This bakemeat to Vitelli?

MANTO: With much ease:
30 I am familiar with the guard; beside,
It being known it was I that betrayed him,
My entrance hardly will of them be questioned!

PAULINA: About it then. Say that it was sent to him
From his Donusa; bid him search the midst of't.
He there shall find a cordial.

35 MANTO: What I do
Shall speak my care and faith.   *Exit.*

DONUSA: Good fortune with thee!

---

24 **Troth**] Truly.
29 **bakemeat**] meat pie.
35 **cordial**] remedy.

PAULINA: You cannot eat?

DONUSA: The time we thus abuse
We might employ much better.

PAULINA: I am glad
To hear this from you. As for you, Carazie,
40   If our intents do prosper, make choice whether
You'll steal away with your two mistresses
Or take your fortune.

CARAZIE: I'll be gelded twice first;
Hang him that stays behind.

PAULINA: I wait you, madam.
Were but my brother off, by the command
45   Of the doting viceroy there's no guard dare stay me;
And I will safely bring you to the place
Where we must expect him.

DONUSA: Heaven be gracious to us!   *Exeunt.*

SCENE 6.
A ROOM IN THE BLACK TOWER.

Enter Vitelli, Aga, and Guards.

VITELLI: Paulina, to fall off thus! 'Tis to me
More terrible than death and like an earthquake
Totters this walking building (such I am)
And in my sudden ruin would prevent,
5   By choking up at once my vital spirits,
This pompous preparation for my death.
But I am lost: that good man, good Francisco,
Delivered me a paper, which till now
I wanted leisure to peruse.   *Reads the paper.*

AGA: This Christian
10   Fears not, it seems, the near approaching sun
Whose second rise he never must salute.

---

44 off] away (from here).
6 pompous] ceremonious.

Enter Manto with the baked meat.

FIRST GUARD: Who's that?

SECOND GUARD: Stand.

AGA: Manto!

MANTO: Here's the viceroy's ring
    Gives warrant to my entrance; yet you may
    Partake of anything I shall deliver.
15   'Tis but a present to a dying man,
    Sent from the princess that must suffer with him.

AGA: Use your own freedom.

MANTO: I would not disturb
    This his last contemplation.

VITELLI: O, 'tis well!
    He has restored all, and I at peace again
    With my Paulina.

20 MANTO: Sir, the sad Donusa,
    Grieved for your sufferings more than for her own,
    Knowing the long and tedious pilgrimage
    You are to take, presents you with this cordial,
    Which privately she wishes you should taste of
25   And search the middle part, where you shall find
    Something that hath the operation to
    Make death look lovely.

VITELLI: I will not dispute
    What she commands, but serve it.   *Exit.*

AGA: Prithee, Manto,
    How hath the unfortunate princess spent this night
    Under her proud new mistress?

30 MANTO: With such patience
    As it o'ercomes the other's insolence,
    Nay, triumphs o'er her pride. My much haste now
    Commands me hence; but, the sad tragedy past,
    I'll give you satisfaction to the full
35   Of all hath passed, and a true character
    Of the proud Christian's nature.   *Exit.*

---

19 He] God.
35 **character**] detailed summary or report (of a person's qualities).

AGA: Break the watch up.
What should we fear in the midst of our own strengths?
'Tis but the basha's jealousy. Farewell, soldiers.   *Exeunt.*

SCENE 7.
AN UPPER ROOM IN THE BLACK TOWER.

Enter Vitelli with the baked meats, above.

VITELLI: There's something more in this than means to cloy
    A hungry appetite, which I must discover.
    She willed me search the midst. Thus, thus I pierce it.
    Ha! What is this? A scroll bound up in packthread?
5   What may the mystery be?   *[He reads] the scroll.*
    "Son, let down this packthread at the west window of the castle. By it
    you shall draw up a ladder of ropes, by which you may descend. Your
    dearest Donusa with the rest of your friends below attend you. Heaven
    prosper you. Francisco."
10   O best of men! He that gives up himself
    To a true religious friend leans not upon
    A false deceiving reed but boldly builds
    Upon a rock, which now with joy I find
    In reverend Francisco, whose good vows,
15   Labors, and watchings in my hoped-for freedom
    Appear a pious miracle. I come,
    I come, good man, with confidence. Though the descent
    Were steep as hell, I know I cannot slide,
    Being called down by such a faithful guide.   *Exit.*

SCENE 8.
A ROOM IN ASAMBEG'S PALACE.

Enter Asambeg, Mustapha, and Janissaries.

ASAMBEG: Excuse me, Mustapha, though this night to me
    Appear as tedious as that treble one
    Was to the world when Jove on fair Alcmena

Begot Alcides.° Were you to encounter

5   Those ravishing pleasures which the slow-paced hours
        (To me they are such) bar me from, you would
        With your continued wishes strive to imp
        New feathers to the broken wings of Time
        And chide the amorous sun for too long dalliance
        In Thetis' watery bosom.

10 MUSTAPHA: You are too violent
        In your desires, of which you are yet uncertain;
        Having no more assurance to enjoy 'em,
        Than a weak woman's promise, on which wise men
        Faintly rely.

ASAMBEG: Tush, she is made of truth,
15   And what she says she will do holds as firm
        As laws in brass that know no change. What's this?

                                        The chamber shot off.

        Some new prize brought in, sure.   *Enter Aga.*
                                Why are thy looks
        So ghastly? Villain, speak!

AGA: Great sir, hear me,
        Then after kill me. We are all betrayed!
20   The false Grimaldi, sunk in your disgrace,
        With his confederates has seized his ship
        And those that guarded it stowed under hatches.
        With him the condemned princess and the merchant
        That with a ladder made of ropes descended
25   From the Black Tower in which he was enclosed.
        And your fair mistress—

ASAMBEG: Ha!

AGA: —With all their train
        And choicest jewels are gone safe aboard.
        Their sails spread forth, and with a fore-right gale

---

7 imp] graft.
10 **Thetis' watery bosom**] the ocean, Thetis being an immortal deity of the sea, the most famous of
the Nereids.
s.d. **chamber**] a small cannon used to fire salutes.
28 **fore-right gale**] a wind blowing strongly in line with the intended course.

Leaving our coast, in scorn of all pursuit
30   As a farewell they showed a broadside to us.
ASAMBEG: No more.
MUSTAPHA: Now note your confidence!
ASAMBEG: No more.
    O my credulity! I am too full
    Of grief and rage to speak. Dull, heavy fool,
    Worthy of all the tortures that the frown
35   Of thy incensed master can throw on thee!
    Without one man's compassion, I will hide
    This head among the deserts, or some cave
    Filled with my shame and me, where I alone
    May die without a partner in my moan.   *Exeunt.*

FINIS.

---

30 **showed a broadside**] turned and fired a round from the cannon positioned along the side of the ship.
35 **thy incensed master**] the Ottoman sultan.

Notes

DEDICATION

George Harding, Baron . . . of the Bath.   A patron of various authors and play-wrights, Harding (1601–1658) received other literary dedications, including Robert Burton's *Anatomy of Melancholy* in 1621 and John Webster's *Duchess of Malfi* in 1623.

PREFATORY VERSES

James Shirley   A prominent poet and playwright of the Caroline period, Shirley (1596–1666) began writing plays for Queen Henrietta's company in 1625.

Daniel Lakyn   A physician who is known to have traveled to Morocco, Istanbul, and the Black Sea region. He is the author of a manuscript on the subject of venereal disease (British Museum, Sloan Manuscript 2818).

DRAMATIS PERSONAE

Asembeg, viceroy of Tunis   An early modern spelling (and pronunciation) of "Hassan Bey". There was a Venetian renegade of this name who held the post of Ottoman viceroy in Algiers from 1577 to 1580.

Mustapha, basha of Aleppo   Edwards and Gibson cite George Sandys' *Relation of a Journey* (London, 1615), which reports that ". . . Mustapha and Hadir (two of the Viziers of the Port) have married the Sultan's sister and niece" (74).

ACT ONE, SCENE I

8. **Will swear by Mahomet and Termagant**   The usual oath of the "Saracens" and "pagan Moors" who appear in medieval and early modern romance literature. Terma-gant was often included in a group of pagan idols supposedly worshipped by Saracen knights. Cf. Spenser's *Færie Queene*, in which the pagan knights use the same oath, for example at 6.7.47: "And oftentimes by Turmagant and Mahound swore."

25–32. **I would not . . . Over a hotchpotch.**   This passage refers to the radical Protestant groups of Germany and the Low Countries, especially the Anabaptist sect. The leaders of the famous Anabaptist rebellion at Munster in 1534 included craftsmen and workers. Edwards and Gibson cite Thomas Nashe, *The Unfortunate Traveller:* "entered John Leiden the Botcher into the field . . . his men were all base handicrafts, as cobblers and curriers and tinkers" (*The Works of Thomas Nashe,* McKerrow, ed., 5 vols. [Oxford: 1958], 2:232).

ACT ONE, SCENE 2

63. **takes up the pantofles** Edwards and Gibson refer to the following statement in Sandys, *Relation of a Journey* (1615), p. 74: "Their husbands come not unto them [royal Turkish women] until they be called: if for speech only, their shoes which they put off at the door are there suffered to remain; but if to lie with them, they are laid over the bed by an eunuch, a sign for them to approach."

67. **The most invincible, mightiest Amurath** At the time Massinger wrote *The Renegado,* the Ottoman sultan Amurath (or Murat) IV had recently come to the throne. He ruled from 1623 to 1640 and succeeded in reviving and stabilizing the Turkish imperial state. He is said to have ordered the execution of more than twenty thousand people.

ACT ONE, SCENE 3

52–53. **To spare a . . . Were not improvidence** The Master suggests that they should not spend all their money on a sailor's binge of sex and drink, but rather they should save some to provide for any unexpected mishap (or "after-clap") in the future. A pun on "clap" suggests that they may need to pay for a cure for the "clap" (the venereal disease) contracted while indulging in the "sensual pleasures" anticipated by Grimaldi.

ACT TWO, SCENE 1

70–73. **'Tis but procuring . . . in the field.** A satirical glance at the supposed practice, under the early Stuart monarchs, of promoting to knighthood those royal favorites who arranged sexual liaisons at court (instead of rewarding "service in the field" of battle).

ACT TWO, SCENE 5

24. **Those thieves of Malta** From their base in Malta, the military order of the Knights Hospitallers engaged in piracy, attacking and pillaging Muslim vessels in the Mediterranean. They were also known to prey upon Christian ships from time to time.

54–60. **the bold Maltese . . . and threats deluded.** In 1522 the island fortress of the Knights of St. John at Rhodes was besieged and conquered by an Ottoman force under Suleiman the Magnificent. After nine months under siege, a mutiny by the

inhabitants of the city led to the surrender of the Knights, who departed under a truce
and established their order in Malta.

64–73. These knights of . . . from other nations.   In 1565 the Knights of Malta
withstood a Turkish siege of their fortress, an occasion of great rejoicing throughout
European Christendom. The Turkish elite troops, the janissaries, were bought or captured from Christian peoples ("ravished from other nations") as children and then
trained as Muslims and warriors.

ACT TWO, SCENE 6

9. One, by his . . . some French ambassador   an allusion to the visit of the French
nobleman Cadenet, who was present at the English court from December 1620 to
January 1621. Sir Simonds D'Ewes reports that "many thousands" came to see him and
wrote, "I found him a proper tall man and a gallant courtier . . . his hatband, scarf, and
clothes were so richly set out with diamonds, as they were valued to amount unto
between £30,000 or £40,000" (cited in Edwards and Gibson 2:1).

ACT THREE, SCENE 1

63–68. Stay and stand . . . thy speech forever   Mustapha has forced Manto to
remain behind, perhaps by restraining her physically at first, but then by threatening
her with a sword or dagger. He threatens to kill her, but his aggression is also sexual:
he is driven by frustration and jealousy, as well as wounded honor and thwarted ambition. When he says he will make her "fall" if she does not "stay and stand," he speci-
fies that this will be "Not to firk your belly up, flounder-like, but never / To rise again."
In other words, she is warned to to prepare herself not for sexual intercourse, but to die.

ACT THREE, SCENE 2

48–52. if I, / That . . . of those companies.   Gazet plays upon the notion of
"drinking and whoring" as commercial activities represented by legitimate mercantile
"companies" or guild organizations. If he were to forgo these "charters," that is, the
legal rights to do business, Gazet suggests, then no self-respecting practitioner of the
business of drinking and whoring would pity his abstinence ("liveries" are the members
of the city guilds or "companies," who are privileged to wear the "livery" of their organizations). The word "livery" also glances at the sense of "liver" as the seat of love
and violent passion.

ACT THREE, SCENE 4

38. your sanzacke.   a Turkish title mentioned in Sandys' *Relation* (an important
source for Massinger), where "Sanziaks" are "governors of cities . . . with their territories and forces" (47).

39. **Your chiaus.** A Turkish diplomatic title (from "chaush," meaning "messenger") but understood by Gazet to mean a swindler or cheat. The English word "chause" originated in the scheme of a fraudulent Turk who arrived in London in 1609, claiming to have come as a "chiaus" or messenger from the Turkish court. He was received royally and succeeded in swindling London merchants.

ACT THREE, SCENE 5

65–66. **if Hippolytus and . . . kiss together.** Hippolytus, who rejected the love of his stepmother, Phaedra, and was killed as a result and Diana, the classical goddess of chastity and the moon, represent male and female chastity, respectively. For them to kiss would be either completely innocent and harmless, or a shocking violation of their chastity.

ACT FOUR, SCENE 1

49–61. **For theft! He . . . A sad account!** Grimaldi is reading from the Bible. The passages to which he refers are Exodus 22:1–3 and 21:23–24.

72. **s.d. in a cope, like a bishop.** It was extremely rare for a Jesuit to become a bishop. Massinger is probably thinking of Cervantes' *Life in Algiers*, in which a bishop, Jorge D'Oliveres, arrives to ransom Christian captives.

99–104. **I, that have sold . . . and loathe it.** Many captives sold by Muslim pirates into bondage became galley slaves. Grimaldi's eye-for-an-eye sense of self-loathing and retribution has been amended. His paralysis and despair have been cured, and he is now committed to virtuous action and to the conversion of Muslims to Christianity. His new purpose is to save as many souls as he had made suffer through his piracy.

ACT FOUR, SCENE 2

43. **s.d. Paulina steps aside.** This is the stage direction in the quarto text, but the preceding line spoken by Asembeg, "Above, you shall observe all" and his last words in the scene, "descend, my best Paulina," indicate that at some point, probably soon after she "steps aside," Paulina moves to the upper stage area or "gallery" to observe the trial of Donusa without being seen by the others.

57. **s.d. a black box** A contemporary English source claims that if the Sultan "send a Cappagy, that is, a Pursevant to [a Turk] with his writing, with a black seal in a black box, none of them all dare withstand him, but suffer the base cappagy to strangle him" (Biddulph, *Travels of Certain Englishmen*, 1609, p. 805; cited in Gibson and Edwards).

ACT FOUR, SCENE 3

125–31. **I will not . . . of his Alkoran.** The "seducer" is the Prophet Mohammed, and these accusations are the standard demonizations derived from the anti-Islamic polemical tradition, going back to the medieval period.

ACT FIVE, SCENE 3

152–53. **I will turn . . . begin in whore.**   Paulina pretends to desire conversion to Islam. "To turn Turk" could also signify infidelity or a sexual betrayal (meaning "to turn whore") as Gazet's aside indicates.

170. **the black tower**   Gibson and Edwards refer to Sandys, *Relation of a Journey* (London, 1615, p. 41), who describes a "black Tower . . . a prison for captives of principal quality" and "a certain Hollander, who having been captured by a renegado escaped by means of a rope from this tower."

ACT FIVE, SCENE 8

1–4. **this night . . . Alcmena / Begot Alcides**   Asembeg alludes to classical mythology and the night when Jove delayed the sunrise so that he could enjoy three nights of lovemaking with "fair Alcmena." The result of such a supernatural event was the birth of a hero with superhuman powers, Alcides (or Hercules).

Appendix 1

~

THREE BALLADS

THE SEAMAN'S SONG OF CAPTAIN WARD, THE FAMOUS PIRATE
OF THE WORLD, AND AN ENGLISHMAN BORN.
(To the tune of "The King's going to Bulloigne")

Gallants, you must understand,
Captain Ward of England,
A pirate and a rover on the sea,
Of late a simple fisherman
In the merry town of Feversham,
Grows famous in the world now every day.

From the Bay of Plymouth
Sailed he towards the south,
With many more of courage and of might.
Christian princes have but few
Such seamen, if that he and we were true,
And would but for his King and Country fight.

Lusty Ward adventurously
In the Straits of Barbary
Did make the Turkish galleys for to shake.
Bouncing cannons fiery hot
Spared not the Turks one jot,
But of their lives great slaughter he did make.

The islanders of Malta,
With argosies upon the sea,

Most proudly braved Ward unto his face,
　　But soon their pride was overthrown,
　　And their treasures made his own,
And all their men brought to a woeful case.

　　The wealthy ships of Venice
　　Afforded him great riches;
Both gold and silver won he with his sword.
　　Stately Spain and Portugal
　　Against him dare not bare up sail,
But gave him all the title of a Lord.

　　Golden seated Candy,
　　Famous France and Italy,
With all the countries of the Eastern parts,
　　If once their ships his pride withstood,
　　They surely all were clothed in blood,
Such cruelty was placed within their hearts.

　　The riches he hath gained,
　　And by bloodshed obtained,
Well may suffice for to maintain a king.
　　His fellows all were valiant wights,
　　Fit to be made prince's knights,
But that their lives do base dishonors bring.

　　This wicked-gotten treasure
　　Doth him but little pleasure,
The land consumes what they have got by sea,
　　In drunkenness and letchery,
　　Filthy sins of sodomy,
These evil-gotten goods so waste away.

　　Such as live by thieving
　　Have seldom-times good ending,

Candy] Crete.

As by the deeds of Captain Ward is shown:
  Being drunk amongst his drabs,
  His nearest friends he sometimes stabs;
Such wickedness within his heart is grown.

  When stormy tempest riseth,
  The Causer he despiseth,
Still denies to pray unto the Lord.
  He feareth neither God nor Devil,
  His deeds are bad, his thoughts are evil,
His only trust is still upon his sword.

  Men of his own country
  He still abuseth vilely,
Some back-to-back are cast into the waves;
  Some are hewn in pieces small,
  Some are shot against a wall;
A slender number of their lives he saves.

  Of truth it is reported,
  That he is strongly guarded
By Turks that are not of a good belief;
  Wit and reason tells them
  He trusteth not his countrymen,
But shows the right condition of a thief.

  At Tunis in Barbary
  Now he buildeth stately
A gallant palace and a royal place,
  Decked with delights most trim,
  Fitter for a prince then him,
The which at last will prove to his disgrace.

  To make the world to wonder,
  This Captain is commander
Of four-and-twenty mighty ships of sail,
  To bring in treasure from the sea

Into the markets every day:
The which the Turks do buy up without fail.

His name and state so mounteth,
These countrymen accounteth
Him equal to the nobles of that land;
But these his honors we shall find
Shortly blown up with the wind,
Or prove like letters written in the sand.

FINIS.

LONDON:
PRINTED FOR F. COLES, T. VERE, AND WILLIAM GILBERTSON.
[DATE OF FIRST ISSUE, 3 JULY 1609.]

THE SONG OF DANSEKAR THE DUTCHMAN.
(To the tune of "The King [Henry]'s going to Bulloigne.")

Sing we seamen, now and then,
Of Dansekar the Dutchman,
Whose gallant mind hath won him great renown;
To live on land he counts it base,
But seeks to purchase greater grace,
By roving on the ocean up and down.

His heart is so aspiring,
That now his chief desiring
Is for to win himself a worthy name;
The land hath far too little ground,
The sea is of a larger bound,
And of a greater dignity and fame.

Now many a worthy gallant,
Of courage now most valiant,
With him hath put their fortunes to the sea;

All the world about have heard
of Dansekar and English Ward,
And of their proud adventures every day.

There is not any kingdom,
In Turkey or in Christendom,
But by these pirates have received loss;
    Merchantmen of every land
    Do daily in great danger stand,
And fear do much the ocean main to cross.

They make children fatherless,
Woeful widows in distress,
In shedding blood they too much delight;
    Fathers they bereave of sons,
    Regarding neither cries nor moans,
So much they joy to see a bloody fight.

They count it gallant bearing
To hear the cannons roaring,
And musket shot to rattle in the sky;
    Their glories would be at the highest
    To fight against the foes of Christ,
And such as do our Christian faith deny.

But their cursed villanies,
And their bloody piracies,
Are chiefly bent against our Christian friends;
    Some Christians so delight in evils,
    That they become the sons of devils,
And for the same have many shameful ends.

England suffers danger,
As well as any stranger.
Nations are alike unto this company;
    Many English merchantmen,
    And of London now and then,
Have tasted of their vile extremity.

London's *Elizabeth*
Of late these rovers taken hath,
A ship well laden with rich merchandise.
    The nimble *Pearl* and *Charity*,
    All ships of gallant bravery,
Are by these pirates made a lawful prize.

    The *Trojan* of London,
    With other ships many a one,
Hath stooped sail, and yielded out of hand.
    These pirates they have shed their bloods,
    And the Turks have bought their goods,
Being all too weak their power to withstand.

    Of Hull the *Bonaventer*,
    Which was a great frequenter
And passer of the straits to Barbary,
    Both ship and men taken were
    By pirates Ward and Dansekar,
And brought by them into captivity.

    English Ward and Dansekar
    Begin greatly now to jar
About [the true] dividing [of] their goods;
    Both ships and soldiers gather head,
    Dansekar from Ward is fled,
So full of pride and malice are their bloods.

    Ward doth only promise
    To keep about rich Tunis,
And be commander of those Turkish seas;
    But valiant Dutch-land Dansekar
    Doth hover near unto Argier,
And there his threat'ning colors now displays.

    These pirates thus divided,
    By God is soon provided
In secret sort to work each other's woe.
    Such wicked courses cannot stand,

The Devil thus puts in his hand,
And God will give them soon an overthrow.

FINIS.

Printed for F. Coles, T. Vere, and W. Gilbertson.
[Original dated 1609.]

The Famous Sea-Fight between Captain Ward and the Rainbow
(To the tune of "Captain Ward, etc.")

Strike up, you lusty gallants, with music and sound of drum,
For we have descried a rover upon the sea is come;
His name is Captain Ward, right well it doth appear;
There has not been such a rover found out this thousand year.

For he hath sent unto our King, the sixth of January,
Desiring that he might come in, with all his company:
"And if your King will let me come, till I my tale have told,
I will bestow for my ransom full thirty ton of gold."

"O nay! O nay!" then said our King, "O nay, this may not be,
To yield to such a rover myself will not agree;
He hath deceived the Frenchman, likewise the King of Spain,
And how can he be true to me, that hath been false to twain."

With that our King provided a ship of worthy fame,
Rainbow she is called, if you would know her name;
Now the gallant *Rainbow* she rows upon the sea,
Five hundred gallant seamen to bear her company.

The Dutchman and the Spaniard, she made them for to fly,
Also the bonny Frenchman, as she met him on the sea.
When as this gallant *Rainbow* did come where Ward did lie,
"Where is the Captain of the ship?" this gallant *Rainbow* did cry.

"O that am I," says Captain Ward, "there's no man bids me lie;
And if thou art the King's fair ship, thou art welcome unto me."
"I'll tell thee what," says *Rainbow*, "our King is in great grief
That thou should'st lie upon the sea, and play the arrant thief,

"And will not let our merchants' ships pass as they did before,
Such tidings to our King is come, which grieves his heart full sore."
With that this gallant *Rainbow* she shot, out of her pride,
Full fifty gallant brass pieces, charged on every side.

And yet these gallant shooters prevailed not a pin,
Though they were brass on the outside, brave Ward was steel within.
"Shoot on, shoot on!" says Captain Ward, "your sport well pleaseth me;
And he that first gives over, shall yield unto the sea."

"I never wronged an English Ship, but Turk and King of Spain,
For and the jovial Dutchman, as I met on the main.
If I had known your King but one, two years before,
I would have saved brave Essex' life, whose death did grieve me sore."

"Go, tell the King of England, go tell him thus from me,
If he reign King of all the land, I will reign King at sea."
With that the gallant *Rainbow* shot, and shot, and shot in vain,
And left the rover's company, and returned home again.

"Our Royal King of England, your ship's return'd again;
For Ward's ship is so strong, it never will be ta'en."
"O everlasting!" says our King, "I have lost jewels three,
Which would have gone unto the seas, and brought proud Ward to me!"

"The first was Lord Clifford, Earl of Cumberland;
The second was the Lord Mountjoy, as you shall understand;
The third was brave Essex, from field would never flee;
Which would 'a gone unto the seas, and brought proud Ward to me!"

LONDON:

PRINTED BY AND FOR W. ONLEY, AND ARE TO BE SOLD BY THE BOOKSELLERS OF PIE-
CORNER AND LONDON BRIDGE. [ORIGINAL DATE, CIRCA 1620.]

Appendix 2

~

A ROYAL PROCLAMATION

By the King.
A Proclamation against Pirates.
[Whitehall, 8 January 1609.]

The King's Majesty, having been informed through the manifold complaints made to his Highness by his own subjects as others, of the many depredations and piracies committed by lewd and ill disposed persons, accustomed and habituated to spoil and rapine, insensible and desperate of the peril they draw upon themselves, and the imputation they cast upon the honor of their sovereign so precious to him, as for redress thereof he is enforced to reiterate and inculcate his loathing and detestation not only of the crimes, but also to manifest to the world his sincerity and exceeding desires for the due and speedy suppressing of the delinquents; and having lately found, by many pregnant circumstances, that most of these great faults are continued by the connivance or corruption in many [of] the subordinate officers, especially such as are resident in and near the ports and maritime counties. In his princely care to preserve justice, as one of the main pillars of his estate, and for the speedy prevention of such foul crimes, and the severe punishment and extirpation of such enormious offenders (most hateful to his mind, and scandalous to his peaceable government) and for the preservation and continuance of amity and good correspondency with all other princes and states, hath with the advice of the Council thought it necessary at this present, to publish these articles and ordinances ensuing: wherein if any shall be found culpable, refractory, or contemptuous, his Majesty is resolved and hereby declareth, that such punishment shall be inflicted on him or them so offending, that others may be exemplarily forewarned, from committing so odious facts, and be deterred

---

enormious] abnormally wicked.

from aiding, relieving, comforting, or abetting such and so enormious male-factors.

If any person whatsoever shall upon the seas, or in any port or haven, take any ship that doth belong to any of his Majesty's subjects, friends, or allies; or shall take out of it by force, any goods of what nature or quality soever: he or they so offending shall suffer death, with confiscation of lands and goods, according to the law in that case provided.

If any person or persons so offending, do at any time hereafter come into any port or place of his Majesty's dominions, his Majesty expressly chargeth all his officers forthwith to apprehend him and them, and to commit them to prison, without bail or mainprize, and that the name of the person and cause of his imprisonment be forthwith certified into the Admiralty, that speedy order may be taken for further proceeding and execution according to law, and the contents of his Majesty's former proclamations.

All his Majesty's subjects shall forbear from furnishing, victualing, aiding, receiving, relieving, comforting, or abetting, any pirate or sea rover, or any person not being a known merchant, by contracting, buying, selling, barter-ing, or exchanging with him or them, upon peril of his Majesty's heavy indig-nation, and the grievous pains by law belonging to the same.

All admiral causes shall be summarily heard by the Judge of the Admiralty without admitting any unnecessary delay, and no appeal from his shall be allowed to the defendant or defendants in cases of depredations or spoil, ei-ther for the offenders, or their accessories before or after the offense com-mitted, or those in whose possession the goods spoiled are found, unless first by way of provision the sum adjudged be paid to the plaintiff upon sureties to repay it, if the sentence shall be reversed. And no prohibition in such causes of depredation and spoil, and their accessories and dependents shall be here-after granted against the Admiralty.

No ship or goods taken from any his Majesty's friends shall be delivered upon any other order then upon proof made, or certificate exhibited, in the said Court of the Admiralty, to the end that a record may be kept of all such restitutions made to strangers, to serve if occasion shall require.

And for the preventing of future mischiefs, every Vice Admiral is enjoined by the proclamation (whereof he is to take notice at his peril) to certify into the said Court of the Admiralty every quarter of the year, what ship or ships

---

mainprize] release of a prisoner into the friendly custody of one who provides "surety" for the pris-oner's appearance in court.

warlikely appointed, hath gone to the sea, or returned within that time with any goods taken at sea, or the procedure thereof, upon pain to lose to his Majesty (by way of fine) for every such default, forty pound of current money of England, to be answerable into his Majesty's receipt of the Exchequer, by certificate from the said Judge of the Admiralty, under the great seal of that office, to be directed to the Lord Treasurer, and the Barons of the Exchequer.

The Vice Admirals, customers, and other officers of the ports, shall not suffer any ship to go to sea before such time as they respectively in their several ports have duly searched and visited the same, to the intent to stay such as apparently shall be furnished for the wars, and not for merchandising or fishing. And if there shall be cause of suspicion by the provisions, or furniture, or extraordinary number of men, or suspected persons therein, that the said ship and company is otherwise to be employed than in merchandise or fishing: then in such case of suspicion, the Vice Admirals and officers of the ports shall stay and in no wise suffer the said ship to pass to seas, without good bonds with sufficient sureties had in the double value of the ship and her furniture, to use nothing during their said voyage but lawful trade of merchandise or fishing. And if they shall suffer any such persons otherwise to repair to the seas than is above mentioned, they shall suffer imprisonment until the offenders may be apprehended, and shall be answerable to the parties grieved, for their contempt and offense in this behalf committed.

And whereas divers great and enormious spoils and piracies have been heretofore committed within the Straits of Gibraltar and other places by Captain John Ward and his adherents, and other English pirates, and the goods, moneys, and merchandises have been and are sold, dispersed and disposed of, most lewdly and prodigally by the means of their receivers, comforters, and abettors, to the great prejudice of his Majesty's good friends the Venetians, and others in league and amity with his Majesty, whom they have so robbed and spoiled: His Majesty doth hereby expressly charge and command all Lieutenants, deputy Lieutenants, Vice Admirals and their deputies, Justices of Peace, Captains of his Majesty's Ships, and all other officers of the Admiralty, and all mayors, sheriffs, bailiffs, constables, and other his officers whatsoever, as they and every of them tender his Majesty's service, and upon peril of his Majesty's endeavors, in the inquiring, searching for and apprehending of all such pirates, their receivers, comforters, and abettors. And if they shall by their travails and care find any of them, to send them presently to the next common jail, there to remain without bail or mainprize, till the Lord High Admiral of England, or his lieutenant the Judge of the Admiralty may be advertised thereof, and shall dispose of them according to the laws in that case provided.

Lastly, forasmuch as his Majesty is advertised that this pirate Ward and others are made the more able to continue in strength and power, to infest the subjects of all Christian princes and estates, by means of that receipt and protection which is given them in Tunis, Argiers, and the places adjoining, His Majesty doth hereby straitly prohibit all his subjects whatsoever that shall go to sea, that they nor any of them, shall sell, alien, barter, or exchange any ordinance, powder, cordage, or any provision whatsoever, serviceable for the war or shipping, directly or indirectly, to or with the said Ward, or his adherents, or any other pirate or pirates whatsoever, under pain of death as accessories in cases of piracy. Neither shall any of his Majesty's subjects, residing for the time in Tunis, Argiers, or in any other place in Barbary, or the places adjoining, or hereafter resorting thither, dare to buy, barter, exchange, or receive directly or indirectly any goods taken at the seas, upon any pretext whatsoever, under pain of confiscation of his own proper goods, lands, and chattels here in England, and such other punishment as by law may be inflicted upon so contemptuous and grievous an offender.

Given at Whitehall the eighth day of January, in the sixth year of his Majesty's reign of great Britain, France and Ireland.

God save the King.

IMPRINTED AT LONDON BY THE DEPUTIES OF ROBERT BARKER,
PRINTER TO THE KING'S MOST EXCELLENT MAJESTY. ANNO DOM. 1608.

---

alien] transfer property.

A NOTE ON THE TEXTS

The texts of the plays are based primarily on the Folger Shakespeare Library copies of the earliest printed editions. I am indebted to various editors who preceded me, especially Philip Edwards and Colin Gibson, editors of the Clarendon edition of Massinger's plays and poems. Spelling and punctuation have been modernized in the plays and in all quotations from early modern texts. Changes or additions to the original stage directions are placed within brackets. Latin stage directions (except for "exit" and "exeunt") have been translated into modern English. The lists of dramatis personae are based on the original texts, but were rewritten and supplemented by myself, as the lists of characters are not complete or accurate in the originals. Scene divisions follow the original in *Selimus* and *The Renegado*, but they have been added for *A Christian Turned Turk*, where there are none in the 1612 text. The scene headings include a phrase describing the setting for each scene. These descriptions are my own work and sometimes are conjectural, but they are meant to aid, in a small way, the imagination of the reader.

The texts of *Selimus* and *The Renegado* are relatively unproblematic, and emendations are rarely necessary, but the 1612 quarto edition of *A Christian Turned Turk* is a very rough text and extensive emendation and conjectural reconstruction have been necessary to restore the play to readability. Lois Potter recently observed that "It must have been printed from papers nearly as foul as the hero: the list of dramatis personae is incomplete, crucial stage directions are missing, speeches are misattributed."[1] I have sought to straighten out these textual tangles, and I believe the result is the restoration of the "fast-moving and interesting" plot that Potter recognized in Daborne's

---

1. Lois Potter, "Pirates and 'turning Turk' in Renaissance drama," *Travel and Drama in Shakespeare's Time*, Maquerlot and Willems, eds. (Cambridge: Cambridge University Press, 1996), 124–40.

play. Until now, the strength and beauty of that drama has been hidden, like a once vivid oil painting covered by the smoke and dust of time; it has gone unrecognized by readers faced with the murky facsimile that was the only printed version of the play widely available until this edition.

CPSIA information can be obtained
at www.ICGtesting.com
Printed in the USA
LVHW091550231121
704240LV00015B/61

9 780231 110297